CAN'T GIVE IT AWAY ON SEVENTH AVENUE

THE ROLLING STONES AND NEW YORK CITY

CHRISTOPHER McKITTRICK

Post Hill
PRESS

A POST HILL PRESS BOOK

Can't Give It Away on Seventh Avenue:
The Rolling Stones and New York City
© 2019 by Christopher McKittrick
All Rights Reserved

ISBN: 978-1-64293-039-9
ISBN (eBook): 978-1-64293-040-5

Cover art by Cody Corcoran
Interior design and composition by Greg Johnson, Textbook Perfect

Post Hill Press
New York • Nashville
posthillpress.com

Published in the United States of America

CAN'T GIVE IT AWAY ON SEVENTH AVENUE

Cheers to Erin

CONTENTS

"THIS TOWN'S GONNA MAKE IT"

On October 20, 2001, Mick Jagger walked onto the stage at Madison Square Garden—an arena he had performed in as the lead singer of the Rolling Stones eighteen times over the previous thirty-two years. By then "The World's Most Famous Arena" had already played an instrumental role in the legacy of the band. All but one of the songs on their landmark live album *'Get Yer Ya-Ya's Out!' The Rolling Stones in Concert* were recorded during their first concerts there in November 1969, and clips from the same shows were featured in *Gimme Shelter*, the infamous 1970 documentary. Signifying the band's long history with the Garden, in June 1984 the Stones became the first rock group to be inducted into the venue's Hall of Fame.

Jagger, however, was not appearing that night with the band he had fronted since 1962. He had not played with the Stones in over two years, since the conclusion of their No Security Tour. In the months prior, he had been recording and doing preliminary promotional work for his fourth solo album, *Goddess in the Doorway*, which was set to be released in November, but on this night, Jagger was one of the many famous musicians participating in The Concert for New York City, a benefit show in memory of the nearly three thousand New Yorkers

1

who had been killed in the terrorist attacks on the World Trade Center less than six weeks earlier.

Jagger wasn't alone. Keith Richards, his childhood friend and the Stones' guitarist, appeared unannounced at the side of his longtime bandmate, and the "Glimmer Twins" were showered with cheers from an audience made up mostly of hundreds of members of the New York City Fire Department, the New York City Police Department, and their families. After they embraced each other, Richards stepped up to the microphone while strumming his guitar.

"New York. How ya doing, guys? You know, I got a feeling this town's gonna make it."

Coming from the mouth of the quintessential rock 'n' roll survivor—few rockers have been as up close and personal with death as Richards—it was a proclamation of endurance and hope. Richards, Jagger, and the house band then launched into an uplifting rendition of "Salt of the Earth," the rarely performed but poignantly appropriate gospel-influenced final track on *Beggars Banquet*.

Before sliding into the next song—the disco-influenced "Miss You," which celebrates the dirty decadence of '70s Manhattan—Jagger offered his own proclamation on the enduring spirit of New York City: "You know, if there's one thing to be learned from this, if there's one thing to be learned from this whole experience, it's you don't fuck with New York, okay?"

Though Jagger and Richards were born almost six decades earlier, an ocean away in Dartford, England, the pair were speaking on good authority. Besides their intimate history with Madison Square Garden, both Jagger and Richards called New York City home for many years. Despite their English origin, the Rolling Stones can be considered one of the great New York City bands based on their long, colorful history with Gotham in their music, performances, and offstage antics. The band's emotional connection with the city spans decades. A year after the attacks, Jagger allowed a song from *Goddess in the Doorway* titled "Joy" to be used free of charge in a commercial made by the City of New York to thank the rest of country for their aid in the aftermath of the attacks.

When the Rolling Stones began gigging around London in the early 1960s, it was impossible for them to know that their music would take them all over the world many times over for more than five decades. When Jagger and Richards had the fateful chance reunion at the Dartford railway station in 1960 that would eventually alter the course of rock music, neither could have imagined that they would both make New York City their home and that Manhattan would become ingrained in the music and image that their band would create.

Before the 1960s, popular music was rarely globe-spanning, and when the Rolling Stones was formed, English rock 'n' roll bands certainly did not have that reach. While the Stones were devoted fans of American rhythm and blues and rock and roll, British bands that emulated their sound played London and, if they were lucky, perhaps as far as West Germany. At that time the transatlantic pop music exchange from the United States to the United Kingdom was almost exclusively one way, which explains the fascination British Invasion bands had with American music. British pop music fans could easily find their favorite American artists at the local record store, but Americans had yet to show much interest in British artists.

Outside of making a handful of appearances on popular US TV programs, as Lonnie Donegan did on *The Perry Como Show* and *The Paul Winchell Show* in the mid-1950s, followed by his tour of the States in 1956, it was unprecedented for British bands to have sustained success in the United States. Rocker Cliff Richard, popularly regarded as the "British Elvis," did a four-week US and Canadian tour in January and February 1960 and a second tour in August 1962, but he failed to make a major impact. In contrast, American artists toured England with great success. In fact, the Stones supported Bo Diddley, Little Richard, and the Everly Brothers on a fall 1963 UK tour and would later open for New York City natives the Ronettes on their January 1964 UK tour. After all, the United States already had Chuck Berry, Bo Diddley, and Muddy Waters. Why would America ever demand English imitations? "When I was growing up, the idea of leaving England was pretty much remote," Richards wrote in his 2010 autobiography, *Life*. "My dad did it once, but that was in the army to go to Normandy and get his leg blown off. The idea was totally impossible."

At first, New York did not hold the same promise for the young Jagger, Richards, and Brian Jones as another American city. Their love of the blues and Chess Records put Chicago higher on their list of American cities to visit. Though New York is the home of the Brill Building, which was still the center of songwriting and business in American pop music in the early 1960s, all of Jagger and Richards's idols had recorded at Chess Studios in Chicago. It's no surprise that during their first American tour they recorded a few songs at Chess and met Muddy Waters, Chuck Berry, Willie Dixon, and Buddy Guy on the premises. Though the Stones would develop a strong connection with Chicago, in subsequent decades the group would plant stronger roots in New York City and draw influence from the music of 1970s Manhattan.

Of all the Stones, drummer Charlie Watts, who formally joined the group in January 1963, was perhaps the only member who had designs on New York at a young age. Watts had grown up a fan of jazz and had played in numerous jazz clubs in London with local bands. He was devoted to American jazz greats and as a teenager even wrote and illustrated a picture book, *Ode to a Highflying Bird*, as a tribute to Charlie Parker. It was published in 1964. Decades later, Watts recalled his early ambitions to *The Guardian*. "I wanted to be Max Roach or Kenny Clarke playing in New York with Charlie Parker in the front line. Not a bad aspiration. It actually meant a lot of bloody playing, a lot of work. I don't think kids are interested in that. But that may be true of every generation, I don't know. When I was what you'd call a young musician, jazz was very fashionable." By the time Watts joined the Stones, they were already performing bluesman Jimmy Reed's "Going to New York" in their set, though Watts might have been the only one who believed the song's title. Watts's Manhattan jazz club dreams would eventually come true, but only after the Stones became the toast of the city.

It was appropriate then that when the Stones made their first visit to the United States, they arrived in New York, landing at the recently renamed John F. Kennedy International Airport on June 1,

1964. It was less than four months after the Beatles' hugely successful tour, which featured iconic performances on *The Ed Sullivan Show* and ignited Beatlemania in America. Despite their perceived rivalry, in June 1964 the Rolling Stones were no Beatles. Their first American album, *England's Newest Hit Makers*, was released only two days before their arrival, and their first US single, a cover of Buddy Holly's "Not Fade Away," had been released in March in the wake of the Beatles' US debut but failed to make a major splash (reaching only number forty-eight on the Billboard chart). During the tour, their second US single "Tell Me" was released on June 13 and peaked at number twenty-four. Whereas the Beatles came to the US as conquering heroes with "I Want to Hold Your Hand" and "She Loves You" at the top of the Billboard Hot 100 singles chart and *Meet the Beatles!* and *Introducing...The Beatles* at the top of the Billboard albums chart, the Stones were unestablished underdogs. They arrived largely unheralded and departed three weeks later hardly better known.

Yet, on the touring front, the Stones would eventually have a far bigger impact than the Beatles. While the Beatles were truly the first globetrotting pop band, they ceased touring after August 1966. The Stones were just getting started, and their best tours, and in particular, their best concerts in New York, were still ahead of them. After following the Beatles in playing Carnegie Hall, *The Ed Sullivan Show*, and Forest Hills Stadium in the mid-1960s, the Stones would go on to play every major venue in the New York metro area on their box office record-setting tours—including stadium shows in Queens and East Rutherford, New Jersey, arenas in Manhattan and Brooklyn, and theaters and orchestra halls all over Manhattan. The number of stages the members of the Stones have appeared on in New York more than doubles when the members' solo concerts (including the pre-Stones groups of Ronnie Wood and both the pre- and post-Stones groups of Mick Taylor) are taken into account. Counting the number of times a member of the Stones jammed with another artist on a Manhattan stage, particularly in the late '70s and early '80s, there is more Stones history in New York than in any other city in the world. It's no surprise that when the Stones announced the initial dates of their fiftieth-anniversary tour, two were at London's O2 arena and three were in the New York metro area. London might have given birth to the group, but it was in America, and in New York City in particular, where they truly developed into "The World's Greatest Rock 'n' Roll Band."

Indeed, much had changed already for the Stones by the time they arrived in New York for their second American tour on October 23, 1964. Their second US album, *12 x 5*, was released six days earlier and quickly rose to number three on the Billboard charts. The original version of "Time Is on My Side" had been released as a single on September 26 and became the group's first American top-ten hit, reaching number six on the Billboard singles chart. They would play the song along with Chuck Berry's "Around and Around" on *The Ed Sullivan Show* on October 25, the first of a half-dozen appearances the band would make on the career-making program. Much like the Beatles earlier in the year, the Stones' performance was answered by an audience full of girls screaming hysterically, especially when Jagger, dressed casually in a sweater instead of a suit like the Mop Tops, bobbed and weaved during the guitar breaks. America was hooked, and each of the Stones' subsequent studio albums, from 1965's *The Rolling Stones, Now!* through 2016's *Blue & Lonesome*, would reach the top five on the Billboard charts. Fans never stopped screaming for the Stones, especially in New York.

While the Beatles' pop sensibilities remained firmly British despite their early covers of American songs like "Twist and Shout," it was the Stones who more deeply mined American music—blues, rock, country, and even bits of the Great American Songbook—for their sound. As Richards said to *The New York Times* in 2002, "I think that's the difference between us and the Beatles. They were much more homegrown. We were always looking out. It was the difference between Liverpool, which to a Londoner is very provincial, and London, where we came from."

Though the Stones would remain based in England through the end of the 1960s, their connection with New York City would grow each time they returned to the United States for a tour. Starting in late

1965, Brian Jones made several visits to Manhattan until his final one in September 1967. Jagger and Richards would both spend an increasing amount of time in the city, particularly when Jagger became well established in celebrity social circles during the 1972 American Tour. By the late 1970s, Jagger, Richards, and the newest Stones guitarist, Ronnie Wood, all had residences in Manhattan and were common fixtures at nightclubs and social events. Former Stones guitarist Mick Taylor, who played with the group from 1969 to 1974, would begin regularly playing in New York and the metro area in the mid-1980s, and Watts would finally get to embrace his big-band jazz club aspirations by bringing the Charlie Watts Orchestra and his succeeding solo bands to New York starting in 1986. Even bassist Bill Wyman, who officially retired from the Stones in 1993, would return to New York in 2001 to play a concert with his solo band, the Rhythm Kings. In addition to the band's extensive performance history in New York as a whole, New York City is the only city in which every member of the Rolling Stones has played shows with side projects (with the exception of Jones, who never had a solo band). Not even London, the birthplace of the Stones, can claim the same.

As with everything with the Rolling Stones, the band's history in New York City is entwined with some of the most infamous stories of rock 'n' roll decadence. When the Stones first arrived in New York, it was a city in decline. The 1960s and 1970s brought immense social change to New York, much of which was reflected in the Stones' music. During the 1970s and early 1980s, the Stones' changing sound was influenced by the new music of New York City's nightlife, economy, and culture. In the years leading to the twenty-first century, New York City's booming economy paralleled the band's monstrously successful concert tours in the 1990s and 2000s, which fundamentally changed the music business. In an art form where artists are frequently decried by their fans for "selling out," the Stones continue to write the book on marketing a band as a business entity, and have almost inexplicably gained even more popularity and financial rewards to a degree previously unimaginable by pop musicians.

Richards knew that New York City would "make it" after 9/11 simply because it was the city that made the Rolling Stones the wildest, sleaziest, and most exciting rock band in history. While New York can claim dozens of homegrown artists born and bred to sing of the streets and the subways, no band quite matches the spectacle of "The Capital of the World" like "The World's Greatest Rock 'n' Roll Band."

CHAPTER 1

"I'M GOIN' TO NEW YORK"

In the interests of promoting New York City as a modern urban center even in the Space Age, in August 1959 the city announced its intention to host a World's Fair in 1964 in Flushing Meadows Park, the same site in Queens that held the 1939–1940 World's Fair. Thomas J. Deegan Jr., who was chairman of the 1964 World's Fair committee, said the theme of the fair would be "Peace Through Understanding." The objective was to showcase New York to the world and inject billions into local coffers via tourism, an industry that would come to dominate the city's economy by the end of the century. The plan was met with near-universal acclaim from city officials, including Mayor Robert F. Wagner Jr., who had been in office since 1954. Wagner saw it as an opportunity to remake the image of New York and decided to go to battle with the emerging counterculture.

Prior to the announcement, seedier aspects of the city had been creeping into popular culture. The early writings of the Beats—including the 1953 semi-autobiographical novel *Junkie: Confessions of an Unredeemed Drug Addict*, written by William S. Burroughs—offered stark, uncompromising views of the city's drug culture and homelessness, as well as frank depictions of sex, including homosexuality. The

Beat Generation presented dirty truths of the urban landscape that city officials desperately wanted to eliminate.

On March 14, 1960, the story "Life on W. 42nd St. A Study in Decay" appeared on the front page of *The New York Times* calling the block between Seventh and Eighth Avenues "an enigma to New Yorkers concerned with the deterioration of the midway of Manhattan." The article cited the "grind joint" movie theaters open until 4:00 a.m. for their sexual and violent content as a prime draw for "undesirables." The article also decried homosexuality as "an obvious problem," along with loiterers, dropouts, vandals, pickpockets, and drug users, and went into detail about how they congregated around a rock 'n' roll jukebox in the block's subway station. The message was clear: New York City's problems were out in the open for all to see.

To combat these issues, Wagner's administration targeted prostitutes, homosexuals, and beatniks. Officials faced little resistance revoking the liquor licenses of gay bars, while police entrapped, harassed, and arrested homosexuals and prostitutes on charges of indecency. Eliminating the so-called beatniks was another story entirely.

By the end of the 1950s, the American folk music revival was a growing movement in Greenwich Village. While jazz had been the predominant form of music in the area and among the Beat Generation writers, the avant-garde tradition of bohemian artists embraced the stripped-down folk music in nightclubs and coffeehouses, though most events visible to the community were the traditional Sunday gatherings of folk musicians in Washington Square Park. The gatherings began in the 1940s, but by 1960 their popularity had increased a hundredfold and the park was filled with hundreds of musicians arriving from miles away sporting unkempt hair and ragged clothing. To city officials and local residents, these beatniks represented the growing unwashed specter of social disobedience.

In May 1960, former mayoral candidate Newbold Morris was appointed parks commissioner by Mayor Wagner to replace renowned "Master Builder" Robert Moses, the urban planner who had served for twenty-six years and overseen dramatic changes to the city's landscape.

Morris, likely under pressure from Washington Square business owners and residents, began rejecting permits to allow the musicians to play in the park. For more than a decade, permits had been issued with little effort, and the process was such a formality that many musicians didn't even bother applying for them. Initially, the musicians ignored the rejections, but on Sunday, April 9, 1961, Morris filled the park with police officers to prevent them from playing. Nearly three thousand folk musicians showed up anyway, and when they started singing "My Country 'Tis of Thee" and "The Star-Spangled Banner" in protest, cops arrested ten performers.

The overly large headline of the *New York Mirror* the next day read "3000 Beatniks Riot in Village," which embellished the few rowdy incidents of the mostly non-violent protest. Yet not all in the media were against the gatherings. In his nationally syndicated "These Days" column, journalist George E. Sokolsky decried the decision, remarking, "For 17 years, these songfests continued and nobody much bothered about it. The Beatniks came with their whiskers and their gals wore long hair and all their faces were grubby which is their symbol of revolt—but it is better to rebel by not using lipstick than to rebel by throwing bombs." He questioned the hypocrisy of Cold War-era America's boasting of its freedoms of expression in the face of communism when photos of peaceful musicians being arrested were being circulated, ending his column with "God save us from the stuffed-shirts."

On April 12, Mayor Wagner announced his support of Morris and suggested that the musicians take Morris's offer to use the amphitheater in East River Park two miles away instead. Six other demonstrations followed, including one outside Morris's East 72nd Street apartment. (A New York University student who was arrested at a demonstration on April 30 later hired lawyer Ed Koch, future mayor of New York, to represent him in a case against the NYPD for assault charges.) On May 4, the state supreme court upheld the ban, saying that the musicians were banned not "upon any distaste for folk singing" but because hundreds of musicians playing prevented others from using the park for "sitting, resting, relaxation and meditation." Shortly afterward, the folkies realized that there was actually no law against singing in the park without a permit, only against playing instruments. Because of that loophole, seven hundred musicians packed the park on May 7 to sing unaccompanied, with police unable to arrest anyone. It was clear that the beatniks were not budging.

Bowing to public pressure, Mayor Wagner announced on Friday, May 12, that the ban on music in Washington Square Park would be lifted on a "controlled basis" between 3:00 p.m. and 6:00 p.m. on the north side of the park the following Sunday. The return of the folkies on May 14 went off without incident, though *The Times* reported that the hundreds of musicians left behind "a landscape of ice-cream wrappers and beer cans." J. Owen Grundy, the editor of *The Villager* in Greenwich Village, wrote a letter to the editor of *The Times* that decried the decision because it brought "an extraordinary invasion of homosexual and professional beatniks, mostly from outside, who seem to take especial pride in appearing in public in the dirtiest and most unkempt attire conceivable." But on July 6, the Appellate Division of the New York State Supreme Court reversed the ruling that supported the ban. For seemingly the first time, the stuffed shirts lost.

Shortly thereafter, the folk music revival, practically personified by Village resident Bob Dylan, who had moved to New York shortly before the Washington Square protests, exploded, and Greenwich Village became a tourist attraction and an entertainment destination that rivaled the popularity of the World's Fair. It was indeed "Peace Through Understanding."

* * * * *

Though trying to fight against the beatniks who had invaded the East Village proved futile, as the opening of the World's Fair approached, New York officials became increasingly dedicated to cleaning up the city's image. On December 17, 1963, *The New York Times* published an article titled "Growth of Overt Homosexuality in City Provokes Wide Concern" by Robert C. Doty on its front page. The article detailed the New York

State Liquor Authority's and the NYPD's efforts to shut down gay bars, which operated in secret and were run mostly by the mafia. However, the article was also an in-depth analysis of the legal, moral, and image issues confronted by the city. Doty wrote, "The city's homosexual community acts as a lodestar, attracting others from all over the country. More than a thousand inverts are arrested here annually for public misdeeds." Three years after the concerned article in *The Times* about the state of 42nd Street, Doty wrote that the "undesirable" population of the area was still a problem: "In a fairly restricted area around Eighth Avenue and 42d Street there congregate those who are universally regarded as the dregs of the invert world—the male prostitutes—the painted, grossly effeminate 'queens' and those who prey on them."

The image problems that officials were trying to control in advance of the World's Fair faced an even bigger setback when one of the most infamous crimes to ever happen in New York occurred four months later. In the early morning of March 13, 1964, twenty-eight-year-old Catherine "Kitty" Genovese was murdered near her home in Kew Gardens, Queens, just two miles away from the site of Flushing Meadows Park, where the World's Fair was less than six weeks from opening. The story initially made little noise. But over the next two weeks, metropolitan editor A. M. Rosenthal of *The New York Times* saw chilling angles of the crime. Genovese had been attacked outside her building by Winston Moseley, a twenty-nine-year-old man from South Ozone Park, Queens. Moseley initially stabbed Genovese twice in the back, seriously injuring her, but fled when one of Genovese's neighbors shouted out his window at Moseley in response to Genovese's screams of pain. Moseley returned ten minutes later to find Genovese lying in the building's vestibule, unable to get into her building. Over the next twenty minutes he continued to stab her, and then raped her as she was dying. He was arrested six days later when he was caught by police during an unrelated burglary. He confessed to the murder while in custody, saying his only motivation was to murder a woman.

What struck Rosenthal about the story was that there were many residents of the building within earshot of the murder, yet none of them did anything to prevent the second (and fatal) attack. He assigned reporter Martin Gansberg to the story, and on March 27 it became a front-page headline in *The Times*: "37 Who Saw Murder Didn't Call the Police." The article was a damning portrayal of Genovese's neighbors, and the neighbor who finally called the police offered an indifferent explanation to officers as to why he didn't do it sooner: "I didn't want to get involved."

The shocking story launched into the national consciousness, and to many it became the prime illustration of urban apathy toward crime. Later studies revealed that the number of witnesses to the crime as cited by Gansberg was a gross exaggeration and that much of the narrative presented in the article was inaccurate. Yet the damage was done to New York's reputation. This was not the image that New York wanted to project just weeks before the Fair.

* * * * *

As popular as the folk revival was in the early 1960s, it could not compare to the pop music revolution that was to take place in 1964. On December 10, 1963, the *CBS Evening News* aired a leftover story about a long-haired rock 'n' roll group called the Beatles who had achieved unprecedented sales and popularity in their native Great Britain. The piece—which originally aired on *CBS Morning News* on November 22, 1963; it was withheld from the evening broadcast because of that day's assassination of President John F. Kennedy—was the first one on national American television to report on the Beatles. In less than two months, the Beatles would become the most popular rock 'n' roll group in history. After their massive success in Great Britain, concert promoter Sid Bernstein, a New York native, was convinced that he could promote the Beatles in the United States and arranged for a promotional tour. The city's battle with youth music was over the moment the Beatles stepped onto the stage of CBS-TV Studio 50 at 1697 Broadway on February 9 to perform on *The Ed Sullivan Show* before a television audience of seventy-three million, over twenty million more than the total number of people who attended the 1964–1965 World's Fair, which for all of New York's efforts turned out to be a colossal financial failure. (Coincidentally, one of the major events of the 1964–1965 World's Fair was the burying of a time capsule that is scheduled to be opened in 6939, five thousand years after the 1939 World's Fair time capsule was buried. One item that was included was the Beatles' *A Hard Day's Night* LP.)

The Beatles' arrival in America was a perfect storm of media coverage, public relations, and marketing. In contrast, the arrival of the Rolling Stones could not have been more opposite.

The Rolling Stones had been a group for a little over eighteen months by the time the Beatles first appeared on *The Ed Sullivan Show*, though twenty-seven-year-old bassist Bill Wyman (announced as twenty-one to the press) and drummer Charlie Watts (who arrived in New York the day before his twenty-third birthday, though it was announced as his twenty-second to the press) had been in the lineup for only a little over a year. After passing on the Beatles, Decca Records signed the Rolling Stones to a three-year recording contract in May 1963 and distributed the band's records in the United States through its American subsidiary, London Records. The group enjoyed popularity in the London music scene, partially fueled by the publicity drummed up by the band's twenty-year-old manager, Andrew Loog Oldham. Oldham decided to exploit the group's image as one with a rougher edge than the Beatles and cultivated this "bad boy" image through the press, believing that it harked back to the rebellious nature of the early American rock and roll that teenagers had embraced to the chagrin of their parents. Prior to the Stones' arrival, some of this found its way into the American press. Manhattan journalist Dorothy Kilgallen wrote in a May 1964 edition of her nationally syndicated column,

> *"Those who think the Beatles caused too much of an uproar when they arrived here had better take to the bomb shelters when a new British group, The Rolling Stones, arrives next month. They are hard to describe—well, hard to describe without seeming offensive: they*

don't believe in bathing ('it's bad for your health'), they wear dirty old clothes, their hair is twice as long as the Beatles' and they never comb it, they've been thrown out of the best London restaurants for refusing to wear ties. But London Records, regarded as a conservative firm, has invested $85,000 in the quintet, and the English teenagers are wild about them."

"English teenagers are wild about them" was something of an exaggeration, though the Stones were indeed gaining popularity in England. Their third single, "Not Fade Away," which was released on February 21 in the UK and peaked at number three on the charts, was the group's first UK top-ten hit. By that time the Beatles already had four top-ten hits on the UK charts, including three number ones. Yet Oldham kept up the Beatles comparisons in the June 3 Associated Press report that announced the Stones' arrival to the United States. The article quoted one nameless "detractor" who said, "They are dirtier, wilder, freakier and more disheveled than the Beatles and in some places they're more popular than the Beatles." Eric Easton—the Stones' business manager, who co-managed the band with Oldham—dismissed the criticism by saying "The Rolling Stones are not dirty. It's true that they appear to conform to a certain image. They are independent and they dress as they please, but they're not dirty." The rest of the article contained hackneyed statements from the band members about their ambitions, clothes, and interests. But the hook was there—if your parents didn't like the Beatles, they *really* wouldn't like the Rolling Stones.

This marketing was precisely what distinguished the Stones from the Beatles and the dozen other British Invasion bands who attempted to storm the American market in the mid-1960s. But when the Stones first arrived on June 1, all the press in the world wouldn't have bought them what they sorely needed—a hit. It isn't clear what the Rolling Stones imagined would be waiting for them when they boarded a plane in Heathrow Airport for New York City. *The Times* identified them as "young men with shoulder-length haircuts," which would become a point of fascination for the newspaper (over the summer of 1964, they published three articles about longer men's hairstyles in England using the members of the Stones as examples). Unfortunately for the Stones, their hair would make more news than they would during the first American tour, as evidenced by the Stones' being greeted by two English sheepdogs upon their arrival at Kennedy in a ridiculous unplanned publicity stunt. *The Times* reported that about five hundred teenage girls were at Kennedy Airport and were kept in check by about fifty Port Authority and New York policemen. It was a sizable crowd, but a small fraction of the number of fans who had greeted the Beatles just four months earlier and even a fraction of the crowd that had greeted the Dave Clark Five, who had a top-ten hit with "Glad All Over" when they arrived in the US in March. With their reputation preceding them, the band had to undergo a health check at the airport, "something that no other English group had been subjected to," Wyman wrote in his autobiography.

The Stones' visit went downhill soon afterward when it became apparent that few people outside of New York had heard of the band. Oldham later recalled, "Once we left the airport we were invisible; not a soul knew who we were." While Oldham was exaggerating—Wyman recalled that the lobby of the Hotel Astor in Times Square was an "insane asylum," with seventy screaming girls and dozens more outside as they tried to check in—the rest of the American tour was indeed a difficult experience. When the Beatles had visited in February, the band really played only two concerts—the Washington Coliseum in Washington, DC, and Carnegie Hall in New York (a third live performance—a six-song set at the Deauville Hotel in Miami—was broadcast on *The Ed Sullivan Show*). Though the Beatles were far more popular, they had yet to attempt a tour of the US, and the Stones were doing it with little airplay. The Dave Clark Five were finishing a tour as the Stones arrived and had not gone west of the Mississippi or south of Washington, DC. The Stones were venturing all the way west to California and all the way south to Texas.

The band spent their first two days doing media in Manhattan, including hosting a press conference at the Hotel Astor and making a three-hour appearance on Murray the K's *Swingin' Soiree* radio show. In 1964, disc jockey Murray Kaufman was a forty-two-year-old, decade-long veteran of New York radio. In 1958 he began hosting *Swingin' Soiree* on WINS, which was dedicated to pop music. He also promoted seasonal rock concerts in Brooklyn that featured artists he heavily played on his show, including New York natives the Ronettes. Kaufman's rock 'n' roll roots were undeniable—famously, he was credited under a pseudonym as co-writer of Bobby Darin's 1958 number-three pop hit "Splish Splash" when Kaufman challenged Darin to write a song that began with the line "Splish splash, I was takin' a bath." After befriending the Beatles during their first visit to America and extensively covering their tour, Kaufman was heavily promoted by his station and himself as the "Fifth Beatle," a nickname he variously claimed was given to him by George Harrison or Ringo Starr (footage in the documentary *The Beatles: The First US Visit* suggests that Kaufman actually gave himself the title). Though Kaufman's goofy and energetic broadcasts made him a popular radio personality, to the Rolling Stones he seemed something of a dinosaur, though Wyman called him "a great champion of British pop" in his autobiography.

The Murray the K interview ended up changing the fortunes of the Stones when Murray introduced them to a song by the Valentinos titled "It's All Over Now," a song they would record in Chicago just nine days later. Jagger would later recall, "Murray The K gave us 'It's All Over Now' which was great because we used to think he was a cunt but he turned us on to something good. It was a great record by the Valentinos but it wasn't a hit." When released in the UK a little over two weeks after it was recorded, it became the group's first number-one single. The jockey took the group out to the famous Peppermint Lounge after the interview. Located at 128 West 45th Street, the Peppermint Lounge was a small dance club whose popularity had taken off several years earlier when the twist became a national phenomenon. It became the unofficial headquarters of the dance craze and a hangout for celebrities. The Ronettes had actually gotten their big break there in 1961 when Ronnie and Estelle Bennett and their cousin Nedra Talley were waiting in line and the manager mistook them as the dancers he had hired for the evening. They ended up dancing onstage behind the famed house band, Joey Dee and the Starliters, and Ronnie even sang Ray Charles's "What'd I Say" with the band. The future Ronettes were hired immediately and performed at the club in their early years. The Beatles had been filmed there as they hung out during their New York visit in February, so a visit by "England's Newest Hit Makers" seemed equally appropriate. Though the Peppermint Lounge closed in 1965 after losing its liquor license (investigators discovered the club was owned by Genovese crime family boss Matty "the Horse" Ianniello, who was convicted of skimming from the Peppermint Lounge and several other bars and restaurants he owned), the club reopened under new management in November 1980 before moving downtown in 1982. During the short revival at the original location, Jagger was spotted at the club.

The Stones also made their first US television appearance on *The Les Crane Show*, though it was only an interview that included numerous comments from the host about Brian Jones's hair. Oldham later called Crane a "stagger-brained, lacquered pimp with a smile and demeanor so cut out and fake we felt like we'd stopped off on the wrong set and were in *Hogan's Heroes* meets *The Twilight Zone*."

The Stones found time to explore New York the next day. Watts visited the Metropole Cafe, a famed Times Square jazz club, and Charlie Parker's Birdland in its original location on Broadway. Over the first few US tours, Watts saw Gene Krupa, Sonny Rollins (who would later play sax on three tracks on the Stones' *Tattoo You* album), and Charles Mingus perform in New York clubs. Richards and Oldham visited the nearby Colony Records (where Richards bought Lenny Bruce records) and the Brill Building, where they were denied a meeting with Elvis Presley songwriter Jerry Leiber. According to Oldham, "The Brill Building and its great writer/producers like Leiber and Stoller had not yet gotten over the 'British Invasion,' even though most of the writers were doing fine by us." They were, however, given a song written by Leiber and Brill Building mainstay Artie Butler titled "Down Home Girl," which they would record in Los Angeles during their second American visit. It appeared on the UK album *The Rolling Stones No. 2* and on the US album *The Rolling Stones, Now!* That evening the Stones attended a party at the Dakota Building on 72nd Street thrown for them by Bob Crewe, the New Jersey-born producer who helped make the Four Seasons superstars. At the party, Murray the K reiterated his suggestion that the Stones record "It's All Over Now," and gave Oldham a copy of the single.

Outside of New York and other big cities, they found a different America. Richards wrote in *Life*, "There was the stark thing you discovered about America—it was civilized round the edges, but fifty miles inland from any major American city, whether it was New York, Chicago, L.A. or Washington, you really did go into another world." Being relatively unknown didn't help matters, with Richards adding, "Back in England we had a number one album, but out in the middle of America nobody knew who we were. They were more aware of the Dave Clark Five and the Swinging Blue Jeans. In some towns we got some real hostility, real killer looks in our direction. Sometimes we got the sense that an exemplary lesson was about to be taught us, right then and there."

Jagger felt the same. "New York was wonderful and so on, and L.A. was also kind of interesting. But outside of that we found it the most repressive society, very prejudiced in every way. There was still segregation. And the attitudes were fantastically old-fashioned. Americans shocked me by their behavior and their narrow-mindedness."

The tour started in California on June 5 and featured eleven concerts in eight cities, concluding with two shows at Carnegie Hall in New York on June 20.

Early on June 20, the Stones appeared on *The Clay Cole Show* on a special episode called "The Beatles vs. The Rolling Stones." Cole's rock music television show had launched in 1959 and had aired on local station WPIX since 1963. Previously, he'd hosted the show during the summer from New Jersey's Palisades Amusement Park, the subject of Freddy Cannon's 1962 hit song "Palisades Park." With the move to WPIX, Cole moved to a Manhattan studio. When Cole was offered the opportunity to host a special edition of his show featuring both the Stones and the Beatles, he obviously saw it as a huge opportunity. Cole had the Stones live in his studio and received a satellite feed from Chicago of concert footage of the Beatles. (Though Cole claimed in his autobiography that the footage aired on a live feed, the Beatles did not perform in Chicago until September 5, 1964. On June 20, 1964, the Beatles were performing in Sydney, Australia. Exactly when the footage of the Beatles was taped remains unknown, and tapes of Cole's broadcasts have long been lost.) In his autobiography *Sh-Boom!: The Explosion of Rock 'n' Roll (1953–1968)*, Cole recalls: "When we brought girls to the stage for some one-on-one questioning, the segment fell apart— the girls were dumbstruck and giddy, and the Stones were preoccupied bird watching, soaking up their first whiff of teenage America." He also criticized the Stones for their lack of personal hygiene. The band mimed "Tell Me," "Carol," and "Not Fade Away" while Jagger sang live. The program was the highest-rated episode of *The Clay Cole Show* ever, and WPIX aired it three more times that week. That success only hinted at what the band was to expect at their two shows at Carnegie Hall later that day.

Built in 1891 on Seventh Avenue between West 56th Street and West 57th Street, Carnegie Hall is renowned for both its internal and external architecture and has always been regarded as having some of the best acoustics in the city, making it the premier stage for classical concerts for decades. In 1962, the New York Philharmonic, which had been the resident company of the hall since shortly after it opened, left for the newly constructed Lincoln Center. That same year the venue was declared a National Historic Landmark, protecting it from demolition, a fate it nearly faced in the 1950s. By that time, Carnegie Hall hosted events ranging from classical to country music.

A National Historic Landmark might seem like an awkward fit for the Stones, but Carnegie Hall had infrequently hosted rock concerts since Bill Haley & His Comets played there in May 1955. The Beatles played there on February 12, 1964, and the Dave Clark Five followed with two shows in May. The response to the Stones in New York was again far more positive than on the rest of their tour. "The temperature was 92 degrees," Wyman recalls, "and nobody, including the police, thought the fans would come early, but when we arrived we were confronted by dozens outside. We were eventually dragged into the stage entrance by the police. The compere, Murray the K, introduced us individually to the audience, which went crazy." The audience at the first show nearly rushed the stage. Carnegie Hall management and the police requested that the Stones cancel the second show. The Stones refused. The audience at the evening performance wasn't any better behaved. Wyman would later remark that the mainly female crowd was whipped into such a frenzy by the Stones' performances that rock concerts were banned from the venue for a year. Rock journalist Al Aronowitz confirmed the insanity when he wrote in his obituary of Jones several years later, "To walk into Carnegie Hall to hear them for the first time was to have a bucket of sound splashed into your face. The Stones didn't play concerts in those days. What they played were riots." None other than Chuck Berry would bring rock and roll back to Carnegie Hall with a series of concerts in June 1965. Not surprisingly, the Stones were never invited back.

The relative failure of the Stones' first US tour was a consequence of timing. When the band returned for its second tour in October, the landscape had changed dramatically. On September 9, the Associated Press reported the shocker that the Rolling Stones had replaced the Beatles as the most popular band on the weekly *Melody Maker* poll in the UK. The Stones released their fourth US single, "Time Is on My Side," on September 26 and their second US album, *12 X 5*, on October 17. Their cover of the jazz song "Time Is on My Side" became the band's first top-ten US hit, peaking at number six, while the album became the group's first top-ten album by reaching number three on the Billboard charts (their first album peaked at number eleven). When the Stones arrived at Kennedy airport on October 23 for their second American tour, they had something they lacked the first time around—momentum. As Wyman put it, "The huge interest in British pop that was building up over there meant we anticipated much greater success than our first mediocre trip, which we now realized had been premature. On our last trip people were curious. This time there was excitement: we were knocked sideways with the news that our American fan club had grown to 52,000-strong."

The Stones gave a requisite press conference at Kennedy, and having a hit record made all the difference. The "insane asylum" that had met the band at their hotel during the first arrival had multiplied a hundredfold. The Stones' hotel press conference—their second press conference of the day—became a mob scene when teenager girls posing as "high school press representatives" flooded the event. Shortly afterward the Stones split for rehearsals for their most important television appearance yet and then attempted to relax at the Peppermint Lounge, which proved impossible once they were swarmed by fans.

October 24, the first day of the tour, held a full schedule, starting with their second appearances on Murray the K's show and *The Clay Cole Show*. The band followed these with two performances at the Academy of Music. Located on East 14th Street between Irving Place and Third Avenue, the venue was opened as a movie palace in 1927 and, despite its name, still operated primarily as a movie theater, though it was increasingly becoming popular for rock concerts. A second show was added that evening after the original quickly sold out. As promoter Sid Bernstein wrote in his autobiography about the Stones' performance at the Academy of Music later, in May 1965:

> On the day of the Stones concerts, I arrived at the theater early and visited with the band.... Before leaving the guys prior to showtime, I said, "Listen, take it easy out there. We don't want to get thrown out of here, too!" Take it easy? Not for a minute.
>
> The Academy of Music was an old vaudeville house with an orchestra pit separating the audience from the stage, and the kids got so excited they began to rush the stage, trying to leap over the chasm of the pit. There were so many bodies pushing in the same direction that they overwhelmed the security men, and [co-promoter Billy Fields] and I found ourselves flat on our fannies. Bodies were flying all over the place, and some kids landed right in the pit, one on top of another.

Tiny, our six-foot six-inch lead security man, jumped right in there and started throwing the kids back out. It had to be an act of God that no one got hurt. Fortunately for the Stones, they had their own security men, who blocked off stage right and left.

It was something to behold—that day in May 1965 when the Rolling Stones rocked the Academy of Music.

The Stones would play the Academy four more times in 1965, and then again when it was known as the Palladium in 1979. Regardless of how the audience acted at the two Academy shows, the Stones' first national television appearance the next day was even more monumental.

After the Beatles' appearance on *The Ed Sullivan Show* made them household names, the Stones' management worked hard to secure a spot on the program, which finally paid off in the fall of 1964 once "Time Is on My Side" became a hit. Sullivan hosted some of the greatest entertainers of the mid-twentieth century. His family-friendly evening program aired Sunday evenings and was frequently the top-watched program in the country, making an appearance by a band a huge opportunity. Elvis's first appearance in 1956 had had sixty million viewers (which accounted for over 80 percent of the televisions in the US at the time), and the Beatles' first appearance in February had seventy-three million.

Sullivan was notorious for his harsh temper. Bo Diddley was banned from the program after he played a different song than he had agreed to play in his November 1955 appearance. Buddy Holly was banned after his second appearance in January 1958 when he similarly disagreed with Sullivan over what song he should perform. (Sullivan begrudgingly invited Holly back due to his significant popularity, but Holly turned him down.) Bob Dylan never even made it on the program for his scheduled May 1963 appearance when he was told during rehearsals that he couldn't perform the politically charged "Talkin' John Birch Paranoid Blues." He walked out.

Wyman recalled that once they arrived at CBS-TV Studio 50 on October 25—now known as the Ed Sullivan Theater and home to *The Late Show*—the Stones "were prisoners for the whole day" because they could not leave the building due to the masses of fans outside.

Prior to the Stones' taking the stage, the mostly teenage audience sat through the husband-and-wife comedy team Stiller and Meara, followed by nineteen-year-old Itzhak Perlman, the famed Israeli violinist whom Sullivan had introduced to the American public in 1958. When it was time, the Stones emerged from behind a rising curtain playing Chuck Berry's "Around and Around," eliciting shrieks and wails from the girls. Unlike the Beatles and the Dave Clark Five, who all wore matching suits on their appearances, only Richards, Watts, and Jones wore suits, and they didn't match—Watts wore a lighter jacket than the others and Richards didn't wear a tie. Wyman wore a pair of light slacks and a vest, while Jagger looked casual in a simple sweater and uncombed hair.

Jagger showed off his James Brown-inspired toe-tapping dance moves during Richards's two guitar solos. Repeated shots of the audience showed bobbing, screaming, and even crying girls. When the song ended and Sullivan returned to the stage, he rolled his eyes at the commotion and pleaded with the audience to quiet down for the next, far less exciting acts.

The Stones returned in the second half of the show to perform "Time Is on My Side." Even without dancing, Jagger's spoken monologue during the guitar solo sent the audience into hysterics. When the camera returned to Sullivan, he seemed at a total loss for words, and the shrieks drowned out his attempt to interview Jagger. It was like the Beatles all over again, except this group of musicians wasn't as cheerfully likable.

The next day Sullivan told the press that not only would he never have the Stones on again—"So help me, the untidy Rolling Stones will never again darken our portals," he said—but that he'd also no longer feature rock 'n' roll bands or have teenagers in the audience. That sentiment did not last long, or it was simply a ploy to save face with angry

25

parents. Wyman revealed that the band received a message from Sullivan several days later that said, "Received hundreds of letters from parents complaining about you, but thousands from teenagers saying how much they enjoyed your performance."

The Stones' second US tour was the complete opposite of the first. The band played to rioting crowds all across the country, and even headlined a festival in Santa Monica, California, with James Brown, the Beach Boys, and Chuck Berry that was filmed and later released as the movie *T.A.M.I. Show* in December. The tour included a near riot in Providence, Rhode Island, on November 4 when girls would not stop rushing the stage, causing the temporary cover over the theater's orchestra pit to collapse. The Stones left after only five songs.

The band then took an all-night train back to New York that arrived at Grand Central Terminal—a location that would play an important part in Stones history more than twenty years later. With a few days off, Watts continued spending late nights in jazz clubs, while Wyman and Jones spent time with WINS disc jockey Scott Ross. Though Ross was born in Scotland, his family had moved to Maryland when he was a boy. In the 1960s he began working at WINS, and he took over the emcee duties of the Stones' New York concerts from Murray the K. He was far closer in age to the Stones than Kaufman and, being a fellow Brit, he struck up a fast friendship with them as well as the Beatles (he also later married Nedra Talley of the Ronettes).

Jagger and Richards spent one of the off days with the Ronettes at Jones Beach on Long Island, despite the fall weather, and then went with Oldham to the Apollo Theater in Harlem to see James Brown. "James Brown had the whole week there at the Apollo," Richards wrote in his book. "Go to the Apollo and see James Brown, damn fucking right. I mean, who would turn that down?" Brown noticed Jagger and Richards in the audience and asked them to come onstage for a bow.

Ronnie Bennett, later known as Ronnie Spector, brought Jagger and Richards backstage to meet Brown and his band. (She recalls, "I remember Mick standing there shaking when we passed James Brown's room.") Jagger and Richards spent the night at Ronnie and

Estelle's mother's home in Spanish Harlem, where an on-again, off-again romance between Richards and Ronnie began.

Wyman, Jones, and Ross wound up seeing bluesman John Hammond at the Village Gate, the famed Greenwich Village nightclub on the corner of Thompson and Bleecker Streets. The group had arrived too late for Dizzy Gillespie's performance. A number of live albums, such as future Stones collaborator Sonny Rollins' 1962 album *Our Man in Jazz*, were recorded in the club, and Bob Dylan wrote his song "A Hard Rain's A-Gonna Fall" in the basement apartment. Despite the Village Gate's closing in 1993, its sign still hangs above the former location.

In the early morning of November 8, the band flew to Chicago to record tracks at Chess Studios, and after going out on the road in the Midwest, the band returned to Chicago on November 15 for the final show of their second American tour. The year 1964 turned out to be extraordinary for the Stones. The band went from being virtually unknown in America to being one of the top-selling bands in the country with only one top-ten single and one top-ten album to its name. By the time the Stones returned to North America in April 1965, they would have their first top-ten US single written by Jagger and Richards, "The Last Time," and would be weeks away from achieving their first number-one single on both sides of the Atlantic. If the Stones thought they had faced pandemonium in 1964, they were unprepared for what the rest of the 1960s would bring them.

CHAPTER 2

"LET'S SPEND SOME TIME TOGETHER"

Ed Sullivan's promise to American parents lasted just six months. The band's third US album, *The Rolling Stones, Now!*, was released in February 1965 and peaked at number five on the album charts. In December the album's single, the Jagger-Richards-penned ballad "Heart of Stone," was released and peaked at number nineteen in the United States.

After playing a few shows in Canada to start their 1965 North American tour, the Stones returned to New York on April 27 and went with Scott Ross to Bob Crewe's apartment again. Jones, feeling increasingly persona non grata within the band he founded, spent a few days at Ross's West 85th Street apartment and discussed quitting the Stones and being a no-show at the band's upcoming recording sessions in Chicago. Ross recalls in Wyman's autobiography,

> "I tried to talk him out of it, and at least realize that it was a pretty big decision with big implications if he didn't show up at the sessions. But he didn't care. He just said he couldn't do it, wasn't in the frame of mind to record. He was angry, despondent, so he came to New York and stayed with me for about three days. He talked about it a lot, how he was on his own, and felt like he was being cut out."

Nothing came of it for several years, but the internal strife between Jones and the rest of the band, particularly Jagger and Richards, would eventually come to a head.

The next day the Stones rehearsed at CBS-TV Studio 50 for their appearance on *The Ed Sullivan Show* four days later. After the rehearsal, Jagger, Richards, and Jones saw Wilson Pickett perform at the Apollo. The group was back on the road early the next morning to arrive in time for two shows upstate at the Palace Theatre in Albany.

The Stones returned to Manhattan on May 1 to play an afternoon show at the Academy of Music and then hustled out to play an evening show in Philadelphia as part of a festival hosted by *American Bandstand*'s Dick Clark. The band members returned to New York to play *The Ed Sullivan Show*, and to indicate their rise in popularity, played twice as many songs this time: "The Last Time," "Little Red Rooster," "Everybody Needs Somebody to Love," and "2120 South Michigan Avenue," which was played as the show ended. To assuage complaints about the clothing they wore during their first appearance, they all wore suit jackets, although they didn't match (especially with Jagger wearing a checkered button-down shirt with no tie). The band performed "The Last Time" in a set filled with lamps, and the show featured a great angled shot that had Jagger, Richards, and a surprisingly smiling Watts all in the frame.

The screams were less pronounced this time until Jagger started pointing to the audience as he sang "you, you, you" during "Everybody Needs Somebody to Love," which set the audience into a frenzy. Unlike with the first appearance, there were no shots of the hysterical audience. Sullivan's team obviously made some tweaks to the formula, but the sheer popularity of the band was impossible to ignore.

That night, the Stones attended a press reception for them and Welsh singer Tom Jones, who had also appeared on the show that night, at the Playboy Club on East 59th Street, opposite the southeast corner of Central Park. On the way to the club, Jagger, Richards, and Jones got into a fight with a group of men in a convertible who called the Stones faggots. (In his autobiography, Wyman recounts that one of his girlfriends "vividly remembers Keith booting one of them in the mouth.")

The next day the Stones recorded an appearance on *The Clay Cole Show*, which aired on May 29. Some sources claim that this was the episode when Cole presented the "Beatles vs. the Rolling Stones" special, though Cole's autobiography and numerous Cole obituaries say that it was during the Stones' first appearance on the program in 1964. Because the tapes of Cole's shows are long gone, there is no way to verify when "Beatles vs. the Rolling Stones" actually aired.

On May 4, the Stones were back on the road, this time touring the South. It was on this trip that Richards composed the riff to "(I Can't Get No) Satisfaction," which the band started recording when the tour swung up to Chicago. The Stones finished the song in Los Angeles on May 12 when they arrived for the California portion of their tour. The tour ended on May 29 back in New York City with three shows at the Academy of Music, followed by a party at Ondine, a small nightclub on 59th Street between First and Second Avenues that catered to the celebrity crowd. That night Jones dropped acid with Eric Burdon and Hilton Valentine of the Animals, another popular British Invasion band.

After the Stones were back in England, "(I Can't Get No) Satisfaction" was released in the US on June 6. After immediately entering the charts, the single hit number one on July 10, stayed there for four weeks, and soon became the Stones' first gold single. The incendiary lyrics shouted by Jagger were a modern take on classic blues themes (the title recalls Muddy Waters' classic "I Can't Be Satisfied"), while Richards's commanding riff played on a Gibson Maestro fuzz box was like something from another world. Notably, New York's WABC aired an edited version of "Satisfaction" that excised the "trying to make some girl" line. It made little difference. With "Satisfaction," the Stones finally created their own sound and anthem, and the band's popularity continued to explode.

* * * * *

As Wyman details extensively in his autobiography, despite the Stones' being one of the most famous pop bands in the world, the members' bank accounts were shockingly low. In fact, the band's finances were a wreck. Oldham might have succeeded in breaking the Stones, but he didn't know the first thing about handling money. Oldham thought he had found the solution when he met Allen Klein, a New Jersey-born businessman who caused ripples throughout the music industry when he renegotiated singer Sam Cooke's contract with RCA. Executives had refused to perform an audit despite Cooke's repeated requests. Klein got RCA to open their books and then negotiated a groundbreaking deal that secured Cooke a nearly half-million-dollar advance. Klein's work for Cooke as well as bands like the Dave Clark Five, the Animals, and Herman's Hermits gave him a reputation for being an artist-friendly negotiator who got artists maximum money with a minimal tax burden by orchestrating deferred payments from the labels and, in turn, from his New York office. The deals were beneficial to the artists but even more beneficial to Klein, who profited on the money he held.

To Oldham, Klein was the answer to the Stones' business problems. Shortly after they met, Oldham hired Klein to negotiate a new contract with Decca Records. On July 26, Jagger's twenty-sixth birthday, the Stones met Klein in London to discuss hiring him as their business manager. Of course, Oldham had already hired him and two days earlier, in a private meeting, had convinced Jagger and Richards to support him on the matter. Over the summer Klein negotiated a lucrative new deal, which would pay the Stones $3 million over the next five years. The Stones were so thrilled that Klein soon replaced Eric Easton as the band's co-manager.

Klein began planning and promoting the Stones' next American tour, which was to begin at the end of October.

In the midst of these financial and management issues, Jagger, Richards, and Oldham flew to New York to attend the Beatles' historic concert at Shea Stadium on August 15. The two stayed at the luxurious Drake Hotel at Park Avenue and 56th Street. Jagger and Richards first conducted a small press conference on Klein's yacht on the Hudson River. That day Klein asked his nephew, Ron Schneider, to accompany the Stones on future tours to manage the group's finances. Schneider then attended the concert with Jagger, Richards, Oldham, Klein, and promoter Peter Bennett. The group sat in the visitors' dugout and were blown away by the sheer size of the venue and the fifty-five thousand screaming fans, though in a 2015 interview with the *Daily News*, Richards dismissed the performance, saying, "As a band, they weren't in sync with each other." Little did Jagger and Richards know that they would perform in the same venue nearly twenty-five years later.

The Beatles' first concert at Shea Stadium entered the annals of rock legend the moment the last fan exited the stadium. Even riding on the top of "Satisfaction," which was released as a single in the UK in August and quickly repeated its number-one success, the Stones were not at the level of the Beatles in the United States. Whereas the Beatles played forty-thousand-plus-seat stadiums or two shows in fifteen-thousand-plus-seat arenas during their 1965 tour, the Stones tour that started less than two months later was booked into a mixture of twelve-thousand-plus-seat arenas and theaters that had fewer than five thousand seats. Yet again the Stones were scheduled to play New York's Academy of Music (this time with a concert at Philadelphia's Convention Hall later on the same day) on November 6, followed by two shows the next day at Newark, New Jersey's three-thousand-seat Symphony Hall. The number of people at all four shows totaled barely half of the people at Shea Stadium. However, the lower attendance wasn't a result of a lack of fans. The Stones' follow-up single, "Get Off of My Cloud," became the band's second number-one US hit during the tour, and their July 1965 album, *Out of Our Heads,* and December 1965 album, *December's Children (And Everybody's),* hit number one and number four, respectively, on the album charts. The Stones were selling thousands of albums and singles, but the 1965 US tour was booked as if the band's managers were unsure about their drawing power. The Stones felt that signing with the well-connected Klein would lead them to bookings in larger venues for future tours. Even more important, the Stones realized that arena shows would give them more space from the wild audiences that were constantly threatening to tear them apart.

When the Stones arrived in New York on October 27 for their fourth American tour, they were greeted by a gigantic billboard in Times Square paid for by Klein promoting *December's Children (And Everybody's)*. The band stayed at the City Squire Hotel on Seventh Avenue between 52nd and 53rd Streets (now the Sheraton New York hotel) after having been turned down by the 54th Street Warwick Hotel. Being rejected by New York hotels would become something of a problem for the band on their next tour.

The next day the Stones held a press conference in the penthouse of the New York Hilton, the Sixth Avenue Midtown hotel that had opened in 1963 (at the time, it was the largest hotel in the city) and had already made rock history as the hotel where the Beatles stayed during their first visit to New York. Like their last New York press conference, this one was hijacked by the teenage girl "reporters" who ended up in the press pool. When asked if the unmarried Stones—Jagger, Richards, and Jones—dated their fans, Jagger said yes. When asked how old they had to be, Jagger quipped, "Sixteen or eighteen, depending on which state we are in."

After the press conference, Watts went to Manny's Music on West 48th Street between Sixth and Seventh Avenues—the street was called "Music Row" for its number of instrument retailers, most of which are gone now—and bought a set of drums that he shipped back to England. The legendary shop, founded in 1933, was considered one of the premier music shops in the world for its seventy-six-year existence until 2009. The store was founded by Manny Goldrich, who operated the store until his death in 1969, when the store moved to its third and final location on the same block at 156 West 48th Street. In his autobiography, Wyman records that Watts made sure to send his wife, Shirley, flowers along with the drums. Wyman also marks that night as the first time Brian Jones met Bob Dylan, an acquaintanceship that reached several different levels over the last four years of Jones's life.

The tour began the next day, October 29, in Montreal. As with the previous North American tour, the Stones were greeted by hysterical fans and sometimes violence wherever they went. The Stones' angry response to the local police during their November 1 concert in Rochester, New York, went out as an Associated Press report. The police ended the show after the Stones played only seven songs because of the raucous crowd, leading to Richards's shouting at the authorities, "This is a hick town. They were twice as wild in Montreal. They won't get hurt. You're too hard with them." Despite the strong-armed shutdown, there were only two people with reported injuries, including one police officer, out of the 3,500 attendees.

The tour made its way back to New York on November 6 for the Academy of Music concert. Then the band members rushed off for the Philadelphia show immediately afterward, before returning to New York for three days before their next date on November 10 in North Carolina. The three days in New York City turned out to be eventful.

The night of November 6, the whole band met up with Bob Dylan at a nightclub called the Phone Booth at 152 East 55th Street between Third and Lexington Avenues. The club's gimmick was that each table had a working telephone that could be used to order table service. At the club, Jones was accompanied by Nico, the German-born singer, model, and actress who had previously recorded a cover of Gordon Lightfoot's "I'm Not Sayin,'" featuring guitar by Jimmy Page for Andrew Loog Oldham's independent record label Immediate Records. Jones had produced the song, and the two had an on-again, off-again sexual relationship. At the Phone Booth, Jones introduced Nico to pop artist Andy Warhol. Nico would become one of Warhol's famed "Superstars" and Warhol would later arrange the famed collaboration album between Nico and the Velvet Underground. Warhol himself would cross paths with the Stones many times over the next two decades. After getting into a bar fight, Jones left with Dylan to hop the clubs in Greenwich Village and, according to Wyman, Jones ended up recording a song with Wilson Pickett and Bob Dylan in a studio early on the morning of November 7, although the song in question has never surfaced. As usual, Watts went on his normal Manhattan jazz odyssey.

The Stones played two shows on November 7 at the Newark Symphony Hall, a historic theater built in 1925 that was used mainly for classical music and opera performances but had begun to be used for popular music concerts and comedy shows once it was purchased by the City of Newark in 1964. Both performances were delayed because the Stones showed up late (the blame was attributed to Jones, who was paranoid that he was a wanted man because of the previous night's fight). Afterward, the Stones returned to Manhattan and remained in town for one of the most notable events of the 1960s—the November 9 blackout.

"Where were you when the lights went out?" became a popular question (and the title of a 1968 Doris Day film) after a power surge at 5:16 p.m. overloaded power lines and caused most of the northeastern United States—including nearly all of New York City—and Ontario, Canada, to lose power over the next ten minutes. Most of NYC remained powerless for more than twelve hours. Despite the nearly citywide blackout, police reported a remarkably low level of crime, as residents remained mostly indoors. Since the blackout occurred shortly after the workday ended, thousands of commuters turned to Manhattan hotel rooms for the night or simply walked across the bridges when traffic became impossible. The Stones had already checked out of the City Squire when the hotel kindly requested they find different accommodations because the massive number of fans crowding the lobby made it impossible for the hotel to operate. The band moved to the Lincoln Square Motor Inn at 66th Street and Broadway.

During the blackout, Wyman and his friends managed to accidentally set fire to his room with the hotel-supplied candles. Wyman recalls that it was the first night he smoked pot. Bob Dylan visited Jones's room, and legend has it that Dylan greeted Jones with the enigmatic question, "Hey, Brian, how's your paranoia meter running now?" Along with Robbie Robertson of the Band and folk musician Bob Neuwirth, the group smoked joints and jammed among a bevy of naked women.

The Stones made a quick trip to Raleigh, North Carolina, for a concert on November 10, and despite having a show in Greensboro, North Carolina, on November 12 the band used the off day to return to New York to record an appearance on the short-lived prime-time music variety show *Hullabaloo*, which NBC had launched in January. Unlike the group's 1964 and 1965 appearances on *The Ed Sullivan Show*, the performances of "She Said Yeah" and "Get Off of My Cloud" were mimed by the band, with only the vocals being live. It was remarkable how much more casual the Stones were dressed compared to their last Sullivan appearance, with only Watts wearing a suit. Richards wore eyeglasses, a rare look for him, and Jones was dressed completely in black, so the camera barely showed him because he blended in with the background. The performance aired on November 15. After that, the Stones were done with New York City for the tour, which ended on December 5 in Los Angeles and was followed by a few days of recording at RCA Studios in Hollywood.

Though the band broke for much of December, Jones returned to New York City and spent more time with Bob Dylan. Jones and Dylan had a curious relationship. Jones idolized Dylan. According to Wyman, Dylan told the audience at his October 1, 1965, concert at Carnegie Hall that he wrote the song "Like a Rolling Stone" about Jones. Although many others have been identified as possible subjects of the song (its true subject is a matter of dispute), many of the lyrics could be a reflection of Jones's state of mind in 1965 as he contemplated leaving the Stones. Wyman also claims that Jones was paranoid about the fact that the lyrics of "Ballad of a Thin Man" were about him.

Rock journalist Al Aronowitz, who became acquainted with Jones during his New York visits, wrote in the *New York Herald Tribune* about a wild night he spent hanging with Dylan, Jones, Robbie Robertson, and Bob Neuwirth. The night involved the group's riding around in Jones's limousine barhopping, including another visit to the Phone Booth and a visit to an underground movie theater on Lafayette Street. Aronowitz recorded Dylan's cryptic off-the-cuff remarks and noted that the entire time, Dylan kept a Temptations album tucked inside his jacket.

Dylan's interactions with Jones weren't always friendly. An oft-repeated tale that has been recorded in numerous sources involves Dylan insulting Jones one night at Max's Kansas City, the Park Avenue South nightclub that opened in December 1965 and became a favorite hangout of celebrities and musicians. Founder Mickey Ruskin, who had previously operated several coffeehouses and bars, opened Max's as a venue for music and art, and the stage would eventually be graced by the likes of the Velvet Underground, Aerosmith, Bob Marley & the Wailers, Tom Waits, New York Dolls, the Ramones, Blondie, Bruce Springsteen, and Sid Vicious. Dylan mocked Jones by telling him the Stones were awful, ridiculed him for his poor singing skills, and declared Jones as the weak link in the Stones. Once Jones was in tears, Dylan told him to cheer up and offered Jones a spot in his band, an offer that Jones took seriously, according to Wyman, though Jones never had the chance to take Dylan up on it.

* * * * *

The end of 1965 brought the end of Mayor Wagner's term in office. Republican US congressman John Lindsay, a Yale-educated World War II veteran highly regarded by New Yorkers for his liberal voting record in Congress, was elected mayor. He had been a leading voice of support for the Civil Rights Act of 1964. Lindsay, however, had what was perhaps the worst first day a New York City mayor ever faced. The two major transportation unions, the Transport Workers Union (TWU) and the Amalgamated Transit Union (ATU), went on a citywide strike the morning of New Year's Day that halted all subway and bus service for twelve days. The workers were eventually given higher wages and additional benefits. Although Lindsay was initially hailed by the press for ending the strike, the terms of the settlement with the transit unions forced him to seek additional tax revenue from city residents and commuters to the city. His administration saw several strikes by public workers over the next five years, further crushing his popularity.

The Rolling Stones began 1966 with two hit singles in the US. Their version of "As Tears Go By," which had been written by Jagger, Richards, and Oldham and become a top-ten hit in the UK when it was previously recorded by Marianne Faithfull, was released in December 1965 in the US. It peaked at number six on the US charts. In February, the Stones released "19th Nervous Breakdown," which peaked at number two. One of the reasons why "19th Nervous Breakdown" vaulted up the charts is that the Stones flew to New York to appear on *The Ed Sullivan Show* for the third time on February 13 while en route to Australia for a tour. The Stones arrived for rehearsals early in the day, but were forced to stay in the theater for nine hours because the number of fans amassed outside made it too dangerous for them to leave.

The Stones opened with "Satisfaction" to the shrieks of the audience. All the Stones wore jackets except for Jagger, who wore a bright red dress shirt. (This was the band's first appearance on *Sullivan* in color, after all.) There wasn't a tie in sight. Jagger was far more animated in his movements than he'd been in their prior appearances, swinging his microphone stand back and forth. He changed into a white dress shirt and a jacket for "As Tears Go By." Jagger and Richards (on acoustic guitar) performed the song accompanied only by a track of the string arrangement. The audience's continuing shrieks seem completely out of place during the subdued ballad. Jagger was even more energetic during "19th Nervous Breakdown," and that energy almost took the single to the top of the US charts.

Between the end of recording in Los Angeles on March 9 and the start of the band's 1966 European tour on March 26, Jones visited New York again. A cheeky article in Britain's *New Musical Express* described Jones's arriving in England four days later than his fellow Stones "due to the fact that clubs in New York [are] open 24 hours a day and he had been in one four days with an insane Welsh harpist called 'Hari Hari' waiting for it to close!" The story offered a peek into Jones's increasing interest in both Eastern music and drugs, two issues that would eventually drive him out of the band.

In a move that was at least partially fueled by public relations, in late June the Stones sued fourteen of the most elite hotels in New York City for $5 million ($1 million for each Stone) for refusing to book the band in mid-June before their 1966 American tour. The Stones claimed they were being discriminated against "on account of their national origin." Considering that the Stones had trashed nearly every hotel room they had ever slept in throughout Manhattan and that their fans flooded the lobbies of every hotel they stayed at, the hotels' refusal to book them was not surprising. In his syndicated column "It Happened Last Night," *New York Post* gossip columnist Earl Wilson wrote that the Stones solved their lodging issues by staying on a yacht on the East River. However, Wyman's autobiography says that when the group arrived on June 23, they stayed at the Holiday Inn (presumably the one by Kennedy Airport), calling it "the only decent hotel that would have us." That suggests the East River yacht story was a cover to dissuade fans from trying to track them down in the only hotel that would give them beds. In his column the previous week, Wilson reported that residents were petitioning Mayor Lindsay to cancel the Stones concert that was scheduled at the Forest Hills Stadium in Queens. This forced the Stones to hire extra security to dispel concerns about potentially rowdy crowds.

The night of the Stones' arrival, Wyman received a call from bluesman John Hammond, who asked him to come to A&R Recording Studios at 112 West 48th Street to play bass on a few tracks. Jones and Ian Stewart accompanied Wyman to the session (though they didn't participate), and the tracks were released on Hammond's 1967 album *I Can Tell*. The group hung out with Hammond afterward.

The following morning, the Stones held a press function on the S.S. *Sea Panther* as the yacht cruised around Manhattan, to promote the recently released US version of *Aftermath* as well as the tour, which would begin that evening with a show at the Manning Bowl in Lynn, Massachusetts. On the *Sea Panther* was Linda Eastman, a budding photographer for *Town & Country* magazine. It was her first rock photography assignment, and her photos of the band in various relaxed poses brought her instant recognition. Jagger invited Eastman to a party the following week in New York hosted by photographer Jerry Schatzberg, whom the Stones would work with later. After bedding Jagger, Eastman would write about her "date" with the rock star for the teen magazine *Datebook*. Less than a year later she would meet Paul McCartney when she took photos of the Beatles during the *Sgt. Pepper's Lonely Hearts Club Band* press tour. The two would marry in 1969, remaining together until her death in 1998.

The Times appeared to have not warmed up to the Stones by the time they returned for their sole New York appearance at the Forest Hills Stadium in Queens, a stadium the Beatles had played twice in August 1964. It was the band's largest New York show to date, and their first outside of Manhattan. Though the Stones had certainly played upscale venues before in New York, it's still somewhat surprising that the West Side Tennis Club allowed the raucous Stones to play. The venue, which is surrounded by Tudor-style houses in the exclusive Forest Hills Gardens private neighborhood, had hosted the US Open Tennis Championships from 1915 to 1920 and then from 1924 on (during the interval it was played in Philadelphia). In the 1950s, the stadium began hosting concerts. Early performers included Judy Garland, Barbra Streisand, and Frank Sinatra, but rock performers started appearing at the fourteen-thousand-seat venue in the early 1960s, including Ray Charles, Bob Dylan, and the Beatles. The tennis scenes in Alfred Hitchcock's 1951 film *Strangers on a Train* were also filmed at the stadium.

The US Open moved to its present location, the USTA Billie Jean King National Tennis Center, in 1977. The complex is less than three miles away from Forest Hills and was built adjacent to Shea Stadium in Flushing Meadows–Corona Park on the former grounds of the 1964–1965 World's Fair. Forest Hills continued hosting concerts until 1984, and aside from a brief return in 1997, the stadium did not return to hosting concerts on a regular basis until 2013. Nearly fifty years later, the Rolling Stones concert at Forest Hills would provide the setting for a 2012 episode of the 1960s-set television series *Mad Men* titled "Tea Leaves."

The 9,400 fans (not including 250 police officers and 125 security officers) who came to Forest Hills on July 2 for the 1966 music festival headlined by the Stones were apparently not enough of an audience to impress reporter Robert Shelton. The heading for *The Times'* review reads "Middling Turnout Fails to Dull Teen-Age Excitement," and the piece notes the smaller-than-expected turnout several times. The Stones were characteristically late—their helicopter did not arrive until 10:15—and played only a thirty-five-minute set. Nonetheless, Shelton remarks that the Stones "were completely charming and very disciplined musicians" and calls Jagger "a fascinating performer to watch. He does a nimble rock 'n' roll ballet, dancing around alone or with the microphone in another grand old Negro performing tradition."

Variety published an analytical piece wondering whether the Stones and other British Invasion bands had run their course based on their failure to fill even 70 percent of the venue. *The Times* remarked, "The middling attendance at a stadium that seats 14,000 was attributed by some to the heat. Others believed that interest in British rock groups is declining and the scaling of tickets from $5 to $12.50 has simply become too much for the young fans." Of course, the "others" who believed that the Stones' popularity was waning seem like awful assessors of popularity in retrospect, but even in the context of July 1966 it was a poor choice of words. The Stones had five US top-ten singles in the previous year and would have another number-one hit less than six months later. The low attendance could have been from a combination of the upper-nineties-degree heat or the more-expensive-than-usual tickets—the two Beatles shows at Forest Hills in August 1964 sold all sixteen thousand tickets for both shows, with prices ranging from $1.95 to $7.50—but it certainly wasn't a case of diminishing popularity. After all, the Stones completely sold out the 17,500 tickets to the July 25 Hollywood Bowl show and the sixteen thousand tickets for the June 24 Manning Bowl show.

That night the Stones went into Manhattan and saw a much-buzzed-about band, Jimmy James and the Blue Flames. The bandleader would eventually be better known as Jimi Hendrix. Sources differ on where the Stones saw James that night. Many claim it was at Cafe Wha?, the Greenwich Village institution at 115 MacDougal Street that was founded by Manny Roth, uncle of later Van Halen frontman, David Lee Roth. The club opened in 1959 and saw numerous famous musicians and comedians grace its stage, including Bob Dylan. Although the original Cafe Wha? closed in 1968, it was reopened in the same location in 1987 and remains a popular club today. At the time, Jimmy James and the Blue Flames had a residency at Café Wha?. Other sources, however, including Richards himself in a 1971 interview with *Rolling Stone*, claim the band saw Hendrix at Ondine, the 59th Street club where the Stones had celebrated the end of the 1965 American tour. It's possible that Richards saw Hendrix multiple times, particularly because his girlfriend at the time, Linda Keith, helped Hendrix get discovered. Keith and her friend Roberta Goldstein had first seen Hendrix perform on June 24 as a backing musician for Curtis Knight and the Squires at the Cheetah Club, a nightclub that had recently opened at 53rd and Broadway, while the Stones were performing at the Manning Bowl. She immediately wondered why such a talented guitarist and performer was a virtual unknown.

When Hendrix had to pawn his guitar for money, Keith lent him Richards's white Fender Stratocaster, which Hendrix damaged during his performance at the Cafe Au Go-Go that evening. Keith had brought Andrew Loog Oldham to the club to scout Hendrix, but Oldham passed. According to a perhaps apocryphal story recounted by one of Hendrix's girlfriends, Carol Shiroky, in *Becoming Jimi Hendrix*, Richards later went down to Cafe Wha? with a gun to confront Hendrix about stealing the attention of his girl and his guitar. Other sources don't mention the gun incident, despite Richards's well-known fondness for firearms, and the Stones' future association with Hendrix—Jagger and Wyman would both become acquainted with Hendrix to some degree, and he became close friends with Jones—suggests it was unlikely. Regardless,

Hendrix held on to Richards's white Fender Stratocaster, though contrary to some sources it wasn't the white Fender Stratocaster that Hendrix played at Woodstock, which was a 1968 model.

In his autobiography, Richards takes credit for lending more than just a guitar to Hendrix. "[Linda Keith] also picked up a copy of a demo I had of Tim Rose singing a song called 'Hey Joe.' And took that round to Roberta Goldstein's, where Jimi was, and played it to him. This is rock 'n' roll history. So he got the song from me, apparently."

The 1966 North American tour continued on July 28 with the band's first-ever show in Hawaii. Afterward they flew to Los Angeles, where they worked on several tracks including their next two singles, "Have You Seen Your Mother, Baby, Standing in the Shadow?" and "Let's Spend the Night Together." The 1966 tour would be the last time the Stones played in North America for three years and, more significantly, the last time the band would tour this side of the Atlantic with Brian Jones.

On July 29, shortly after the release of his double LP *Blonde on Blonde*, Bob Dylan was involved in a motorcycle accident in Woodstock and broke several vertebrae in his neck. Dylan had recently finished an exhausting tour of Europe and was still being criticized by some for "going electric." After the accident, Dylan stopped performing live for eight years aside from a handful of one-off performances. The crash also brought an abrupt end to Dylan's friendship with Jones. After all their adventures in the Village, Dylan and Jones never saw each other again. Dylan's first one-off comeback concert at the 1969 Isle of Wight Festival was only eight weeks after Jones's death.

The Stones returned to New York for their fourth appearance on *The Ed Sullivan Show* on September 11, 1966. The day before, the Stones posed for photographer Jerry Schatzberg to shoot the memorable cover art for the "Have You Seen Your Mother, Baby, Standing in the Shadow?" single. They met at Schatzberg's studio at 333 Park Avenue South, changed into drag, and walked around the corner to 24th Street and Lexington Avenue, across from Baruch College. There they posed as "Sarah" Jagger, "Molly" Richards, "Millicent" Watts, "Penelope" Wyman, and "Flossie" Jones. Later, when *New Musical Express* asked if the Stones intended the sleeve to have any "meaning," Richards remarked, "The photograph was just a laugh. There's no deeper interpretation to be placed on it than that. A photographer in New York took the picture as a giggle. We intend to bring it out in the US as cover for the single and on the flipside a photo of all of us dressed normally." Still in drag, the band went to a bar and had a round of drinks, though nobody made a move on surely the five ugliest women in the joint.

For the first time on Sullivan, the whole band mimed to pre-recorded tracks because Jones was unable to play. He had broken his wrist in late August when he tried to punch his then-girlfriend, Anita Pallenberg, but hit a wall instead. Jagger's vocals were live. During the first performance of "Paint It, Black," Jones was dressed in white like an Eastern mystic and mimed playing a sitar. The Stones then followed with "Lady Jane" and "Have You Seen Your Mother..." Memorably, Richards wore a Nazi uniform jacket during the final two songs, which must have somehow gotten past Sullivan's censors, and his lip-syncing was horribly off cue. The shrieking crowd was far less pronounced than during the band's previous appearances. In fairness to the audience, this was a lackluster performance. Jones awkwardly "strummed" his instruments while moving his wrapped, still-healing left hand as little as possible, nearly dropping his dulcimer several times during "Lady Jane," while Watts awkwardly stood in the back pretending to play his cymbals at seemingly random moments. Regardless of the quality of the performances, "Have You Seen Your Mother..." would peak at number nine, making it the band's eighth top-ten single in the US.

In November, the Stones returned to the studio in London to work on their next album. On January 14, 1967, they released the double A-side single "Let's Spend the Night Together" and "Ruby Tuesday" in the US. While both sides reached number three on the UK charts, in the more conservative US the lyrics of "Let's Spend the Night Together" were considered too sexually suggestive for radio play. Many stations refused to play it, and some that did censored the word "Night" in the chorus. More disc jockeys ended up playing "Ruby Tuesday" to avoid the controversy altogether. "Let's Spend the Night Together" peaked at fifty-five, while "Ruby Tuesday" hit number one.

Though the Stones had appeared on *The Ed Sullivan Show* four months prior, they returned to the show to promote their new singles. Richards, Watts, Wyman, and Jones arrived in New York on January 10 to enjoy a few days in Manhattan before the January 15 broadcast. Jagger arrived on January 13. When they arrived at CBS-TV Studio 50 for rehearsals, the doorman refused to let them enter. The group broke one of the front glass doors, and Jagger cut his hand open. It was an omen of the battle to come.

Though the Stones made several appearances on the show, the group never had a strong relationship with Sullivan. Two days before their performance, he told them there was something he would not tolerate—the title lyrics of their newest single. "Either the song goes, or the Stones go," Sullivan said.

The Stones had specifically come to Sullivan's show to showcase the new single and were not prepared to perform anything else. As in the previous performance, the Stones were miming to a track with live vocals. Oldham pressured the band to do whatever Sullivan asked, and a compromise was struck. Jagger agreed to sing the lyric "Let's spend some time together" instead. While the compromise seemed out of character, it ultimately was the right business decision, especially since it has remained one of the most famous anecdotes about that era of the Stones. Richards claimed it was thought of as a big joke amongst the band, saying, "Talk about shades and nuances. What does that mean, especially to CBS? A night is not allowed. Unbelievable. It used to make us laugh. It was pure Lenny Bruce—'Tittie' is a dirty word? What's dirty? The word or the tittie?"

Many sources claim that the Stones were told to change the lyric when they arrived at the theater on January 15, but the altered song title was already mentioned in the January 14 UPI report. The report included a statement from Klein about the censorship: "We've taken out the objectionable words, not that we like it. We see nothing objectionable in the original song. Anyone can read into the words what he pleases." It also included Sullivan's retort: "I've hundreds of thousands of kids watching my show. I won't stand for anything like that with a double meaning."

For the performance of "Ruby Tuesday," Richards mimed playing piano and sang backing vocals, while Jones, wearing a stylish white hat, pretended to play recorder. Wyman mimed playing a cello with a bow, and Watts looked even more bored than usual since the only drum parts in the song were during the chorus. Of course, with Jagger standing at least fifteen feet in front of the band and strutting in a sparkling jacket, it's likely audiences didn't even notice that the band was only pretending to play. For "Let's Spend Some Time Together," Jones took a seat at the piano while Richards switched to guitar. Famously, Jagger punctuated most of the times he sang "some time" by shifting his eyes upward in a "Can you believe this shit?" fashion.

In a later interview with *Rolling Stone*, Jagger claimed, "I never said 'time.' I really didn't. I said mumble. 'Let's spend some mmmmm together, let's spend some mmmmm together.' They would have cut it off if I had said 'night.'" Of course, anyone watching the footage can hear Jagger say "time" plenty of times, although he definitely managed to slip in "night" at least once. It wouldn't even be the last time the Stones censored their music in New York—twenty-nine years later, Jagger would conspicuously drop the controversial "Black girls just wanna get fucked all night" lyric from "Some Girls" at the November 1, 2006, Beacon Theatre show filmed for the *Shine a Light* concert film.

The 1981 rock encyclopedia *Dick Clark's The First 25 Years of Rock & Roll* claimed that the Stones went backstage and changed into Nazi uniforms to protest the lyric change and an angry Sullivan wouldn't allow them back onstage. The far-fetched story has been cited many times since, but it appears to be a complete fabrication and is most likely a story stemming from the Stones' dissatisfaction with having to change the lyric and Richards's wearing a Nazi jacket during the band's previous appearance on the program. Regardless, the Stones would not appear on *The Ed Sullivan Show* again for nearly three years, and when they did, it was specifically on their own terms.

* * * * *

On February 12, Jagger and Richards were arrested in the infamous police raid of Redlands—Richards's estate in Sussex—for drug possession. Jagger was charged with possession of four Benzedrine tablets found in his coat pocket, while Richards was booked on the more serious charge of allowing drug use on his property. At the end of June, Jagger was sentenced to three months in prison, while Richards was sentenced to one year. Despite the Stones' reputation, Jagger and Richards had a strong amount of public support—in fact, UPI reported that on July 6 a "delegation" of "long-haired hippies from Greenwich Village's East Village" met with the British vice consul in New York regarding the imprisonment of Jagger and Richards. The article largely mocked the protestors. However, the next month the pair's convictions were overturned.

Though Jagger and Richards avoided serious prison time, there was no doubt that the increasing drug intake was seriously affecting the band's output and performance schedule. During the interim between Jagger and Richards's arrest and release, Jones was hospitalized several times and his relationship with the band, and Richards in particular, began to break down. Jones's girlfriend, Anita Pallenberg, soon left him for Richards once her relationship with Jones became abusive. She became Richards's long-term partner until the end of the 1970s. The 1967 European tour, which ran from late March until mid-April, was particularly difficult for the band. Following the tour, Jones was arrested for possessing cocaine, marijuana, and methamphetamine on May 10, the same day that Jagger and Richards were formally charged in connection with the Redlands bust. During all this trouble, the band members were recording their latest album at Olympic Sound Studios in London, which would become *Their Satanic Majesties Request*. The album was the band's first and only foray into psychedelic rock. The recording sessions were fractured and piecemeal due to their legal issues and the drug use of Jagger, Richards, and Jones. As a result, Wyman even had his first and only lead vocal on a Rolling Stones album, "In Another Land," which was written by him and was released as the album's first single. By that point Oldham had finally quit the group as well—the announcement was not formally made until September—so the Stones self-produced the album.

Late in the production of the album, the group flew to New York to shoot the cover photo. Wyman recalled in his autobiography that Richards faced problems entering the United States on September 13, writing, "He was taken to a private room and grilled for half an hour before they allowed him a 'deferred entry' examination, answering questions about his drugs trial at the immigration offices on Broadway next morning." Jagger, who came on a later flight, also faced thorough questioning.

The album cover for *Their Satanic Majesties Request* is a lenticular image that appears to parody the cover of the Beatles' *Sgt. Pepper's Lonely Hearts Club Band*, which was released earlier that year. In fact, both photos were taken by Michael Cooper. Cooper had been a longtime acquaintance of the band, and was even present during the Redlands drug bust, though he escaped charges. Years later, Jagger recalled, "The whole thing, we were on acid. We were on acid doing the cover picture. I always remember doing that. It was like being at school, you know, sticking on the bits of colored paper and things. It was really silly. But we enjoyed it. Also, we did it to piss Andrew [Loog Oldham] off, because he was such a pain in the neck. Because he didn't understand it." (The following day, the band met with Klein in New York to tell him that they were splitting with Oldham.) In a 1971 interview with *Rolling Stone*, Richards recalls that the entire photographic process was rather silly. "Michael Cooper was in charge of the whole thing, under his leadership. It was handicrafts day...you make Saturn, and I'll make the rings.... It was really funny...we should have done a gig that night." The inside of the album jacket features, among many other trippy images, an illustration of the New York City skyline with Saturn floating dangerously close.

Jagger and Richards returned to New York at the end of October to master the album, which included trimming the length of several songs. Richards and Jagger were also guests at a Halloween party at the psychedelic Greenwich Village nightclub the Electric Circus—known for advertising 50 cents off the admission price if you came barefoot—which had opened at 23 St. Mark's Place in June. At the same time, Jones sat trial for his drug possession charges and was sentenced to a year in prison. While Jones appealed the conviction, he was unable to leave England, making plans for a world tour impossible (at the time, Jagger told *Rolling Stone*: "We want to do something really different, visiting everywhere we can. Not even a concert tour, in the real sense of the word, something far more exciting").

The Stones almost immediately distanced themselves from the album. When *Their Satanic Majesties Request* was released in early December 1967, the critical reaction to the album was largely negative, and it failed to generate a hit single in either the UK or the US ("She's a Rainbow" peaked at number twenty-five on the Billboard chart). It led to the Stones' stepping back and regrouping. Overall, the group has been dismissive of the album since its release. Only two songs—"2000 Light Years From Home" and "She's a Rainbow"—have ever been performed live by the group, and not until more than two decades after their release. In 2015, when the Stones played *Let It Bleed* in its entirety at a secret warm-up gig in Los Angeles, Jagger joked that the band would return the following year and give *Their Satanic Majesties Request* the same treatment. Nonetheless, the album still is influential. For example, the song "2000 Man" would later become a signature song of Bronx-born guitarist Ace Frehley of KISS after he performed a cover of the song on the band's 1979 *Dynasty* album.

However, one of the album's other tracks might be notable for being the first Rolling Stones song that is possibly about New York. The lyrics of the grungy track "Citadel," which reflect an almost apocalyptic narrative, were cited by transsexual Warhol superstar, Candy Darling, as being about New York City. From that point of view some of the lyrics do depict an urban landscape ("Screaming people fly so fast / In their shiny metal cars / Through the woods of steel and glass"). Candy also claimed that the "Candy and Taffy" mentioned in the chorus refer to her and her friend, a transvestite known as Taffy Tits. This is the same Candy mentioned in the Velvet Underground's "Candy Says" and Lou Reed's "Walk on the Wild Side." Darling said she had met Jagger in 1967 at the Hotel Albert on Tenth Street and Fifth Avenue, a run-down building known for housing writers like Hart Crane and Thomas Wolfe; it was also where the rock group The Mamas & the Papas wrote the song "California Dreamin.'" The hotel was popular with musicians during the 1960s, though there is no record of Jagger or the Stones ever staying there.

On December 12, Jones's jail sentence was dismissed, but he was put on probation for three years and ordered to seek treatment for his addiction. The very next day, Jones was hospitalized following a drug overdose. Though he recovered, on May 21, 1968, Jones was arrested again at his apartment for possession of cannabis. The judge spared Jones from prison but told him it was his final chance. Jones might have been able to walk the streets as a free man, but his legal troubles meant that the Stones would not be able to tour the US. The Stones occupied their time by recording, with Jones only sporadically appearing. His days in the band were numbered.

* * * * *

Being away from New York for the entirety of 1968 and nearly all of 1969, the Stones avoided two of the most tumultuous years in the city's political history. In February, a nine-day sanitation strike left the city buried in garbage stacked up on the city streets. Photos of the refuse covering sidewalks were widely distributed in the national media. In March, Upper Manhattan was beset by a number of demonstrations by students of Columbia University. The protests soon expanded to include non-students. Protests continued for weeks, culminating in the acting dean of the university's being held hostage and a violent dispersal of protestors by the NYPD. Shortly afterward, the United Federation of Teachers went on a seven-month strike that inflamed racial tensions between Jewish educators and the parents of minority students over the quality of education in schools with student bodies made up of minority students. Quality of life in New York City was rapidly declining, and these issues were regularly attracting national attention. Though the Stones' "Street Fighting Man" peaked at only number forty-eight when it was released as a single on August 31, 1968, in the US, it captured the attitude of social and political unrest throughout the world, including in New York.

Mayor Lindsay's most visible failure of his first term was the February 1969 nor'easter that dumped fifteen inches of snow on the city. Though New York had experienced far worse snowstorms in the past, the snowfall crippled city services and transportation for days and resulted in forty-two deaths. Lindsay shouldered the blame for the city's being unprepared, especially regarding Queens residents, whose streets were not plowed for days. The episode became an example of how significantly a public official's response to severe weather could impact his or her popularity. Lindsay lost the 1969 Republican mayoral primary, initially ending his hopes for a second term. However, Lindsay ran as the candidate of the New York Liberal Party, and by mounting a campaign that highlighted New York's accomplishment of largely avoiding the destructive race riots that plagued other major cities in the late 1960s—along with an apology for his mistakes—he won the November 1969 election.

Closer to the Stones' world, on June 3, 1968, pop artist Andy Warhol was shot by Valerie Solanas, a writer who believed that Warhol, with whom she unsuccessfully sought to collaborate, was conspiring to steal her work. Solanas opened fire on Warhol at The Factory, and Warhol nearly died on the operating table. Warhol would soon collaborate with the Stones again on the band's most famous album cover.

* * * * *

In August 1968, Jimi Hendrix was a featured artist in the New York Rock Festival concert series at the Singer Bowl in Flushing Meadows Park in Queens, an eighteen-thousand-seat venue that had been built for the 1964–1965 World's Fair. While the Singer Bowl still exists, it has largely been rebuilt into the USTA National Tennis Center and is now two separate stadiums, the Louis Armstrong Memorial Stadium and the Grandstand.

In *The New York Times* write-up of the Hendrix concert, Robert Shelton says that next year's series would be headlined by "the long-absent Bob Dylan and the Rolling Stones." While none of that turned out to be true, in fall 1969 a profoundly changed Rolling Stones did finally return to the United States for a tour for the first time since 1966. For the first time, they were worthy of the name that would soon be bestowed on them—"The World's Greatest Rock 'n' Roll Band."

CHAPTER 3

"GET YER YA-YA'S OUT!"

On June 8, 1969, Rolling Stones founding member Brian Jones left the band. His replacement, the twenty-year-old Mick Taylor, formerly the guitarist for John Mayall & the Bluesbreakers, had already been recording with the Stones for a week. Over the previous two years, Jones had been in and out of treatment and courtrooms in England because of his drug addictions. The Stones were planning an American tour in the fall of 1969, and because of his legal issues, Jones would be unable to secure a visa. Jones was in no condition to tour and was perhaps disinterested anyway. Regardless, there was no way Jones could continue with the group. Jagger, Richards, and Watts visited him to inform him that he was out of the band that he had co-founded. Jones released an official statement that diplomatically said, "I no longer see eye-to-eye with the others over the discs we are cutting."

Though Jones did not leave the band until June 1969, he had hardly been a contributing member since the 1967 European tour ended. Jones was notably absent for many of the sessions for *Beggars Banquet*, contributing guitar on just one song, the acoustic slide on "No Expectations." Jagger said, "That was the last time I remember Brian really being totally involved in something that was really worth doing.

He was there with everyone else. It's funny how you remember—but that was the last moment I remember him doing that, because he had just lost interest in everything." Jones's other contributions included playing Mellotron on "Jigsaw Puzzle," playing the sitar and tambura on "Street Fighting Man," and singing backing vocals on "Sympathy for the Devil." Jones's contributions to the *Let It Bleed* sessions were nominal as well, consisting of playing the congas on "Midnight Rambler" and autoharp on "You Got the Silver." Jones recorded guitar for "Honky Tonk Women" in his final session with the band in March 1969, but his work was later overdubbed by Taylor.

Around midnight on July 2, 1969, Jones was found dead by his girlfriend at the bottom of his swimming pool. Though the death was ruled accidental, the circumstances remain both suspicious and mysterious and, in the over forty years since, investigations into his death have yielded nothing conclusive. In a way, the mystery surrounding Jones's death reflects the mysterious nature of his life. He was one of the founders of the Rolling Stones, but in little over a year his role as band leader was overtaken by Jagger, Richards, and manager Andrew Loog Oldham. He was devoted to the blues and was uncomfortable as the band progressed toward pop, yet, of all the Stones, he was the one who embraced the hippie counterculture the most, straying from the blues himself in a different way. By the end of his life, he had almost completely lost interest in playing guitar and instead studied Eastern music. Jones's bandmates and acquaintances have spoken over the years about his difficult personality, ranging from charming to sadistic and everything in between. How much of this can be blamed on his drug intake or his difficulty with coping with his diminishing role in the band has been guessed at by critics, analysts, and journalists for more than four decades.

What's more, Jones seemed at times not to recognize—or at least refused to acknowledge—that he was in one of the biggest pop bands in the world. During a January 1967 interview with *New Musical Express*, Jones said: "Our real followers have moved on with us—some of those we like most are the hippies in New York, but nearly all of them think like us and are questioning some of the basic immoralities which are tolerated in present day society—the war in Vietnam, persecution of homosexuals, illegality of abortion, drug taking. All these things are immoral. We are making our own statement—others are making more intellectual ones." He went on to discuss pop music's role in questioning "the wisdom of an almost blind acceptance of religion" and how the world was about to enter the enlightened "Age of Aquarius." Of course, these words certainly sound odd coming out the mouth of a member of a band that had recently released a song titled "Let's Spend the Night Together." Also odd is Jones's calling drug taking immoral when he was a drug abuser who would face his first drug-related arrest just four months after the interview. In his memoir *Up and Down with the Rolling Stones*, Richards's former assistant "Spanish" Tony Sanchez claims that interviews with Jones such as these were set up by the band completely unbeknownst to Jones to boost his confidence by making him feel as if he was the band's "spokesman" as his musical and leadership roles diminished.

Even if this particular interview was a setup, it does indicate the affinity Jones had for New York. In his obituary of Jones in the *New York Post*, famed rock journalist Al Aronowitz wrote about Jones's final visit to Manhattan in late 1967, "Although Brian has always hated New York, he keeps telling me he'll be back in a month, after he takes care of his dope busts. Of course, he never returns." Nonetheless, in those early years Jones spent more time than any of the other Stones in New York, and even told the *Daily Mail* in 1964 that he hoped to move there someday. Aronowitz also memorialized Jones with yet another contradiction, remarking, "If he gave nothing else to this world, Brian Jones was the first heterosexual male to start wearing costume jewelry from Saks Fifth Avenue."

The Stones already had scheduled a free concert in London's Hyde Park on July 5 to debut Mick Taylor. The performance, which was attended by a quarter of a million people, became an impromptu memorial to Jones.

* * * * *

Mick Taylor was no stranger to New York. As a member of the Blues-breakers, Taylor first visited the city during the group's extended concert run at the Cafe Au Go-Go in January 1968. The 375-seat Greenwich Village club, located in the basement of 152 Bleecker Street across the street from famed club The Bitter End, had a brief but influential existence in the city's music history. After the club opened in February 1964, its stage was graced by many stars, such as Jimi Hendrix, Van Morrison, Joni Mitchell, Cream, and Jefferson Airplane as well as blues legends like Howlin' Wolf, Son House, Bukka White, B.B. King, Muddy Waters, and John Lee Hooker. Most notably, the Grateful Dead played their first-ever New York show there on June 1, 1967, and revisited several times. The club even played a role in New York State legal history when comedian Lenny Bruce was arrested on obscenity charges there in April 1964. Bruce and Cafe Au Go-Go owner, Howard Solomon, were found guilty of obscenity on November 4, though Solomon's conviction was eventually overturned on appeal and Bruce died while awaiting his appeal. (Bruce received a posthumous pardon in 2003, from New York State governor and Stones fan George Pataki). The Blues Project—featuring Al Kooper, who later played piano, organ and French horn on the Stones' "You Can't Always Get What You Want"—recorded the album *Live at the Cafe Au Go Go* in November 1965. Despite its popularity, the club closed in October 1969.

John Mayall returned to New York in October 1968 to play four shows in two days at the Fillmore East (playing two shows per night was tradition at the venue), the legendary theater opened by rock promoter Bill Graham, who would later promote the Stones' 1972, 1975, 1978, and 1981 US tours. Born in Germany and given the name Wulf Wolodia Grajonca, he had escaped the Holocaust when his mother placed him in foster care. (He later discovered his mother had died at Auschwitz.) In the early days of World War II he escaped to France, then the United States, eventually ending up in a foster home in the Bronx. Grajonca changed his name to Bill Graham, and, after a stint in the US Army and working in the resort community in New York's Catskill Mountains, moved to San Francisco and began promoting concerts, soon promoting shows at the Fillmore Auditorium in San Francisco, which was succeeded by the Fillmore West a mile away in 1968. His success led Graham to open the Fillmore East at 105 Second Avenue in the East Village, the former site of a Yiddish theater. Though the venue operated only as the Fillmore East for three years, a multitude of live albums were recorded there, including ones by Jimi Hendrix, the Allman Brothers, Miles Davis, Derek and the Dominos, and the Grateful Dead. Graham closed both the Fillmore East and the Fillmore West in 1971 and turned to promoting rock tours instead. The East location would briefly operate as a concert venue again under new management in 1974–1975. The lobby of the former Fillmore East is currently a bank, though the bank features an exhibit about the hallowed rock venue.

Mayall's band's going from a 350-seat club to a 2,700-seat theater in only ten months shows its remarkable growth in popularity. Mayall returned to the Fillmore East for four more shows on February 28 and March 1. Taylor began working with the Stones less than three months later.

* * * * *

On September 17, ABKCO, Allen Klein's label, announced that the Stones would tour the United States in November and December for the first time since 1966. Their popularity hadn't waned at all during their three-year absence. In fact, it had grown. Since then, the Stones had had two number-one hits ("Ruby Tuesday" and "Honky Tonk Women") as well as a number-three hit ("Jumpin' Jack Flash") and two other top-forty hits ("Dandelion" and "She's a Rainbow"). Though the Stones had played a mix of theaters and arena-sized venues on the 1966 tour, they tackled larger venues this time around, with some locations getting both matinee and evening shows. Years later, Richards recalled, "It had gotten to the point by 1969 where to satisfy all our fans in a city, we had to play six or eight shows. We just didn't have enough nights. So we either had to disappoint people or move up to bigger places."

The tour would include three concerts in two days in Manhattan, and those would be the band's largest yet in New York City. For the Stones, it showed the surge of popularity the band had experienced over the previous three years. After drawing a crowd of nine thousand to the Forest Hills Stadium in 1966, the Stones were planning to play three shows—one on Thanksgiving, November 27, and two on November 28—at Madison Square Garden, an arena that had broken ground just four days after the Stones' first appearance on *The Ed Sullivan Show*.

The history of Madison Square Garden, which has branded itself "The World's Most Famous Arena" for decades, tells the story of popular entertainment in New York over the last century and a half. The arena where the Stones played three shows in 1969—and have played more than a dozen times since—is actually the fourth version of the Garden. Three previous arenas bearing the name—the first two located adjacent to Madison Square Park, hence the name—had been operating in Manhattan since 1879. By the time the fourth Garden opened in February 1968, the arena was an entertainment destination known as the premier sporting complex in the country. The previous Garden, which was located a block west of Times Square on Eighth Avenue between 49th and 50th Streets until the new arena took its place, was Manhattan's indoor sports hub and was home to the New York Rangers, the New York Knicks, college basketball, and dozens of high-profile boxing matches.

Controversially, the site selected for the new Garden was between Seventh and Eighth Avenues from 31st to 33rd Streets, and required the demolition of Pennsylvania Station, which was moved underground and below the Garden. The demolition of the historic railroad station spurned a movement to save New York's Grand Central Terminal from a similar fate and began a preservation movement for historical buildings, including several historic venues the Stones members would later play with their solo bands. The Stones would take advantage of the historic nature of Grand Central decades later when announcing their 1989 world tour.

It's hard to find an athlete or a performer who doesn't hold Madison Square Garden in awe. Countless historical moments, including several involving the Rolling Stones, have happened at the arena. The Garden is celebrated for its superior sound and atmosphere. As rock journalist Al Aronowitz wrote about the arena in his 1972 review of a Stones show, "The structure is built sort of like a trampoline hanging from cables that stretch across the ceiling and the hotter the rock show, the more it bounces." Many musicians consider headlining the Garden the true measure of "making it." The new Garden quickly became a popular stop for top rock acts, and since opening it had already hosted several concerts, including Cream on November 2, 1968 (the first rock concert at the Garden), the Doors on January 24, 1969, and Jimi Hendrix on May 18, 1969. The Stones would be the first rock band to perform multiple shows at the arena.

Though the Garden could hold more than twenty thousand people for concerts, the Stones capped the capacity between sixteen and seventeen thousand. While planning the tour, Richards explained to *Rolling Stone*, "In all the future gigs, we want to keep the audiences as small as possible. We'd rather play to four shows of 5,000 people each, than one mammoth 50,000 sort of number. I think we're playing at Madison Square Garden in New York, but it will be a reduced audience, because we're not going to allow them to sell all the seats."

It was also the first tour on which the Stones played an extended set. In previous tours, the sets had not been much longer than a half hour and ten songs or less, which was a standard length for most touring rock groups at the time. By the end of the 1960s that had changed, and groups like Cream were playing an hour to ninety minutes. The Stones followed suit by playing a fourteen-song set at Hyde Park, and would generally play thirteen to fifteen songs per concert during the US tour.

Despite the band's hell-raising reputation, once the tour began with a warm-up show in Fort Collins, Colorado, on November 7, the Stones had relatively few issues through the New York dates at the end of November. There were some complaints about ticket prices—mostly ranging from $4.50 to $8—though in the case of New York, that was cheaper than the $5 to $12.50 that was charged for the 1966 Forest

Hills concert. However, Bill Graham, who promoted the California shows, was reportedly unhappy with the concerts' grosses. Nonetheless, Graham worked with the Stones on future tours because he believed in them. In a post-tour interview with *Rolling Stone*, Graham compared the Rolling Stones to the 1969 "Miracle" New York Mets, a team that had been a perennial loser since its first season in 1962 but that went on to win the World Series in 1969. Graham said, "What I hope the Stones do is turn the whole country on, do what the Mets did for New York, wake 'em up. And I think the Stones can do it. Mick Jagger is the greatest fucking performer in the whole fucking world."

The Stones also taped performances of "Gimme Shelter," "Love in Vain," and "Honky Tonk Women" for *The Ed Sullivan Show* on November 18, and Jagger also taped a short interview. All of these aired on November 23. Unlike with their previous appearances, however, the Stones were recorded in Los Angeles at CBS Television City studios. Sullivan told the Associated Press that he traveled cross-country because "these boys are hot, especially with the younger crowd. They're on a concert tour, so I decided to come here and tape them. They cost a lot of money, but they're worth it." *The Ed Sullivan Show* had suffered declining ratings over the past several years, and the Stones were a proven draw. Nevertheless, this was the band's final appearance on Sullivan's show, which ended its lengthy run in June 1971.

The Stones hosted the only official press conference of the tour at the Rainbow Grill in Rockefeller Center on November 26, just hours before they were to play the Civic Center in Baltimore, Maryland, two hundred miles away. The *Washington Post* set the scene as: "After being submitted to a security check unrivaled at the Pentagon, journalists were given drinks and canapés while a string quartet played Haydn." In contrast to how the Stones had been depicted in the media for the previous five years, the AP report said that the Stones were "the most polite persons there." There was pandemonium among the press trying to get their questions in, leading Jagger to ask, "Shall we scream at you like you're screaming at us?" Jagger was also asked his opinion of New York City, to which he responded, "It's great. It changes. It explodes." He was also asked if he had yet felt satisfied, to which he responded, "Financially dissatisfied, sexually satisfied, philosophically trying." The most notable thing to come out of the press conference was the announcement that the group would be headlining a daylong free concert in Golden Gate Park in San Francisco, though the group also shot down longstanding rumors that they would do a similar free show in Central Park. ("Now is too cold," Jagger said. "We've got to do it outside. And San Francisco is really into that sort of thing.") Part of the Stones' motivation for doing a free performance in the US was to fight back against criticism that the ticket prices for the 1969 tour were too high. After twenty-five minutes of mostly inane questions, the Stones were off to Baltimore.

The day after the Baltimore concert was Thanksgiving, and that night was the Stones' first-ever performance at Madison Square Garden. While New York is known for the Macy's Thanksgiving Day Parade, the most anticipated event in Manhattan that day was the Stones concert. Six thousand people had stood in line at the Garden box office to buy tickets when they went on sale on November 6, and both evening performances were sold out (the matinee performance still had "a couple of hundred" empty seats, according to *Rolling Stone*).

All three Garden shows had the same set list, though the order differed for the first show. Each started with the same four songs: "Jumpin' Jack Flash," "Carol," "Sympathy for the Devil," and "Stray Cat Blues." They also ended with the same six: "Midnight Rambler," "Live with Me," "Little Queenie," "Satisfaction," "Honky Tonk Women," and "Street Fighting Man." For the middle portion, the Stones played "Love in Vain," "Prodigal Son," "You Gotta Move," and a medley of "Under My Thumb" and "I'm Free." The Garden shows were recorded for both a potential live album and by filmmaking brothers Albert and David Maysles for a possible documentary.

In his review of the first show for *The Times*, Mike Jahn praised Jagger, writing that he "snarls and howls in the finest man-woman blues tradition," and that the concert was "an enthusiastic reading of some of a fine group's finest material." However, he complained about the layout of the bill. The Stones did not take the stage until 11:00

p.m., three hours after the concert started. Terry Reid opened the show, followed by B.B. King and then Ike and Tina Turner (the Turners were joined by a very inebriated Janis Joplin at the first show for their set-ending "Land of a Thousand Dances"). A second report in *The Times* by Francis X. Clines noted that that the NYPD wasn't overly concerned with security because it believed that "the basically middle-class audience had only holiday entertainment in mind." The AP report was complimentary to the band in general, but seemed turned off by Jagger's antics and remarked, "The biggest hits with the audience were those songs that put down women: 'Under My Thumb,' 'Satisfaction' and 'Honky Tonk Women.' Teenage girls apparently wouldn't mind being dominated by Jagger."

The Garden shows were far more remembered for their musical quality than any onstage scandals. Nine of the ten tracks on the band's first live album, *'Get Yer Ya-Ya's Out!' The Rolling Stones in Concert*, which was released the following September, came from these three shows. The original release included "Jumpin' Jack Flash" and "Honky Tonk Women" from the November 27 show; "Carol," "Stray Cat Blues," "Sympathy for the Devil," "Little Queenie," and "Street Fighting Man" from the November 28 matinee show; and "Midnight Rambler" and "Live with Me" from the evening show (the tenth track, "Love in Vain," was recorded at the November 26 Baltimore concert). Jagger and Richards re-recorded some of the vocal tracks in London in January and February 1970, though in 2009 the album was re-released with unaltered bonus tracks, featuring "Under My Thumb" and "I'm Free" from November 27, "Satisfaction" from the November 28 matinee show, and "Prodigal Son" and "You Gotta Move" from the evening show. An accompanying DVD also included footage of the November 27 performances of "Prodigal Son," "You Gotta Move," and "Satisfaction" and November 28 matinee performances of "Under My Thumb" and "I'm Free."

Jagger's attire was much noted for a long red scarf that he wore, which one eager New York fan managed to grab, nearly pulling him off the stage. Jagger also had something of a wardrobe malfunction during one of the November 28 shows, and teased the audience by saying, "I think I've busted a button on me trousers and me trousers are going to fall down. You don't want me trousers to fall down, do you?" The third show ended with five thousand rose petals raining from the ceiling to send the Stones off.

As the NYPD predicted, the shows were without incident aside from scalpers outside charging up to $40 for a pair of tickets that cost $3.50. In fact, the biggest scandal involving the Madison Square Garden shows did not even involve the Stones at all. Gossip columnist Steven A. Brandt, who wrote for *Photoplay* magazine, attended the November 27 show with several friends, including Ultra Violet, an actress who appeared in several of Andy Warhol's films. Brandt left the concert early ("The concert was so lively, so opposite himself," Violet told the Associated Press) and returned to his room at the Hotel Chelsea, the famed 23rd Street building that was a haven for artists, musicians, and writers; at one time or another, Bob Dylan, Janis Joplin, Tom Waits, Patti Smith, Leonard Cohen, and Iggy Pop all called it home. Violet called Brandt after the concert, and he told her that he had taken twenty-two pills. She called the Chelsea's night clerk, who found Brandt on the floor. Medical help was unable to get to Brandt before he died of an overdose.

November 27 was also Jimi Hendrix's twenty-seventh (and notably last) birthday. He attended the show that night and hung out with the group backstage. Interestingly enough, at an after-party for Hendrix's birthday uptown, a moment between Jagger and Hendrix's then-girlfriend, Devon Wilson, inspired a lyric to one of Hendrix's final songs. Jagger had previously been involved with Wilson, and Hendrix had previously tried to steal Marianne Faithfull from Jagger while he was dating her, so there was a level of animosity between the pair. Jagger cut his finger at the party, and while a bandage was sought, Wilson grabbed Jagger's finger and began sucking it. The moment inspired the lyric "She drinks her blood from a jagged edge," in Hendrix's song about Wilson, "Dolly Dagger." The song was not released until October 1971, which was not only after Hendrix's death but also after Wilson's. She died on February 19, 1971, after plunging to her death out of a ninth-floor window at the Hotel Chelsea under mysterious circumstances.

The 1969 tour wrapped up with two shows in Boston on November 29. The Stones grossed around $2 million from the tour, with $286,542 of that from the three Garden shows alone, which the Garden touted in advertisements. The tour was immediately followed by a November 30 festival appearance at the Palm Beach International Raceway, which also included Janis Joplin, Sly & the Family Stone, and Jefferson Airplane. The festival had few problems outside of some crowd control issues with the forty thousand patrons and some minor arrests. However, tight security kept away many of those who didn't purchase the then-steep twenty-dollar tickets.

The December 6 Altamont festival was another story entirely.

Much has been written about the disastrous Altamont Speedway Free Festival and how for many the violence and chaos of that Saturday marked the polar opposite of New York's celebrated Woodstock Festival, which happened less than four months prior. By the end of the festival, four people had been killed (coincidentally, there were also four births). The most shocking death was that of Meredith Hunter, a black teenager who was stabbed to death while he was high on drugs by Hells Angel Alan Passaro after he saw Hunter pull out a revolver. Hunter's death was captured on film by Eric Saarinen, who was filming the concert for the Maysles brothers' documentary, which was released the next year as *Gimme Shelter* and focuses on circumstances surrounding Hunter's death.

The effects of Altamont remained a popular topic in the press for months to come. In February, Columbia pop culture professor Albert Goldman wrote a highly critical piece in *The Times*, labeling bands like the Stones "rock bandits" that betrayed the ethical ideals of counterculture. The media generally portrayed a narrative that Altamont represented the death of 1960s counterculture, a thread that was continued when the documentary shot at Altamont featuring footage of Hunter's death was released exactly one year after Altamont under the title *Gimme Shelter*.

Gimme Shelter opened at the Plaza Theatre in New York, an East 58th Street movie theater. In his review for the *Village Voice*, writer and filmmaker Howard Smith continued the publication's earlier disgust at the events of the film and called Altamont "a coda for the '60s. It was the last real 'scene' of the decade—somehow not a very fitting end to the decade that brought us flower-power and peace groups." There was agreement even on the opposite end of the cultural spectrum. New York-based conservative columnist William F. Buckley Jr. wrote about the film in his twice-weekly "On the Right" syndicated column. While Buckley says little about the quality of the film, he recounts the events surrounding the death of Hunter with obvious disgust for the Stones and Jagger in particular (on Jagger's musical ability, Buckley wrote, "His voice couldn't be better than that of, say, every fourth person listed in the telephone directory"). Like Smith, he ended his column calling the film an end to the hippie era, writing that the Stones "crowd like sardines into the helicopter, and fly out of the lonely crowd, leaving behind them the corpse of Woodstock Nation."

In an article about the film titled "Making Murder Pay?," *Times* film critic Vincent Canby wrote about how the film and its release disturbed him: "To be perfectly blunt about it, *Gimme Shelter*, in spite of the skill with which it was photographed and edited...is one of the most unpleasant, bleak, depressing movies I've ever encountered." Canby called the film "a kind of quasi-fact" that "exploits the events, much as the people within the movie exploit the Stones (with the Stones' whole-hearted cooperation), and as the Stones exploit their public." The Maysles brothers and co-director Charlotte Zwerin actually responded to Canby with a letter to the editor published on December 27 defending their film, arguing that featuring the killing in *Gimme Shelter* could not be exploitive since it was a factual event that was captured by their cameras, and adding that the Hells Angel who killed Hunter had not yet been found guilty of murder because Hunter had been handling a gun, making the title of Canby's piece inaccurate (ultimately the Hells Angel was acquitted on grounds of self-defense).

* * * * *

Between Altamont and the launch of a 1972 tour, the Stones spent very little time in the United States. Part of the reason was that the band faced pressing business matters. Despite massive sales of records and tickets and the large advance on their latest recording contract, the band was constantly struggling with money and was unable to receive cash in a timely fashion from Klein's New York office. Jagger enlisted Prince Rupert Loewenstein, a German aristocrat banker who became the band's new business manager, to examine the band's finances and find out just what they had agreed to with Klein. In February 1970, the Stones discovered that not only had they not paid taxes on their earnings in the UK over the previous five years—and as a result had tax bills that collectively amounted to millions of pounds—but the contract they signed with Klein in 1965 indicated that they owned neither the publishing rights nor the masters of any of the music they had ever produced. While the group worked on the follow-up to *Let It Bleed* in London, the band's management prepared the group's new recording contract with Atlantic Records without Klein. In September, the band released *'Get Yer Ya-Ya's Out!' The Rolling Stones in Concert*, a live album that featured nine songs recorded during the 1969 Madison Square Garden concerts. It was their last album for Decca. The band undertook a fall 1970 tour of England, and then a March 1971 "farewell" tour of England and Scotland as they packed up their operations for France.

In April 1970, the Stones launched their own record label, Rolling Stones Records, as a subsidiary of Atlantic Records. Although much of the new activity in the US music business was taking place on the West Coast, New York's Atlantic Records was an emerging powerhouse. The label was formed in New York in 1947 by Turkish-born Ahmet Ertegun, son of the first Turkish ambassador to the United States, Munir Ertegun, and former A&R manager for National Records Herb Abramson. The pair built the company up from an operation run by a handful of people to one of the largest labels in the country in less than ten years because of their ear for talent and their loyalty to their roster of recording artists (Atlantic was one of the few labels of the era to pay artists royalties), including the label's black artists, whom Ertegun held in high esteem. In his biography, Richards recalls of Ertegun, "Ahmet encouraged talent. He was very much hands-on. It wasn't like an EMI or a Decca, some huge conglomerate. That company was born and built up out of love of music, not business." With a roster that included at one point or another the Coasters, the Drifters, Ray Charles, Bobby Darin, Phil Spector, Buffalo Springfield, Cream, Aretha Franklin, Led Zeppelin, Wilson Pickett, and the writing team of Jerry Leiber and Mike Stoller, Atlantic had a pedigree that attracted the Stones. Along with Marshall Chess (son of Leonard Chess, who founded the legendary Chess record label that recorded most of the Stones' favorite artists), who was hired to serve as president of Rolling Stones Records, the band released their first post-Decca album, *Sticky Fingers*, in April 1971 with an iconic cover designed by Andy Warhol.

The cover art for *Sticky Fingers* features the fly of jeans with a working zipper worn by a well-endowed man. Pulling it down exposed the model's underwear. The model's name is debated still—Warhol shot photos of several men at the Decker Building at 33 Union Square West, which housed The Factory at the time, and he never revealed who it was. The album, with its lead single "Brown Sugar" quickly hitting number one in the US, was a massive critical and commercial hit. Its second single, the ballad "Wild Horses," reached only number twenty-eight but later became one of the band's most enduring songs.

The Stones then turned their attention to France to record their next album, the most expansive of their career. Though Richards was soon consumed by his heroin addiction and Taylor had his own drug issues, this period of recording was extremely fertile, resulting in the band's first double album, *Exile on Main St.*, believed by many to be their masterpiece. The album not only contained some of the finest music the Stones ever produced, but it and the following tour turned the band into worldwide superstars. Despite appearing on the scene almost a decade before as a band that didn't have enough sense to shower, the Stones were becoming the object of affection for upper-crust celebrities and socialites, particularly those in New York.

CHAPTER 4

"IF I EVER GET BACK TO FUN CITY"

In January 1972, the *Wall Street Journal* reported that Jagger was named on the International Best-Dressed List for the previous year, solidifying his increasing stature in popular culture. When they had first arrived in America, the Rolling Stones could barely get recognition from the American press—and certainly not from the *Wall Street Journal*—but now Jagger was being counted among the beautiful jet-set fashion plates. The now married Jagger—he had wed Nicaraguan socialite Bianca Pérez-Mora Macías in May 1971—soon became entrenched in celebrity culture, a marked change from the Stones' outsider status that had stuck to them since Altamont and their self-imposed exile from England. Even with Altamont's being singled out by many as the end of the hippie era, much of America had stopped seeing the Stones as the downfall of Western civilization. Jagger was even featured on the cover of the July 14, 1972, issue of *Life* magazine. Thomas Thompson's story on the Stones summed up the changes in the rock scene since the 1969 Stones tour best: "Haight-Ashbury is just another San Francisco intersection now (though tourists keep stealing the street sign as a souvenir), and the windows of psychedelia are boarded up. Bill Graham closed both Fillmores East and West, the twin temples of rock music. Underground newspapers by the scores shriveled and died. The streets and the campuses became silent but for the swish of the Frisbee."

After a long period of recording in France, Jagger, Richards, and Taylor spent the first three months of 1972 in Los Angeles finishing *Exile on Main St*. Jagger added gospel-influenced vocal overdubs on "Tumbling Dice," "Loving Cup," "Let It Loose," and "Shine a Light." Wyman and Watts joined them in February, as the Stones had legal meetings regarding their disputes with Allen Klein. Klein's company was busy releasing compilations of the Stones' pre-1970 catalog. Since ABKCO owned the rights to the Stones' catalog, the label released compilation albums of older Stones tracks practically every six months, often coinciding with official band releases or tour announcements. The seemingly endless series of repackages infuriated the Stones. In order to finally remove themselves from Klein, the Stones agreed to a paltry settlement and gave him control of the band's entire back catalog through 1969, including sharing ownership of the *Sticky Fingers* tracks "Brown Sugar" and "Wild Horses," which Klein demanded because they had been recorded in December 1969, before his contract with the Stones ended. Since they were the two singles off *Sticky Fingers* and thus the most successful and valuable tracks, ownership of them was something of a final slap in the face from Klein to the Stones. In May, the Stones announced they had settled their legal issues with Klein, but Klein's control over the band's early catalog would cause headaches for the Stones for decades afterward, with Klein continuing to issue repackaged Stones compilations throughout the 1970s and 1980s.

In March, Richards and Pallenberg went for drug treatment in Switzerland in order to clean up for the tour, with Richards later remarking, "I'd rather clean up before I went on the road. It's bad enough cleaning up by yourself, but the idea of putting the whole tour on the line because I couldn't make it was too much, even for me." This was the first of several rehab stints that Richards underwent in order to kick his heroin addiction, though they were unsuccessful at keeping him off the drug, which he continued to use throughout the '70s.

Afterward, the Stones prepared for the release of *Exile* in late May and then immediately turned their attention to tour rehearsals in Los Angeles. Following the model of the band's 1970 European tour and short 1971 UK tour, pianist Nicky Hopkins, saxophonist Bobby Keys, and trumpeter Jim Price joined the band for the tour, with Ian Stewart stepping in for Hopkins for some songs. Stevie Wonder was selected to be the opening act for the entire tour.

Exile had already yielded a top-ten single ("Tumbling Dice") in both the US and UK before it was released. The album reached number one in both the US and UK, with the album going gold in the US almost immediately. Despite near-universal acclaim today, however, *Exile* was released to mixed reviews. Though in subsequent years band members, especially Richards, were quick to mention that the cold critical reception proves the worth of rock critics, most New York critics actually gave the double album positive reviews. Don Heckman in *The Times* called *Exile* "perhaps the best cross-section yet of the unique elements that make up the Stones' music." Robert Christgau called it "incontrovertibly the year's best" in *Newsday*. Outside of New York, critics were less enthusiastic. *Rolling Stone*'s Lenny Kaye was the most critical in an overly long 2,300-word review, remarking, "*Exile on Main Street* spends its four sides shading the same song in as many variations as there are Rolling Stones readymades to fill them, and if on the one hand they prove the group's eternal constancy and appeal, it's on the other that you can leave the album and still feel vaguely unsatisfied, not quite brought to the peaks that this band of bands has always held out as a special prize in the past." Kaye's criticism of the album's being "the same song" seems indefensible in light of the diversity of the album's tracks. As expected, once the Stones reissued the album, *Rolling Stone* took the time to revise its original review to recognize it as one of the top albums of all time.

Aside from its content, one of the most iconic elements of *Exile on Main St.* is the packaging. The cover of the album features numerous photographs of human sideshow attractions in what appears to be a collage. The cover is actually a shot of a photo-covered wall claimed to have been in a New York City Eighth Avenue tattoo parlor whose name has been lost to time. The photographer, Robert Frank, is a celebrated Swiss photographer whose 1958 photo book *The Americans* depicts the post-war lives of ordinary Americans in stark contrast to the typical glowing images of 1950s American popular culture. He worked closely with the Beat writers—Jack Kerouac wrote the introduction to *The Americans*—which raised him in esteem with the Stones. Though then middle-aged, Frank became acquainted with the Stones and shot Super 8 footage of the band in Los Angeles along with other footage shot in the Bowery in New York without the band, which was collectively used to create the images in the gatefold packaging. As for the cover of *Exile*, in *The Times* Heckman described it as "a collection of candid photos of human 'freaks,' midgets, fat women, cripples, etc." Graphic designer John Van Hamersveld, who previously had done art for Hendrix and the Beatles, selected the image for the cover.

Several of the photos in the collage were taken by New York photographer Diane Arbus of the attractions at Hubert's Dime Museum and Flea Circus, a Times Square curiosity museum that included a "freak show." Located at 228–232 West 42nd Street, Hubert's entertained New Yorkers and tourists from the 1920s until 1965, when many of the exhibits were removed. (Hubert's remained open until 1969. The marquee can be glimpsed in the movie *Midnight Cowboy*, which was shot in 1968.) Appropriately, a Ripley's Believe It or Not! museum now occupies the 42nd Street space of the former Hubert's. Arbus was recognized for her photography of disabled and marginalized people, including those who would typically be featured as sideshow attractions. Some of Arbus's photos were published in *Esquire* in July 1960 in a photo essay entitled "The Vertical Journey: Six Movements of a Moment Within the Heart of the City." The 1960 publishing date of the *Esquire* photos calls into question Frank's 1951 date of his tattoo wall photo, and it has actually been disputed whether the fabled Eighth Avenue tattoo parlor even existed. Coincidentally, Hubert's was located between Broadway and Eighth Avenue.

After a long struggle with depression, Arbus committed suicide in July 1971 while a resident of the Westbeth artists community in the West Village. Had she still been living upon the release of *Exile on Main St.*, it's possible that she could have taken legal action against the band for using her photos in advertising without her consent. In fact, when *Exile* was re-released in a deluxe edition in 2010, Arbus's photo of Hezekiah Trambles, "The Jungle Creep," was used extensively in the marketing of the reissued album. In 2010, both Arbus and Trambles were long dead (a death certificate record gives Hezekiah Trambles of New York County's date of death as January 1, 1979).

* * * * *

Chief among the changing face of New York City was the changing of Times Square from New York's entertainment destination to a haven of crime and prostitution. While a sideshow attraction like Hubert's seemed out of place after the social and political movements of the late 1960s, it was at its heart a family circus attraction. That sort of entertainment had no place in the seedy Times Square of the 1970s.

The 1969 film *Midnight Cowboy*—filmed on location in New York in 1968—depicted the area as home to both heterosexual and homosexual prostitutes and other "undesirables." These problems only became more visible as the 1970s began. The crime rate—specifically the murder rate—continued to increase, with murders more than doubling from 1967 to 1972. As families continued to leave the city for the suburbs and the rise of criminal activity like drug use and underage prostitution increased, New York City increasingly appeared to outsiders to be a city lacking moral values. The city's traditional print media embracing a rock band known for its past drug arrests must have seemed completely fitting in the eyes of outsiders.

* * * * *

The Stones' 1972 tour was the stuff of legend even before it reached the four-night stand at Madison Square Garden that concluded the two-month trek (with the final show falling on Jagger's twenty-ninth birthday). The tour was promoted by Bill Graham, who had recently closed his Fillmore East and West venues to reinvent himself as the ultimate rock concert tour promoter, and naturally the Stones became his premier clients. To say the tour was unruly would be an understatement unworthy of the Stones. The band members traveled on a private jet with sixty people in their entourage. Fans were arrested at every tour stop, mostly for drug possession or trying to get into the shows without tickets. The Stones spent a few nights at the Playboy Mansion in Chicago as guests of Hugh Hefner. Richards and Stephen Stills nearly got into a knife fight in Denver. The Stones' equipment van was bombed in Montreal (Quebec separatists were suspected). Finally, Jagger and Richards were arrested in Rhode Island when Richards assaulted a photographer but were released because Boston mayor, Kevin White, pleaded with authorities to free the Glimmer Twins, fearing that canceling that night's Stones concert would result in rioting in Boston (the concert went on, but the Stones took the stage five hours late). The tour was documented by Robert Frank, who was making a film titled *Cocksucker Blues*. Due to the debauchery depicted, the film has never been officially released, though the band gave tacit approval for it to be screened during New York's Museum of Modern Art retrospective *The Rolling Stones: 50 Years on Film* in November 2012.

Their 1969 tour might have set the standard for rock tours, but the Stones' 1972 tour and the shows at Madison Square Garden would set the standard for pop culture events. After initially scheduling three shows in New York and then adding a fourth, the Stones realized that the demand far outweighed the supply. They decided to distribute tickets via a postcard lottery, a system they would continue to use in New York over the next several tours. New Yorkers had to mail requests for tickets from June 11 to June 16, and the Garden staff (supervised by an accounting firm) selected twenty thousand winners from the more than half a million submissions. Winners could buy up to four tickets at $6.50 each. Most bought the maximum, and many scalped their extra tickets for as high as seventy-five dollars each. Though the system was meant to eliminate long lines at ticket windows, when the Garden box office opened on July 10, lines had already been forming for hours. Not all of the fans in line were winners, and some had to leave empty-handed. A spokesperson for the Garden told UPI, "From a standpoint of demand I would say it is one of the hottest attractions we've ever had." In reference to a four-show stand at the Garden by Elvis Presley in early June—the only time Presley ever played concerts in New York City—the spokesman added, "Even Elvis Presley didn't generate as much excitement as the Stones." The Stones explored the option of ending the tour with a free outdoor concert in New York to meet demand, but with Altamont still fresh in people's minds, the plan was scrapped.

More than a week before the Stones arrived in New York, the press was already covering the mania surrounding their visit. Don Heckman wrote a glorifying multi-page review of the band's June 19 show in Chicago for *The New York Times* Sunday magazine that seemed to elevate Jagger and Richards to the status of Greek gods, even focusing on how Jagger's pants were "tailored of a silk-like material that clings so tightly that his genitalia are pushed up and out—a sexual display as aggressively protuberant as a fifties teen-age girl in a point bra." Aside from Jagger's member, the article also examined how the Stones organization had changed since the troubled 1969 tour. On the topic of the Garden postcard lottery, Richards remarked, "You know, they told us that a million people had written in for tickets in New York City. Which means we'd have to do something like 50 shows if we were to play for them all. That's almost unbelievable, and I have to admit I'm turned on by it. Any audience, when you're playing for them, can turn you on, but when you think of that million—and maybe another two or three million that didn't get around to sending in the applications—it's incredible." Both Heckman and *Rolling Stone* also covered the story of Cynthia Sagittarius, a spacey twenty-one-year-old woman who hitchhiked from New York to Vancouver for the first show and proceeded to hitchhike to almost every show on the tour on its way back to New York (the band eventually gave her a VIP pass). As if the hype for the New York shows wasn't big enough, Jagger boasted to the press that he might strip nude onstage for his birthday performance, which would also occur on the night of a full moon. *Variety* reported that the band wanted to release five hundred chickens into the audience or bring an elephant out onstage, but those plans were nixed by Garden management.

The day before the first show, July 23, was a rare off day. Mick and Bianca Jagger visited Princess Lee Radziwill's home in the affluent community of Southampton, Long Island. Radziwill, the younger sister of former first lady Jacqueline Kennedy Onassis, had spent several days on tour with the Stones earlier that month. Radziwill was acquainted with New York writer Truman Capote, who was commissioned to write about the tour for *Rolling Stone*, an assignment he ultimately never finished (*Rolling Stone* ended up featuring an interview with a drunken Capote conducted by Andy Warhol about the tour to roughly complete the assignment). Capote left the tour halfway, but both he and Radziwill were backstage at the Garden concerts. Not all of the Stones were as enamored of the presence of celebrities as Jagger was. Wyman later recalled a particular episode when the band was sitting backstage at the Garden with Radziwill, Capote, and talk show host Dick Cavett (who recorded interviews with Jagger and Wyman for a one-hour television special that aired on August 11). When it was time to hit the stage, Ian Stewart—never one for fussiness—entered the room and in front of all said to the Stones, "All right, my little shower of shit, you're on."

As anticipated, the opening night of the Stones at the Garden on July 24 resulted in some minor crowd control trouble, though five hundred police officers and security guards ensured that the spectacle did not get out of hand and blocked off Seventh and Eighth Avenues between 31st and 33rd Streets. Several hundred ticketless fans gathered on Seventh Avenue demanding entry, resulting in the arrests of several people for throwing objects at police or ticket scalping. *The Times* captured the bizarre circumstances, reporting, "There were weird outfits of satin and feathers, body paint and frosted sparkles. On the streets surrounding the Garden, drug dealers whispered their wares to passers-by while peddlers sold shirts emblazoned with the Rolling Stones emblem, a huge, lascivious red tongue." *The Times* also profiled the crew, who began assembling the stage and lighting at seven o'clock in the morning on the day of the first show. The article boasted of the Stones' $115,000, sixteen-thousand-watt sound system, which was 60 percent louder than the 1969 tour's amplification (the article claimed it had been measured at 136 decibels).

Heckman did not offer the same level of praise as he had for the Stones' Chicago performance when he reviewed the first Garden concert for *The Times*, which he blamed on the band's feeling anxious. He said, "For the Stones, the tensions of a New York opening may or may not have had their effects, but as Stones shows have gone on this particular tour, the performance was no better than average." In contrast, among three glowing write-ups about the first show in the *Village Voice*, Ira Mayer declared, "[We] may well take the title away from another (faltering) Garden attraction, the Ringling Brothers, Barnum and Bailey Circus. Yes, the Rolling Stones just may be the Greatest Show on Earth." Heckman had better things to say about both shows on June 25, claiming that the evening performance marked "the first time since they hit New York [that] the Stones found their stride, stopped relying on reputation and image, and played some tough-as-nails rock 'n' roll." The following day, he declared the tour-ending fourth concert the best of them all, "probably the most emotionally charged program in the Stones' long, two-month trek across the United States and Canada." Nearly every media outlet responded to the concerts with an overflow of praise, with the *New York Post*'s Al Aronowitz going as far as to say, "Ah, thank you Stones for giving New York the best of you. You put us first on your list by making us last on your tour." The few naysayers included New Jersey's *Free Aquarian*, an independent periodical, which said,

> *"The Stones, as usual, were pure excitement. But musically, they were dull and unimaginative. Except for Taylor's beautiful solo in 'Love in Vain,' there was no improvisation, no long jams. Everything was set beforehand, every guitar note and drum beat was planned. Maybe*

they feel as if they don't have to prove themselves anymore, maybe they're just tired of it all, but it still would be real nice if the Stones, just once, came onstage in dungarees and sacrificed a little sparkle and excitement for music. It would make a whole lot of people feel a little better about them."

The *Aquarian* was right about the tour's being too rehearsed. Even more so than the 1969 tour, the Stones did not stray from the tour's set list. In fact, after making some small changes during the first month of the tour, by the beginning of July the Stones did not make any changes to the set list. The sixteen-song set included six songs from *Exile on Main St.*, "Rocks Off," "Happy," "Tumbling Dice," "Sweet Virginia," "All Down the Line," and "Rip This Joint," and two from *Sticky Fingers*, "Brown Sugar" and "Bitch." For the encores, the Stones were joined by Stevie Wonder and his band for a medley of Wonder's 1966 hit song "Uptight (Everything's Alright)" and "Satisfaction," the only pre-1968 Stones song in the set. Richards later claimed that Klein's ownership of the Stones' pre-1971 catalog prevented them from using more classics. Those rights issues also prevented the band from releasing a live album.

The final concert also featured a rendition of "Happy Birthday" dedicated to Jagger, after which he was presented with a two-tier birthday cake. Bianca came onstage and handed him a stuffed panda while the crew wheeled out 150 lemon meringue pies. Naturally, the pies became weapons in a huge onstage pie fight among the band and crew.

The first concert was followed by a six-hundred-person party at the Four Seasons, where Jagger notably stayed for less than ten minutes. The big blowout to celebrate Jagger's birthday was saved for after the fourth show, hosted by Ahmet Ertegun on the roof of the St. Regis hotel.

The St. Regis remains one of the most prestigious of Manhattan's early-twentieth-century luxury hotels. Located just two blocks south of Central Park at 55th Street between Madison and Fifth Avenues, the St. Regis was built by the Astor family and opened in 1904. More than twenty years later, new owners built two more stories on the previously eighteen-floor hotel, including adding a grand ballroom on the roof. The hotel is most notable for claiming to have created a morning cocktail called the Red Snapper, though it is now known worldwide by its far more popular name, the Bloody Mary. The hotel already had a solid rock 'n' roll pedigree. The previous year, John Lennon and Yoko Ono were living in the hotel, and, in October 1971, Lennon recorded the demo version of "Happy Xmas (War Is Over)" in his room. Lennon recorded the single at the Record Plant just one week later.

The five-hundred-person guest list included many New York social-ites. Other guests included Stevie Wonder, Tennessee Williams, Woody Allen, Diane Keaton, George Plimpton, Carly Simon, Andy Warhol, Bob Dylan (who also attended the June 24 concert), and Zsa Zsa Gabor. Stripper and Warhol pal Geri Miller, described by the *Daily News* as "a young lady with about five pounds of silicone in each breast" popped out of a giant birthday cake. Also entertaining the guests were Count Basie, Muddy Waters (Jagger and Wonder briefly jammed with Waters), and a tap-dancing troupe from Harlem. Years later, Jagger would recall, "The two bands that Ahmet had booked for my birthday party was Count Basie and Muddy Waters. I thought I'd died and gone to heaven, really." The admiration wasn't entirely mutual. In an interview with the *Washington Post* a few weeks later, Waters said of performing with the lead singer of the band that was named in tribute to him, "We had a ball there, drinking and singing with—now what's that boy's name?"

Though the party was thrown for Jagger, the gossip columns in New York's papers and magazines barely mentioned the Stones. Tour manager Peter Rudge told *Rolling Stone* that the mix of society and tour personnel at the party was uncomfortable. "The party was depressing. It was a very nice gesture, a party thrown for Mick and the group, but it was really very, very difficult for anyone on the tour to relate to those people. You know—what does princess so-and-so have to do with the assistant electrician sitting at the next table? No one could really enjoy themselves in that kind of environment." When he was interviewed on the road by *New Musical Express*, Richards also expressed annoyance at the Stones' celebrity hangers-on. He said,

"It's a difficult thing to handle anyway, because it starts with things like—'Oh, Truman Capote is going to come along and write something on the Stones'—and he comes along and brings along Princess Lee Radziwill and some other socialites from New York and you're surrounded by those people. And it just takes one guy like Capote to trigger it off. I mean, all those jet-setters must be bored or something. They seem to be on this massive ego trip anyway, which I just don't want to know about. All I can say is—those people will not be around a second time. There's no way they're going to be in our company ever again."

Richards also added that this wasn't the first time that they had been objects of the upper class's affection. "But that situation was nothing new for us. I mean, back in 1964 when we were touring the States, we'd been invited to parties by all these 'socially important' people. Back then we'd just tell 'em where to go."

Indeed, critics wondered what it was about the band that now made them so acceptable to the upper crust of society. The following month, critic Peter Schjeldahl wrote a *Times* editorial suggesting that the near-universal praise for the Stones in New York media could be because rock journalists who had grown up with the band's music had a soft spot for the group (though he himself praised the performances). But the change in public perception of the Stones was clear. As Lisa Robinson wrote in the UK music magazine *Disc* in her review of the Garden concerts, "Once a scruffy band of outlaws, the Rolling Stones are the darlings of the jet-set, international society, and big names now—and all of this has said a lot more about them in New York than anything else this week, including their four sold-out concerts."

Regardless of the changing opinion in the media and among celebrities, fans still flocked to see the band, especially in New York. Of the tour's almost $4-million gross, nearly $500,000 of it came from the Garden concerts.

* * * * *

After the tour, the Stones took an extended break, which included several of the members country-hopping to avoid British taxes, as well as French authorities, who were also after them for taxes regarding their time spent in France. The band and Anita Pallenberg were also facing drug charges by French authorities, which were later tossed out for everyone except Richards and Pallenberg, who in 1973 were barred from entering France for two years. In late November Jagger made a brief stop in New York to visit John Lennon and Yoko Ono at the Record Plant studio to play guitar on Ono's "Is Winter Here to Stay?" The song was released on her 1973 album *Approximately Infinite Universe*. (In an interview with *New Musical Express*, Jagger explained with the air of a backhanded compliment, "I just went in there and disrupted it, really. I started playing the guitar very loudly with John. Actually, it was Yoko's record they were doing. She's doing very straight things and trying to sing properly. She's not screaming, she's really trying to sing. You know, carrying a tune and that type of thing.")

Afterward he flew to Jamaica, where the Stones started work on the follow-up to *Exile*. In early 1973, the band performed a benefit concert in Los Angeles for the victims of the recent earthquake in Bianca Jagger's home country, Nicaragua, which was followed by a brief tour of Hawaii, New Zealand, and Australia. (A planned tour of Japan was canceled when Japanese officials refused to allow Jagger entry because of his past drug convictions. Australia initially banned the band as well but later relented.) In the meantime, the Stones continued working on songs for the next album, which the band titled *Goats Head Soup*. It was released in August 1973, shortly before the Stones' seven-week tour of Europe. Though certainly not reaching the artistic heights of *Exile*, the album received positive reviews in *Rolling Stone* and *The New York Times*.

Goats Head Soup started a tradition of the Stones' recording songs that mentioned New York City. Previously, the only mention of New York in a Stones lyric was the line "I laid a divorcee in New York City" in "Honky Tonk Women." On *Goats Head Soup* three songs include references to New York. Most similar to the sexual "Honky Tonk Women" lyric is the New York reference in "Starfucker," a song about a groupie (in the US the song's title was censored to "Star Star"). The song generated controversy not only because of its repeated use of "You're a starfucker" in its chorus, but because the lyrics referenced the groupie bedding Steve McQueen and John Wayne. The song includes the couplets: "Baby, baby, I've been so sad since you've been gone / Way back to New York City," and "If I ever get back to Fun City, girl / I'm gonna make you scream all night."

The phrase "Fun City" became a satirical nickname for New York from the first day of Mayor Lindsay's tenure when the Transport Workers Union of America "celebrated" by going on strike. When asked about the strike on live TV, Lindsay responded, "I still think it's a fun city." *New York Herald Tribune* writer Dick Schaap ridiculed Lindsay's softball answer in his January 7 editorial, "The Fun City":

> *Not long after the transit strike began the other day, Mayor John Lindsay went on radio and television to announce that New York is a fun city. He certainly has a wonderful sense of humor. A little while later, Lindsay cheerfully walked four miles from his hotel room to City Hall, a gesture which proved that the fun city had a fun Mayor....*
>
> *The funniest thing was that New Yorkers actually were finding humor in the absence of buses and subways. One citizen was very concerned that the pickpockets and muggers, the true New Yorkers, he called them, would get out of shape. He offered to give them a room where they could practice on each other for the duration of the crisis.*

In short order "Fun City" became the nickname for the seedier side of New York. The question "What's new in Fun City?" would inevitably be answered by stories of crime, civic incompetence, and failing social welfare programs. Since Lindsay's tenure in office was rife with problems, columnists never seemed to run out of new ways to shower abuse on him with stories about "Fun City." As a result, a Rolling Stones song about a promiscuous groupie turning tricks in Fun City released in the final months of Lindsay's tenure as mayor seemed incredibly appropriate in a twisted sort of way, since New York became increasingly more of a "fun" city throughout his time in office.

Another song that captures the danger and seediness of New York is "Dancing with Mr. D," a slow-paced, riff-driven funk song about late-night trysts with "Mr. D," a sinister character who brings death along with him. It's not hard to view the titular Mr. D as the Grim Reaper or the Devil, and the lyrics reflect the many places Mr. D can be found, including "hiding in a corner in New York City." With New York's reputation as "Fun City," anyone hiding in a corner could be perceived as a threat.

"Dancing with Mr. D" was the B-side to the album's second single, the US top-twenty hit "Doo Doo Doo Doo Doo (Heartbreaker)." Based on the somewhat ridiculous title and the word "Heartbreaker," one might assume the song is a doo-wop-style song about a broken heart. However, unlike the other two songs on *Goats Head Soup* that mention New York, "Heartbreaker" appears to be based on a specific incident. In the early morning on April 28, 1973, ten-year-old African American Clifford Glover was walking with his stepfather, Add Armstead, in South Jamaica, Queens. The pair was stopped for questioning by two plainclothes police officers in an unmarked car regarding an earlier taxi robbery, even though Armstead and Glover did not fit the description of the perpetrators. As the officers approached, Armstead and Glover fled. Armstead later said because the officers were not in uniform, they thought the pair was aiming to rob them, especially since one of the cops, Thomas Shea, brandished his weapon. Shea, a thirty-six-year-old white officer, fired and shot Glover in the back, killing him. Shea and his partner were then recorded making disparaging comments toward Glover to a dispatcher. Shea later claimed that he saw Glover carrying a gun, but no weapon was found. When news of the shooting broke, riots erupted in Queens. Shea was charged with murder, and the police union was ridiculed for trying to help Shea beat the charges.

The shooting made headlines not only because of the racial component, but also because of two troubling facts: Glover was the youngest person ever killed by an NYPD officer, and Shea became the first NYPD officer to be tried for murder while on duty. Just the year before, police officers in New York had fired 2,510 bullets in the line of duty, the highest number ever recorded, and it was revealed that Shea had fired his weapon four other times in the previous six years. Coming on the heels of the Knapp Commission investigations, the shooting of Glover added to the distrust the public already had of the NYPD. Shea was eventually declared not guilty in June 1974, leading to more riots and even more reasons for many New Yorkers to feel suspicious of the NYPD.

Jagger has never confirmed or denied that the lyrics of "Heart-breaker" are about Glover, but it's hard to dispute that the first verse was likely influenced by the shooting ("The po-lice in New York City / They chased a boy right through the park / In a case of mistaken iden-tity / They put a bullet through his heart"). The second verse tells the sordid tale of a ten-year-old girl who died in an alleyway of a heroin overdose. Though a real-life equivalent of this story has not been iden-tified, it reflects both the drug culture of "Fun City" and of the Stones themselves. The chorus of the song repeats how these incidents are examples of a "heartbreaker" that can "tear your world apart" and steal "the love right out of your heart." As with the other two songs on *Goats Head Soup*, "Heartbreaker" did not reflect the glitzy Manhattan that had welcomed the Stones in 1972 with open arms and lavish parties. It was the urban decay that inspired them.

* * * * *

Goats Head Soup became a number-one record in both the US and the UK. It quickly went gold in both territories on the strength of its first single, "Angie," which reached number one in the US and number five in the UK. After the fall European tour ended, the band jumped almost immediately into recording its next album in West Germany. Jagger took a break from the sessions to visit New York to attend the open-ing of The Bottom Line, a nightclub on West 4th Street in Greenwich Village. The popular small venue hosted members of the Stones several times. Richards joined Rockpile onstage there on October 25, 1978, to play Chuck Berry's "Let It Rock," which was later aired on the *King Biscuit Flower Hour* radio program. Richards also joined bluesman Robert Cray onstage there on November 21, 1986, saw Billy Connolly's comedy show there on March 24, 1987, and saw Billy Preston perform there on January 21, 1988. Jagger saw Stevie Ray Vaughan play there on May 9, 1983, and he took the stage on January 26, 1988, to perform "Red House" with Joe Satriani, who later became the guitarist of Jagger's solo touring band. Mick Taylor would make the first of several appearances there on August 1, 1986. The venue hosted dozens of notable performers and remained popular with musicians until it closed in 2004.

On Easter Sunday, April 14, 1974, the Ziegfeld Theatre hosted the premiere of *Ladies and Gentlemen: The Rolling Stones*, a concert film that had been recorded during four shows in Texas during the 1972 tour. To celebrate, the band's management planned a massive street fair with live music, sumo wrestling, kung fu demonstrations, sideshow attractions, and circus animals on West 54th Street between Sixth and Seventh Avenues, the block where the Ziegfeld is located. The Ziegfeld opened in 1969 as one of the last single-screen movie theaters (it was the only one-thousand-plus-seat single-screen movie house left in the city until closing in 2016) and was named after the previous Ziegfeld Theatre, a Broadway theater that was located down the street from 1927 to 1966. Radio station WNEW had six hundred tickets to give away for the premiere and received fifty thousand requests. The massive interest made the event seem like a potential disaster in the making, especially once Jagger made several ridiculous announcements that made the festival a must-see, including saying he would arrive in a car covered with rubber ducks.

City officials revoked the permit when police said that the estimated one hundred thousand attendees would overrun the block. Promoters attempted to move the fair to Central Park but ended up canceling both the festival and the red carpet event—at which all the Stones except Richards were scheduled to appear, along with other notable musicians including John Lennon, David Bowie, and Alice Cooper—since thousands of Stones fans would have probably shown up, creating a massive security issue. The Stones had planned to release two thousand white pigeons and one thousand Frisbees into the crowd. The movie still screened that night, but only to the six hundred listeners who had won tickets via WNEW and four hundred members of the press and their guests. The only pageantry was the forty-foot Rolling Stones tongue logo balloon designed by Andy Warhol hanging above the theater, and the free Frisbees. Nevertheless, the premiere proved that New York wasn't any less starved for the Stones than they were in 1972.

New York reviews of the film were positive, especially because the film was released with a unique four-track quadraphonic soundtrack that re-created the audio of the concert (screenings of the film required a sound truck to operate the audio). Patrick Carr of the *Village Voice* beamed, "To watch the Stones in action and on form from as close as a camera can get is to witness the ultimate in rock, and that's what 'Ladies and Gentlemen, the Rolling Stones' does for you." Because of its roadshow presentation, the film did great business in major cities and was eventually converted to mono so it could be screened in any movie theater.

Over the following months, the Stones worked on outside projects. Wyman released his first solo album, *Monkey Grip*, which he promoted on the New York radio program *Speakeasy* with pianist Dr. John, who played on the album. Jagger, Richards, and Taylor worked on solo recordings for Faces guitarist Ronnie Wood. Wood was a longtime friend of Taylor's, and Jagger and Richards had crossed paths with him before. Wood had previously worked with Jagger on the demo version of "It's Only Rock 'n' Roll (But I Like It)," which became the first single and title track of the upcoming Stones album. *It's Only Rock 'n' Roll* was released in October.

New York critics in general reacted negatively to the new album. In *The Times*, John Rockwell wrote that he felt the phrase "it's only rock 'n' roll" served as a putdown to all the artists who sought to use rock and roll as a serious art form. In the *Village Voice*, famed rock critic Lester Bangs accused the Stones of becoming "oblique in their old age" and said the album lacked edge; he included a somewhat vague suggestion that the Stones should just commit suicide. Neither single—"It's Only Rock 'n' Roll (But I Like It)" or the second, a cover of the Temptations' "Ain't Too Proud to Beg"—broke into the top ten in the US, and though the album reached number one in the US and went gold, it was considered a disappointment.

The album included one song that referenced New York. "Till the Next Goodbye," a ballad about a parting couple, features the opening lines, "Honey, is there any place that you would like to eat? / I know a coffee shop down on 52nd Street." The tender invitation turns nasty in the second verse, "Yeah, a movie house on 42nd Street / Ain't a very lovely place for you and I to meet."

"Till the Next Goodbye" would be the last song Taylor recorded with the Stones for several decades, and the 1972 Madison Square Garden shows would be the last time he performed with the Stones in New York City for forty years. In November 1974 he quit the band (the split was announced to the public the following month). Taylor has since given various reasons for leaving the band, but chief among them were his dissatisfaction with the Stones' limited touring schedule, his drug addictions, and not receiving credit for his contributions to songs that he felt warranted songwriting credit, including "Till the Next Goodbye."

The Stones began recording their next album in West Germany shortly after Taylor left, but did the bulk of the recordings in January and February in the Netherlands. The band used the sessions to audition over a half-dozen guitarists for the spot vacated by Taylor. After they had toured the US in 1969 and 1972, another three years had passed and the Stones were already planning to tour again in 1975. In order to do that, they needed to find the right replacement for Taylor.

CHAPTER 5

"BEEN TEN THOUSAND MILES"

Word on the 1975 tour started with rumors in the press that the Stones were preparing a sweep across America. This time, however, the pop music columns were buried beneath article after article about the decline of New York City.

On April 11, John Rockwell of *The New York Times* reported that the Stones were planning a summer US tour that would include shows at both Nassau Coliseum and Madison Square Garden in late June. The Stones ultimately didn't play at the Coliseum (and never have played a show there, although the group used it for rehearsals for the 1989 tour), opting for an extended run at the Garden instead. Rockwell also speculated in his article on who would fill in on guitar after the departure of Mick Taylor in December 1974. Though Rockwell said that his sources were telling him Wayne Perkins of the Muscle Shoals Sound Studio, who had previously played on Bill Wyman's solo album *Monkey Grip* and had contributed to the sessions for the Stones' next album, would be joining the group on tour, he correctly predicted that the position would be filled by Faces guitarist Ronnie Wood.

Twenty-seven-year-old Wood already had been associated with the Rolling Stones for over a year before he was recruited for the job.

Wood had worked with Jagger on the Stones' hit "It's Only Rock 'n' Roll (But I Like It)." The demo version of the song was recorded at Wood's house, and Wood's acoustic guitar from the demo appears on the final track. Jagger and Richards returned the favor by working on Wood's first solo album, 1974's *I've Got My Own Album to Do*. Earlier in 1975 Wood also played guitar and provided backing vocals on several tracks for the recording sessions that would later make up the *Black and Blue* album. Jagger and Richards offered Wood the job if he could work it out with his commitments to the Faces. The Faces had a US tour that ended in mid-March and another US tour that began in August, which allowed Wood to join the Stones. The latter Faces tour ended up being the group's swan song, allowing Wood to join the Stones full-time at the end of 1975.

The announcement of the 1975 tour—named the Tour of the Americas '75, although it never went south of San Antonio—began the longstanding tradition of the Stones' announcing their tours with publicity stunts in New York City. A press conference was scheduled at the Feather Restaurant at the Fifth Avenue Hotel at Ninth Street and Fifth Avenue on May 1. The band arrived in New York on April 26. Jagger and Watts stayed at the Plaza hotel, while Richards, Wood, Wyman, and touring pianist Billy Preston stayed at the Pierre three blocks away. The first indication to the public that something big was happening was when a billboard went up in Times Square announcing the tour, though the billboard initially said "the Rolling Stores" before it was corrected the morning of the press conference.

On May 1, the band and Preston snuck out of the Plaza and traveled via ice cream van to 12th Street and Fifth Avenue, where they hopped aboard a flatbed truck. The truck began driving south on Fifth Avenue, and the Stones launched into "Brown Sugar" as it rolled along. The two hundred members of the international press stationed at the Fifth Avenue Hotel were enjoying complimentary drinks and lunch and a rambling performance by comedian Professor Irwin Corey when they noticed the men they were supposed to be interviewing playing on a flatbed outside the hotel's window. Wood joked that the members of the press were not pleased with the bait and switch, recalling,

> *"Journalists raced after the flatbed, yelling at us, complaining that we'd promised them interviews. And the more they yelled at us, the more we yelled back, 'Fuck you.' We kept right on playing and right on rolling and more and more people going to work followed us on foot, like we were the Pied Piper, which messed up traffic all over that part of Manhattan. Folks came up from the subway, saw us rolling by and God only knows what some of them thought."*

The truck's route took them past the dorms of New York University, full of young students whom the Stones hoped to draw to the concerts.

Most of all, the band was loud during their brief performance. The United Press International report said that "the racket sounded as if every stereo owner in town had conspired to turn his set up full blast simultaneously." After the performance, Jagger threw to the crowd press releases printed on colored paper that announced the tour and the initial dates. The truck moved on to Washington Square Park, where the Stones dismounted and hopped into several limousines. The scheduled press conference never took place, though some radio stations were able to broadcast the performance.

Watts was credited for coming up with the gimmick, having read of jazz bands' doing that as a way to promote themselves. However, it wasn't the first time that a rock band had done that type of promotional performance. The opening credits of the 1958 movie *High School Confidential* feature Jerry Lee Lewis and his band playing the title song on the back of a truck, and the Grateful Dead did an entire concert in San Francisco in March 1968 on a flatbed. The Stones' performance down Fifth Avenue made far more headlines, and because of that it has had lasting influence. Hard rock band AC/DC filmed a music video of the group playing on a flatbed truck driving the streets of Melbourne, Australia, in February 1976. Icelandic singer Björk and rock band U2 would also repeat the stunt in Manhattan for music videos in 1993 and 2004, respectively.

Tour dates had already leaked out before the announcement was made by radio stations across the country at noon, including the band's record-setting run of six shows at Madison Square Garden. Tickets went on sale that day as soon as the announcement aired, with hundreds of fans already in line at the Garden's box office—some having waited as long as two days—to buy tickets at $12.50 each (higher than the $8 to $10 price at other venues across the country). The late announcements didn't hurt ticket sales at all, and tickets for all six concerts were almost entirely sold out by the end of the day.

* * * * *

While the Stones were throwing an impromptu concert down Fifth Avenue, city officials were in the midst of a fiscal crisis unlike any faced by a major American city before. By the end of 1975, New York City was heading towards bankruptcy. The population declined as thousands moved to the suburbs, resulting in a shrinking tax base. The country as a whole was also facing the worst economic recession since the Great Depression and a spike in unemployment. New York City simply did not have enough money to cover its extensive social programs, especially since the poor and the unemployed weren't among those moving away. City agencies slashed their budgets in order to stay afloat. Budget cuts forced the Transit Authority to virtually stop maintaining the subway system, and subway cars and stations were covered with graffiti and fraught with criminal activity.

However, the city's fiscal problems were dwarfed in the news by the escalating crime rate, and particularly gruesome crimes received extensive media coverage. The reputation of New York City as a center of commerce and culture plummeted as crime rates steadily rose. Just weeks before the Stones' promotional gimmick, the murder of a fifteen-year-old prostitute at the Belmore Hotel made headlines. Times Square had long been a haven for drug-related crime and prostitution, and Bryant Park, a formerly celebrated public space just sixteen blocks north of the Fifth Avenue Hotel, was overrun by drug users and homeless people. The year 1975 began in New York City with the January 24 bombing of the historic downtown Fraunces Tavern, which killed four, and ended with the December 29 bombing at LaGuardia Airport, which killed eleven. In June, the New York Police Department laid off fifty thousand employees. (The number of police officers would decline by a third over the next five years.) As the number of police officers decreased, crime rates spiked, resulting in some of the most violent years in the history of the city.

The Rolling Stones were no stranger to headlines about drugs and violence, of course. While the raid on Richards's Redlands home was ancient history by 1975 and the 1972 tour helped to put the harsh memories of Altamont behind them, Richards's London arrest for drug possession in June 1973 and subsequent conviction were still being mentioned in the press. However, aside from Richards's reckless driving arrest in Arkansas, the 1975 tour went on with little trouble with the law. For the first time, it seemed that most people were more scared of walking the streets of Manhattan than of the Rolling Stones. It marked a cultural shift for the Stones, and one that would tie the group closely to New York City's culture scene through the rest of the 1970s.

* * * * *

After the flatbed truck stunt, the Stones were off to Andy Warhol's Eothen estate in Montauk, the easternmost point of Long Island, for rehearsals. Jagger had previously visited Montauk after the conclusion of the 1972 tour and Jagger's wild twenty-ninth-birthday party. Famed photographer Peter Beard—who had accompanied the Stones on the 1972 tour—flew Jagger and his wife to his Montauk estate for a few days.

Beard lived next door to Eothen and rented his house to the group for $5,000 a month while they rehearsed for the 1975 tour at film director Paul Morrissey's house nearby. It was here that Ronnie Wood was given his first contract to become an employee of the Rolling Stones, and also where Jagger and Richards posed shirtless for the famous photo that appeared on the cover of the July 17 issue of *Rolling Stone*. The image was caught by Annie Leibovitz, who would accompany the Stones on the tour.

After throwing a party the next day for Bianca Jagger's thirtieth birthday, the band went to work on rehearsing. The intention was to use the resort town as a quiet place to work with Wood and Preston on the band's set, but word soon got out that the Stones were in town. Groupies and various other hangers-on were attracted to the seaside community with little regard for the normally docile resort.

On May 14, Jagger and his wife did a press conference at LaGuardia Airport in Queens, which they flew to from Montauk on a chartered plane. Jagger spoke to reporters about the stage design for the upcoming tour and dispelled rumors that the tour would be the band's last. However, Jagger did make a statement about the longevity of the band that has gone on to haunt him for decades. When the thirty-one-year-old Jagger was asked about how long the Stones would last, John Rockwell of *The New York Times* quoted his response as, "Will I still be singing when I'm 45? Well, Chuck Berry does, and Dylan could, definitely. It's whether I'll *want* to. I don't think you can go on acting like a 21-year-old. I'd rather be dead than sing 'Satisfaction' when I'm 45." Curiously, "Satisfaction" was left off the set list of the 1975 tour, but Jagger has been asked repeatedly about the quote in dozens, if not hundreds, of interviews since, especially once he started to approach middle age.

The stay in Montauk also inspired the title and lyrics of one of the Stones' most endearing songs, the ballad "Memory Motel." The seven-minute song has been a favorite of Stones fans for its haunting melody and tender lyrics about a man who has a one-night stand with an independent woman who leaves him heartbroken (often speculated to be singer-songwriter Carly Simon, and though Jagger has never confirmed this, he did tell *Rolling Stone*, "Well, the girl in 'Memory Motel' is actually a real, independent American girl. But they are mostly imaginary, you're right....Actually, the girl in 'Memory Motel' is a combination"). Though the music for the song had been recorded earlier in the year during the sessions that would eventually make up the *Black and Blue* album, the final vocals were not added until later in the year after the abrupt end of the Tour of the Americas.

The Memory Motel in Montauk is almost indistinguishable from the many other beach motels that take up most of the real estate in Montauk. It certainly lacks the lavish accommodations that the Stones were used to. Furthermore, there is little truth to the claims that Jagger or any of the other Stones spent much time at the Memory Motel. Most accounts have it that the band was at the motel bar just once and was asked to leave by the owners. The legends often speak about the band's fondness for the hotel bar's piano and pool table, though Jagger spent more time that summer at the seafood restaurant Shagwong a quarter mile up the road. The facts about the Stones' connection with the motel are often embellished, including the oft-repeated "fact" that the Stones wrote "Wild Horses" on the piano in the bar—which would have been very difficult to do in 1975 considering the song was released in 1971, a year before Jagger was the first Stone to visit Montauk. The name of the motel left an impression on Jagger, but other than that, stories of the Stones' time at the real Memory Motel are often as dreamlike as the titular song's melody and lyrics. Today the Memory Motel features a sizable collection of Rolling Stones memorabilia adorning its walls, and it's likely the motel will always be thought of as a landmark for Stones fans.

One very real incident that took place during the Montauk rehearsals almost put the tour in jeopardy. On May 17, Jagger was having dinner with Atlantic Records chairman Ahmet Ertegun at Gosman's restaurant, a Montauk institution. When the pair left the restaurant, Jagger accidentally put his hand through the plate glass door, cutting his wrist open. Despite getting twenty stitches, Jagger had no time to rest—rehearsals were already scheduled to be moved to Stewart Airport in Newburgh, a town in upstate New York about seventy miles north of Manhattan, so the Stones could practice on the tour's stage that had been built in an unused hanger. The band then returned to Montauk on May 26 for final rehearsals before flying to Baton Rouge, Louisiana, for the first two shows on June 1.

The band rehearsed scores of songs in Montauk. Wood has variously claimed he had to learn anywhere between 160 and two hundred songs, though that amounts to more than the Stones' entire recorded output by 1975. Regardless, nearly the entirety of the tour's set list—which had some variations from night to night—were songs the Stones had released on their previous six albums. The only pre-*Beggars Banquet* song that the band played on tour was "Get Off My Cloud" as part of a medley with "If You Can't Rock Me." The set also included the pop standard "That's Life" sung by Billy Preston, along with Preston's 1971 instrumental single "Outa-Space."

Though the New York concerts were in the middle of the tour, both the band's six-night stand at Madison Square Garden and five-night stand at the Los Angeles Forum were treated as marquee social events. On the day of the first show, *The New York Times* published an essay by writer Joyce Maynard about her longtime devotion to the Stones, suggesting that the band's continued appeal for those her age was mainly one of nostalgia. Maynard also wrote a glowing review of the June 12 concert in Boston that *The Times* published on June 29. On June 22, *The Times* published a lengthy essay by writer and jazz pianist Frank Conroy about the rehearsals in Newburgh and Montauk and the first show of the tour in Baton Rouge. The in-depth coverage showed a marked change for a newspaper that a decade prior had found little more to write about the Stones besides their haircuts. Even the *Wall Street Journal*, which had rarely written about the band, published an article on June 20 about tour manager Peter Rudge and the logistics of managing a crew of seventy-eight across North America. The entire city seemed seeped in Stones pandemonium. Ticketless fans roamed the streets outside the Garden looking for sellers, and the Plaza hotel, where the group had been booked to stay, canceled the group's reservations due to security concerns after it leaked that the band was staying there.

The performances at the Garden were indeed events. Compared to the rest of the tour, they featured different stage setups, specials guests, and encore performances of "Sympathy for the Devil," the first time the band performed it live since the song had been misidentified by the *Village Voice* as the song that the band had been playing when Meredith Hunter was murdered at Altamont. The steel Garden stage was twenty-five tons, more than twice the weight of the wooden stage used everywhere else, and took two days to assemble. It retained the lotus-flower design of the everyday touring stage, but it included additional lights and projections. The lighting rigs took another two days to set up. Though the Garden was also decorated with 350 ten-foot gauze leaves hanging from the ceiling, they were removed before the first show, presumably to prevent those in the upper levels—particularly those on mind-altering substances—from trying to reach out and grab them. On Seventh Avenue, the air was electric. In her review for *Sounds*, Barbara Charone remarked, "Outside the Garden you can buy anything except tickets for the show."

Instead of an opening act, the Stones hired over one hundred steel drummers from Brooklyn—a collective known as the Steelbands Association of the Americas—to play throughout the arena to entertain the entering crowds. The drummers would later join the band each night for "Sympathy for the Devil." Also joining the band for the encore were guitarists Eric Clapton on June 22 and Carlos Santana on June 27. (Bob Dylan attended the June 27 concert but didn't appear onstage.) Despite the six shows played, there was little variation in the set list. Richards didn't perform "Happy" on June 24 and 25 (he also did not play on the encore on June 24, due to exhaustion), and the band did not perform "Wild Horses" on June 26. On June 23, the Stones added their cover of the Eric Donaldson song "Cherry Oh Baby" for the first time, which they had recorded for the upcoming *Black and Blue* album. The group played "Cherry Oh Baby" again on June 27.

Despite the increased spectacle and expanded set list, the Garden concerts did not receive the universal praise that the Stones' previous performances at the Garden had garnered. Robert Christgau of the *Village Voice* gave the first Garden show a less-than-stellar review, remarking, "Perhaps because it was opening night in New York, they were working too hard. Not a great show." In particular, he criticized Jagger's stage presence and the choice of Preston as pianist for the tour. John Rockwell of *The New York Times* gave the show a more positive review, but also stated in his lengthy review, "The concert as a whole was neither the firm and final proof that the Stones are washed up nor the greatest pop-music concert in the history of creation," and he complained that the concert was too calculated, though it's worth noting that Rockwell had already seen several performances of the tour. Political speechwriter and journalist Ben Stein, who later parlayed his notoriety into a memorable acting career in the 1980s in films like *Ferris Bueller's Day Off*, attended the first Garden concert and reviewed it for the *Wall Street Journal*. Stein summarized the entire experience as one loud thrashing of noise after another—from the public address system to the steel drummers, to the audience, and to the band members themselves—but praised the spectacle (including his enjoyment of watching various characters in the audience). In *Rolling Stone*, Dave Marsh agreed that the first performance did not go smoothly and blamed the mix and several technical issues with the new stage setup that were figured out by the second concert. Harshest of all, Jan Hodenfield of the *New York Post* declared that the Stones' best days were behind them.

After the first show, the Stones went to the uptown apartment of Earl McGrath, an executive with Atlantic Records, and jammed with Clapton until the early morning. It was said that Jagger and Richards went back to the Garden early the next day to investigate the sound problems. Rockwell attended all of the band's performances at the Garden and declared that June 23, 25, and 27 were the best and opening night on June 22 was the worst, echoing his earlier review. He also wasn't the only reviewer in America to suggest that the Stones might no longer deserve the title of "The World's Greatest Rock 'n' Roll Band" after the 1975 tour.

The mixed reception of the Garden shows and the 1975 tour as a whole served as something of a shift in the Stones' operations. Now that the core members were all in their thirties, the group's longevity both helped and hurt them. The press was already suggesting that the Stones were too old to play rock and roll, and the relatively scandal-less

1975 tour somewhat robbed the band of its hell-raising reputation that it had used as a public relations windfall with younger fans over the previous dozen years. Elton John, Led Zeppelin, and Pink Floyd were the top rock acts of the year in terms of album sales, and even though John and many of the other musicians were contemporaries of the Stones, their music was connecting more with young arena audiences than that of the Stones. It wasn't that the Stones couldn't sell tickets or albums anymore, but with *The New York Times* publishing think pieces about the band's nostalgic appeal, it was understandably difficult to see the group as being on the cutting edge of music. It was a line of thinking that the Stones tried to fight, notably with their set list, which still focused entirely on more recent music and left off the band's biggest hits of the mid-1960s.

* * * * *

The cover of the October 29, 1975, edition of the *New York Daily News* proclaimed "Ford to City: Drop Dead." It was a shorthand description of one of the tensest periods in the history of the city. After years of financial difficulties, New York City officials approached US president Gerald Ford to ask for a bailout. Ford refused and insisted that the city practice more disciplined financial management, inspiring the headline that would rapidly increase Ford's unpopularity in urban areas. Those who saw New York as a failing institution of mismanagement and vice applauded the president's decision. Nonetheless, the looming bankruptcy forced the city government to streamline its budget with cuts and tense negotiations. (Jagger referenced the 1973–1975 US recession and New York's looming financial troubles on the *Black and Blue* track "Hot Stuff" with the lyric "All the people in New York City / I know you all going broke / But I know you're tough, yeah you're hot stuff.")

After witnessing the progress the city had made, Ford asked Congress to approve federal loans to New York. Though it would take two decades to resolve most of the economic problems, the corner had been turned on the city's immediate financial troubles. However, crime and social ills would continue to plague New York, and these troubles would influence the music of the city through the early 1980s. The new sounds of the city would in turn inspire the Stones and transform what might have seemed like a tired band that was out of tricks in 1975 into a group that rediscovered itself as the rock 'n' roll juggernaut that it had been at the end of the 1960s.

The 1975 tour ended on August 8 in Buffalo, New York, instead of ending with proposed dates in Mexico, Brazil, and Venezuela. For the most part, the dates were canceled because it was believed the shows would not be financially profitable. In December, Wood would become a full-time member of the Stones (though not a financial partner) once the Faces disbanded after their final US tour.

In January 1976, Jagger purchased an apartment on West 73rd Street overlooking Central Park and was soon completing the final mixes with the rest of the Stones on the *Black and Blue* album at Atlantic Studios. Before he moved out of Europe, Jagger explained to the Sunday *Times* why he was moving to "Fun City."

> *"Most of the time I'm in the studio or on the road. Rather nomadic, because of the tax thing. France is quiet but there's no music in France, you can't call up a session, so that's why New York is better for me. Oh yeah, we don't like it, it's unsettling, but on the other hand we did get into a bit of a rut in England and I've changed completely since I left. There's only a few things you need: books and clothes. I've got it down to one suitcase and one guitar now, and a few cassette machines."*

Over the next two years, Jagger would become part of New York's social scene, soaking up ideas from the dance music he heard in the nightclubs and the young bands playing in Manhattan. At the same time, Richards's latest problems with the law threatened to end the Stones for good, requiring Jagger to tap into his influences for the Stones' next album, a celebration of the sleaze and sounds of the city. After ten years of flirting, Jagger and Richards were finally realizing that the Stones and New York City were made for each other.

CHAPTER 6

"DON'T MIND THE MAGGOTS"

Jagger spent much of early 1976 meeting with old friends, including fellow New Yorker John Lennon, and working on Stones material. From mid-January to February, the Stones recorded the horns for "Melody" for the upcoming *Black and Blue* LP and mixed the album's eight tracks. During the mixing, Jagger became a popular subject of the city's tabloids as they tracked his nightly whereabouts in the gossip sections.

In March, Bill Wyman released his second solo album, *Stone Alone*. The *Wall Street Journal's* Ben Stein called the album "a dandy" and proclaimed, "Each song is a rock and roll delight." Per the *Journal's* readership, Stein's "review" focused mostly on Wyman's poor upbringing and net worth, including a detail that his girlfriend took a limo from the Plaza hotel to Bloomingdale's and back. One can imagine the notoriously monotone Stein delivering his punchline aloud: "The Plaza is four blocks from the store." *Newsday's* Wayne Robins ran a profile on Wyman that mentioned his alienation from the other members of the Stones, with Wyman remarking, "I'm a different person from the rest of them. I can remove myself when I feel like it. On the road, if everybody wants to party, I can go to bed. In the '60s, I'd like to party. Not so much anymore."

The reviews of *Black and Blue*, released on April 23, were far more detailed. Dave Marsh in his *Rolling Stone* review dismissed the thirty-something Stones as "a different sort of band, playing a different kind of music," and while he gave overall lukewarm praise for the album, he concluded that "the music lacks energy," blaming the album's long gestation period for forcing the Stones to produce weary-sounding tracks. John Rockwell's review of the album in *The Times* was more positive—albeit calling the album "clearly transitional"—praising most of the tracks.

The Stones toured Europe from late April to late June, and though it was rumored that the group would spend the rest of the summer touring the US, the dates never materialized. Jagger and Wood reconvened in late September at Atlantic Studios in New York and spent a month going through live recordings for what would eventually make up most of the band's 1977 live album *Love You Live*, although the album wouldn't be released for another year. On September 28, 1976, Jagger was spotted in the crowd at Yankee Stadium watching Muhammad Ali beat Ken Norton in a controversial decision to retain the World Heavyweight Championship title. Early in 1977, Jagger also joined Peter Frampton at Electric Lady Studios to record backing vocals for two tracks for his *I'm in You* album.

The reason things were so quiet on the Stones front were mostly because of Richards. On February 27, 1977, Richards was staying in the Harbour Castle Hilton in Toronto while the band members rehearsed for the two shows they would be playing in a club that would be recorded as additional material to use on *Love You Live*. Three days earlier at the Toronto airport, hashish and traces of heroin had been found in Anita Pallenberg's luggage. Based on this discovery, law enforcement secured a search warrant for Pallenberg's hotel room, where they found enough heroin to charge Richards with drug trafficking. It seemed likely that Richards could have been sentenced to anywhere from seven years to life in prison. While Pallenberg's luggage issue was cleared up in early March by way of a guilty plea and a fine, Richards was rearrested for the possession of cocaine, which police also found in his room. Richards was unable to leave Canada for over a month until he was granted a visa to seek drug rehabilitation in the United States. Richards then spent three weeks in Paoli, a small town outside Philadelphia, undergoing treatment. Though he initially stayed clean, Richards returned to using heroin at the end of the year. In May, he was allowed to return to New York City to see a psychiatrist.

Two weeks after Richards's arrest, the four other Stones met in New York to discuss the band's future, including their next recording contract. Jagger and Wood continued to mix the live album. While in New York, Wood joined the Eagles onstage for an encore at the group's March 18 Madison Square Garden concert.

In the spring of 1977, Jagger began dating supermodel Jerry Hall shortly after meeting her in Manhattan. The statuesque Texan had been working as a model since she was a teenager and had dated Roxy Music frontman Bryan Ferry (she is pictured on the cover of the group's 1975 album, *Siren*). This led to Mick and Bianca Jagger's getting divorced in 1978. Jagger and Hall would live in New York, become part of the celebrity scene, and have four children together through 1999, though the tabloid press frequently noted that Jagger wasn't any more loyal to Hall than he'd been to Bianca.

* * * * *

While Greenwich Village served as the birthplace of the folk revival in the 1960s, other New York neighborhoods gave birth to the latest musical trends in the mid 1970s that would not only create one of the most fertile periods in New York City music history but also provide key influence for the Stones' next album.

Inspired by 1960s soul music and utilizing new synthesizer technology, American musicians began creating dance music that was soon billed as disco, a shortened version of "discotheque," which was a type of dance nightclub that featured recorded music played by a house deejay instead of a live band. By 1975, disco was a cultural phenomenon and disco clubs were opening in every major city. Disco's popularity crossed not only gender lines but also racial and sexual lines.

New York became a hot spot of the disco movement, with local musicians like Gloria Gaynor, the Village People, and Chic topping the pop charts, and the Manhattan dance club scene drew celebrity attention. The most famous dance club of the 1970s was Studio 54, which opened at 254 West 54th Street in 1977. The building previously had operated as an opera house and a CBS television studio (it was located next door to the Ed Sullivan Theater). When Studio 54 opened, it quickly became the most popular dance club in Manhattan, mostly because of the celebrity clientele and the club's "anything goes" reputation—scantily clad dancers (both male and female) were employed by the club, and drug use and promiscuous sex were said to be rampant both on and off the dance floor. Jagger and Hall were frequent visitors, and mingling in the New York club culture resulted in the couple's frequently appearing in the gossip columns of New York newspapers.

Disco's popularity was so significant that traditional rock artists released disco singles, with some—most notably Rod Stewart, who released the chart-topping "Da Ya Think I'm Sexy?"—facing criticism from their fans for "selling out." In fact, in the late 1970s rock fans began an anti-disco movement, against its emphasis on dancing, its use of synthesized instruments, and the inanity of its lyrical content. For a rock band like the Rolling Stones, treading into disco in the late 1970s was a commercially appealing opportunity, yet could also potentially destroy the band's reputation.

* * * * *

In June, Richards was allowed to leave New Jersey, where he had been living since his Philadelphia-area treatment ended, and moved to a house in South Salem, New York, about fifty miles north of Manhattan. Now that he was legally allowed to work in New York City, Richards spent part of the summer playing with Stephen Stills and John Phillips in separate sessions.

The mixing and overdub sessions for *Love You Live* continued at a tedious pace at Atlantic Studios, with *Rolling Stone* journalist Dave Marsh attending several and noting how long it took the Stones to focus on finishing just a single song. The album was finished by the end of June.

On September 27, the Stones came together publicly for the first time since the Toronto concerts to promote *Love You Live* and held an album release party at Trax, a nightclub on the Upper West Side. Shortly afterward, they were on their way to Paris to record their next album. But even though the Stones were thousands of miles away from Jagger's new hometown, the sessions would be seeped in New York imagery. *Some Girls* is the most New York of Stones albums. Four of the album's ten songs directly reference New York City. When told by *Rolling Stone* interviewer Jonathan Cott that *Some Girls* is "a real New York record," Jagger answered with a laugh, "Hope they like it in south Jersey."

In a 1995 interview with *Rolling Stone*, Jann Wenner asked Jagger to reflect on how New York had influenced the album. Jagger recalled, "I'd moved to New York at that point. The inspiration for the record was really based in New York and the ways of the town. I think that gave it an extra spur and hardness. And then, of course, there was the punk thing that had started in 1976. Punk and disco were going on at the same time, so it was quite an interesting period. New York and London, too. Paris—there was punk there. Lots of dance music. Paris and New York had all this Latin dance music, which was really quite wonderful. Much more interesting than the stuff that came afterward."

In particular, the city's "Latin dance music" influenced the opening track, "Miss You," which was also released a month earlier than the album as the first single. The song was built off an electric keyboard riff that Billy Preston was playing around with during the rehearsals for the March 1977 Toronto gigs, and Jagger was its primary writer, even though Richards received his customary credit. The heavy rhythm of the song was designed to appeal to the disco market—the track features Wyman's perhaps best groove on a Stones single—yet retained enough of a rock edge to not lose the Stones' primary audience. In fact, multiple mixes of the song were released, including a 3:35 single version and an 8:36 extended version. The album track runs 4:48.

The lyrics of "Miss You" tell a tale of a man aching for his lover. Even his friends' calling him up to go meet some "Puerto Rican girls that are just dyin' to meet you" with a case of wine doesn't cheer him up. There is a sinister aspect to the separation—the singer is "haunted" in his sleep, "waiting in the hall," and walking in Central Park after dark to the point that people think he's crazy (in the late '70s, Central Park was not a place one would want to wander around in after dark). Toward the end of the song, the singer attempts to tell himself that he won't miss his love, but ultimately ends by singing, "Lord, I miss you child." As a result, the lyrics hover somewhere between depression, yearning, obsession, denial, and acceptance—in fact, the song grooves its way through all the stages of grief in spite of its upbeat rhythm.

"Miss You" became the Stones last number-one hit in the United States and has remained one of the band's most popular tracks. Richards in particular would later beam with pride that "Miss You" was covered by legendary vocalist Etta James, and he would actually perform the song with James in New York City in February 1981 when he joined her onstage at Lone Star Cafe.

In the years since, *Some Girls* has frequently been pointed at by critics as Jagger's attempt to make a trendy disco album versus Richards's commitment to rock, using "Miss You" as evidence. However, it's something that Jagger has repeatedly denied. As he recalled to Wenner, "I wasn't out to make a disco record...but 'Miss You' really caught the moment, because that was the deal at the time. And that's what made that record take off. It was a really great record.... I wanted to make more of a rock album. I just had one song that had a dance groove: 'Miss You.' But I didn't want to make a disco album. I wrote all these songs—like 'Respectable,' 'Lies,' 'When the Whip Comes Down.'" Richards believed that "Miss You" transcended disco, remarking, "It's a result of all the nights Mick spent at Studio 54 and coming up with that beat, that four on the floor. And he said, add the melody to the beat. We just thought we'd put our oar in on Mick wanting to do some disco shit, keep the man happy. But as we got into it, it became quite an interesting beat. And we realized, maybe we've got a quintessential disco thing here. And out of it we got a huge hit. The rest of the album doesn't sound anything like 'Miss You.'"

"When the Whip Comes Down," which follows "Miss You," illustrates Jagger's ambition to make *Some Girls* a rock album. Accompanied by a hard-edged guitar riff and a driving drumbeat, the lyrics tell a story seeped in sadomasochistic imagery of a gay man who moves to New York and find success as a garbage collector. While he faces discrimination, he sees himself as providing a much-needed service while supporting himself and explains it with a double entendre ("I'm filling a need / I'm plugging a hole / My mama's so glad / I ain't on the dole.") The song also namechecks 53rd Street, which on the East Side had a well-known area for male prostitutes called "The Loop." Just two years earlier, the Ramones had released "53rd and 3rd," a song about being mistaken for a male prostitute. In a 1978 interview with *Rolling Stone*, Jagger seemed unsure of where the song had come from, saying with a laugh, "I don't know why I wrote it. Maybe I came out of the closet." Richards later recalled that the harder-edged songs on the album were an attempt to match the energy of punk, saying, "We were getting a certain kick up the ass from the punks. Not that I'm a really big punk fan, but their energy, and the fact that you realize another generation was coming up on top of you, was a kick up the ass. It felt time to get down to the nuts and bolts of it and not play around with glamorous female voices and horns and stuff."

The album's third song—and the third in a row that mentions New York—is a cover of The Temptations' "Just My Imagination (Running Away With Me)." Though the Stones' version is a mostly faithful cover of the original number-one hit, which depicts a boy wistfully dreaming that the girl of his dreams loves him back, Jagger made several key changes to the lyrics. While the original lyrics express surprise that the singer's girlfriend loves him "out of all the fellas in the world," Jagger switched it to, "And of all the girls in New York she loves me true," switching the perspective to a city that sometimes feels as if it is big enough to encompass the entire world. In a 1978 *Rolling Stone* interview, Jagger admitted he couldn't shake New York City from his mind when working on the album. He said, "Yeah, I added the New York reference in the song. And the album itself is like that because I was staying in New York part of last year, and when I got to Paris and was writing the words, I was thinking about New York."

The last song on the album, "Shattered," is another punk-influenced song with a pulsating bass line and spitfire delivery of lyrics that are steeped in the grime of New York City's streets. The city becomes an empire of "laughter, joy, and loneliness and sex," a battered city in tatters with a rising crime rate and an infestation of vermin. Jagger later claimed he wrote the lyrics while sitting in the back seat of a New York City taxi. Because of that, "Shattered" depicts a filthy, dilapidated town, and when Jagger invites the listener to "bite the Big Apple," he cautions them, "Don't mind the maggots."

The final mixing of *Some Girls* took place in March and April at Atlantic Studios in New York. The album was finally being worked on in the city that inspired it. At that time, Richards began living permanently at his home in South Salem, New York. On May 2, the Stones filmed three music videos in New York, for "Miss You," "Far Away Eyes," and "Respectable." Later that night the band celebrated Bianca Jagger's birthday at Studio 54 with several celebrities, including Stones fan (and previously failed rock journalist) Truman Capote.

When the album was released on June 9, reviews in the New York media were glowing. John Rockwell of *The New York Times* called it "the best Stones record in years," and in *Rolling Stone* Paul Nelson summed up the critical consensus as: "Thus far, the critical line claims that *Some Girls* is the band's finest LP since its certified masterpiece, *Exile on Main Street*, and I'll buy that gladly," though he also insisted that the two albums didn't deserve "to be mentioned in the same breath." Rob Patterson, writing for the Newspaper Enterprise Association, echoed Nelson's praise but far more positively. "*Some Girls* has all the snap, sass, bite, and fury one expected from the Stones. And maybe more."

Most reviewers speculated that the generally harsh portrayal of women in the album's lyrics reflected the splintering marriage between Mick and Bianca Jagger.

By the end of May the group convened in Woodstock, New York, to rehearse for the tour, which was set to start on June 10 in Lakeland, Florida. As per the stripped-down sound of *Some Girls*, the only extra musician joining the group was organist Ian McLagan, Wood's former Faces bandmate (McLagan played electric piano on the studio recording of "Miss You" and organ on "Just My Imagination"). Curiously, the Stones played venues of various sizes on the 1978 US tour, and some of the smallest shows were in the New York area. The band played the 3,200-seat Capitol Theatre in Passaic, New Jersey, on June 14 and the three-thousand-seat Palladium in New York City (formerly the Academy of Music, which the group played multiple times from 1964 to 1965) on June 19. In contrast, between those dates the band played the 1,800-seat Warner Theatre in Washington, DC, and John F. Kennedy Stadium in Philadelphia to a crowd of ninety thousand.

The show in Jersey was presented as a "secret" show, with tickets being sold only at bars, record stores, and head shops. The Capitol Theatre even had a "Closed for Repairs" sign on its doors for much of the day of the show. Music legend Etta James opened the show, though *New York Times* reviewer John Rockwell called her performance of contemporary covers "dated and embarrassing." Although Rockwell said the opening of the show was sonically muddy, once the band launched into songs from the new album, everything was "really first-rate." Rockwell focused much of his praise on Watts, saying "the man's strength, subtlety, and invention were continuously amazing."

The set lists for the New Jersey and New York shows were largely the same, though the Jersey show featured two more songs. The band played "Miss You," "When the Whip Comes Down," "Just My Imagination (Running Away With Me)," "Far Away Eyes," "Respectable," "Shattered," and "Beast of Burden" from the new album at both shows, with the Jersey crowd also getting "Lies." Also in both sets was the opener "Let It Rock," along with "All Down the Line," "Honky Tonk

Women," "Star Star," "Love in Vain," "Sweet Little Sixteen," "Tumbling Dice," "Happy," "Brown Sugar," and "Jumpin' Jack Flash," with Jersey also getting an encore performance of "Street Fighting Man." Naturally, the Manhattan show claimed more star power, with Paul and Linda McCartney, Bob Marley, Todd Rundgren, Warren Beatty, and Diane Keaton all in attendance.

As with the New Jersey show, details of the Palladium show were kept quiet, with most of the band's crew not even knowing the specifics until the day of the show. Tickets were sold via lottery—radio stations like WNEW had listeners send in postcards with their phone number written on them, and the day before the show the winners were called and told where they could buy their tickets. Only then did they find out where and when the concert would be the following day.

Peter Tosh opened the Palladium show. Jagger joined him onstage to perform a duet of "Don't Look Back," a cover of the Temptations song that Tosh had covered with Jagger when Tosh recorded his latest album in May. Tosh opened several shows on the tour, and Jagger made onstage appearances at each venue to accompany him. During the Stones' performance, Jagger acknowledged the Stones' history with the venue by remarking, "We played here once before in 1964. I don't really remember because I was too young then." (Of course, the Stones had played there more than once before.)

Reviews of the Palladium performance were ecstatic, with the Associated Press praising Jagger in particular as "always the eye-riveting showman." Rob Patterson, writing for the Newspaper Enterprise Association, exclaimed, "In a set which included the bulk of *Some Girls*, the very legend of their power and fury was driven home" and "in the smaller hall the Stones were able to seduce each member of the sweat drenched crowd into a pact of rock and roll." In *The Times*, Rockwell said it "was one of those evenings that defines rock 'n' roll.... [T]he concert triumphantly reaffirmed the greatness of rock's most exciting performing band." However, Dave Marsh of *Rolling Stone* sharply disagreed, remarking, "Stripped of their history, the Stones would not be judged a second-rate band, though it is easy to think that when you realize how much their performances have declined in the past few years." Things only got worse between the Stones and *Rolling Stone*—after Jagger and the band's management objected to increasingly negative coverage of the *Some Girls* tour, Jagger decided to kick *Rolling Stone* reporter Chet Flippo off the tour. Jann Wenner eventually published a rebuttal to smooth things over, calling Marsh's review an "ad hominem attack." Wenner praised the Jersey show in particular, but backed up Marsh somewhat by saying that the Stones tour as a whole was disappointing, though he still felt Marsh had an axe to grind.

Later, Richards joked about playing such a small venue in the country's biggest city.

> *"We didn't realize really what we'd done to New York until it was all over. I mean, we realized we'd just blown the biggest market in America and played a 3000-seat (laughs) theater. But that was what we wanted to do and we felt that we needed to do it and that people who dug us would understand it too, you know. I mean, OK, it's a one-shot. We ain't dead yet, we'll be back, you know. We've always been good in the small halls. I mean, (laughs) 'cause we did them for so long and, I guess, in a way, we kind of tested ourselves by doing it. Like going back to playing small places again has always been something like, Come on, let's do it. We should. You know, We used to be great there, you know, we can really turn it on there. 'Cause you have a lot less problems. You know, you don't have to worry too much about amplification 'cause you can feel the hall yourself."*

While the Stones' tour was a hot ticket, the band started to face controversy regarding the lyrics of the title track. In "Some Girls," Jagger sings about women around the world and what he finds annoying about them, including that "black girls just want to get fucked all night." The Stones defended the lyrics as what people stereotypically think about different types of women. Atlantic Records pressured the Stones to remove or edit the song on future pressings. Jagger refused, telling *Rolling Stone*, "I've always been opposed to censorship of any kind, especially by conglomerates. I've always said, if you can't take a joke, it's too fucking bad." Nonetheless, New York City's top black radio station, WBLS, refused to play "Miss You," and a boycott was spearheaded by civil rights leader Jesse Jackson (and now that *Rolling Stone* was back in the band's good graces, it published a lengthy editorial supporting the Stones). It eventually blew over after Rolling Stones Records released a token apology on October 12, though rumors that the album would be recalled led to fans' buying even more copies (*Rolling Stone* reported that the 45th Street flagship location of E. J. Korvette, the discount retail chain, sold nine hundred copies to a single collector). Several months later on *Saturday Night Live*, African American cast member Garrett Morris referenced the controversy when he appeared on the "Weekend Update" segment as a prominent black sociologist and stated, "Now, Mr. Jagger, there is only one question I want to ask you, Jaggs, and you better have the answer, man, you better have the answer, since you have besmirched the character of black women. Therefore, here is my question, Jaggs. Where are all of these black broads, man? Hey, like, where *are* they, baby? You got any phone numbers for me, baby? Please send 'em to me."

Ironically, *Some Girls* was censored and reissued, but not because of offensive lyrics. The original packaging featured the Stones dressed in drag (recalling the US single sleeve of "Have You Seen Your Mother, Baby, Standing in the Shadow?") in mock advertisements alongside celebrities such as Lucille Ball, Jane Fonda, Joan Collins, Farrah Fawcett, Judy Garland, Raquel Welch, and Marilyn Monroe. After being threatened with lawsuits for using the images without permission, the Stones reissued the album with the images removed.

The two-month, twenty-five-date US tour ended on July 26 in Oakland, California. Unlike with previous tours, the Stones did not continue the tour elsewhere. They spent much of the summer pursing other interests. Richards and Wood visited Alice Cooper in New York City while he recorded his *From the Inside* album, and Jagger bought a piece of the New York Cosmos at the height of the professional soccer team's popularity and joined the team's office as an "international consultant" (a large stake in the team was owned by Atlantic

Records' Ahmet Ertegun, whose brother, Nesuhi Ertegun, was chairman of the team), though it isn't clear if Jagger actually did anything beyond attending games. The band spent two weeks in Los Angeles in late August and early September to work on tracks for the follow-up album. It was then when it was announced that the Rolling Stones would appear on the fourth-season premiere of *Saturday Night Live*.

Though it had premiered only in 1975, the live sketch comedy show was already a cultural institution by 1978. During its fourth season, it featured comedy legends like Dan Aykroyd, John Belushi, Gilda Radner, Jane Curtin, and Bill Murray among its cast. The Stones were appearing as the musical guests alongside New York mayor Ed Koch. Much like the Stones, Koch was a pioneer in cultivating a media image. Though Koch had been in office for only ten months, he was already a captivating figure and his profile was expanding nationwide. A native of the Bronx, Koch served in World War II and later became a US congressman. Upon being elected mayor, he received the lion's share of the credit for helping turn the city's beleaguered finances around. Moreover, Koch's unique appearance and New York Jewish accent made him an easily recognizable figure, and it wasn't long before he became a fixture on national news as well as a frequent guest on television talk shows. Like the Stones, Koch realized that he could use his image to sell himself as an iconic figure.

On October 6, the Stones gathered in Westchester, New York, to rehearse for their appearance on *Saturday Night Live* the following day. Though Koch performed the opening monologue—a tongue-in-cheek thanks to the country for bailing out New York—the Stones were technically the guest hosts as well as the musical guests, although they appeared in just two sketches—Jagger was interviewed in a *Tomorrow Show* parody, and Wood and Watts appeared in one of the recurring "Cheeseburger, Cheeseburger" skits. (A sketch that was supposed to feature Richards was removed during dress rehearsal because he was too drunk to deliver his single line.) For their part, the Stones played three songs from *Some Girls*: "Beast of Burden," "Respectable," and "Shattered." Most musical guests played two songs.

The performance is not held in high regard by most Stones fans, because Jagger was extremely hoarse (the hours of rehearsing the day before were the likely cause). The camerawork also didn't do the band any favors, consisting mostly of tight shots of Jagger. With the absence of a screaming crowd, Jagger seemed somewhat lost onstage. Richards appeared to be completely off cue for most of the set, especially on "Shattered," which descended into a kind of rock 'n' roll sludge that Jagger accentuated by ripping his shirt into tatters, fitting the lyrical imagery of the song even if he couldn't hit the notes.

Five days later, archetypal punk rock musician Sid Vicious of the Sex Pistols was arrested for allegedly murdering his girlfriend, Nancy Spungen, at the Hotel Chelsea in Manhattan. The case shocked the music world, and such a horrific crime made even the Stones' worst brushes with the law look relatively tame by comparison. Despite the Sex Pistols' occasionally ripping the Stones and other 1960s British rock bands as dinosaurs, Vicious's bandmate John Lydon (aka Johnny Rotten) revealed in 2013 that Jagger actually paid for Vicious's lawyers. Vicious died in his sleep after a drug overdose in New York before he could stand trial. Jagger himself has never confirmed or denied his involvement, and as a result Lydon has praised Jagger for not trying to use the gesture to promote himself.

Closer to home was Richards's Canadian trial. After many delays, it happened on October 23, 1978. The charge of cocaine possession was dropped, and Richards pleaded guilty to heroin possession but not guilty to trafficking. Richards's prior drug convictions in England were brought up by prosecutors, but his defense team pointed to his ongoing treatment as evidence that he was cleaning up his act. *Saturday Night Live* creator and producer Lorne Michaels, who was born in Canada, spoke as a character witness on Richards's behalf, and Dan Aykroyd, who was also born in Canada, was on standby as a second witness but was not used. More important, Richards had whom he later called his "blind angel" on his behalf—a young, blind Montreal woman named Rita Bedard whom Richards arranged transportation for when he heard she was hitchhiking while following the Stones on tour. The oft-told tale has it that Bedard went to the judge's house and spoke on behalf of Richards.

When it came to sentencing the next day, the judge found Richards guilty. The sentence, however, was lenient—one year of probation, continued treatment and, possibly because of Bedard, Richards and the Stones had to hold a charity concert for the Canadian National Institute for the Blind. Except for a brief relapse in May 1979, Richards finally quit heroin for good.

Jagger made a second appearance on *Saturday Night Live* on December 16—in much better voice this time—to perform "Don't Look Back" with musical guest Peter Tosh, three months after the single was released.

In the June 18 edition of *The New York Times*, Rockwell reflected on the Stones' playing smaller venues on this tour, pointing out that the band had played to 120,000 people with six Madison Square Garden shows during the previous tour in 1975, and played to fewer than ten thousand combined at the Capitol Theatre and Palladium shows. Rockwell speculated that "Gigantic rock concerts, in indoor or outdoor sports arenas, have grown as about as large as they can grow, and pose such obvious difficulties for a proper appreciation of music that many performers are questioning their validity," and that "some rock stars are beginning to realize that enough is enough—that after a certain (and considerable) level of success has been attained, happiness has very little to do with how much money one has." Rockwell obviously couldn't have known it at the time, but he couldn't have been more wrong about just how big Stones concert tours could get and just how much money the Stones could make. By the end of the 1980s, the Rolling Stones revolutionized the way the music industry ran stadium-size concert tours. But before that would happen, the Stones would have to survive the least amicable period in the group's long history.

CHAPTER 7

"WAITING ON A FRIEND"

Now that he was a free man in part because of Lorne Michaels's testimony, Keith Richards began to spend a lot of his time in New York hanging out with Dan Aykroyd and other members of the *Saturday Night Live* cast. Aykroyd invited Richards to his private Blues Bar in downtown Manhattan, where he became acquainted with Aykroyd's fellow *SNL* stars John Belushi and Bill Murray. In particular, Richards would recall memorable times with Belushi, who died in 1982 of a drug overdose. He would later say, "Belushi was an over-the-top man. You can say *that* again. I said to John once, as my father says, there's a difference between scratching your arse and tearing it to bits. John was hilarious, and nuts to hang with. Belushi was an extreme experience even by my standards." In April 1979, Belushi served as the emcee of the band's charity concert in Toronto. Incidentally, Richards's final heroin relapse in May was in Los Angeles while he was hanging out with Belushi.

Another extreme experience for Richards was on July 20, 1979, when Anita Pallenberg's young boyfriend, seventeen-year-old Scott Cantrell, shot himself in the face while playing Russian roulette with one of Richards's guns at Richards's house in South Salem. Richards was in Paris at the time recording with the Stones. Richards and Pallenberg's ten-year-old son, Marlon, was in the house the night of the accident (their seven-year-old daughter was living in England with Richards's mother). It marked the end of any meaningful relationship between Richards and Pallenberg—the two had stopped living together nearly a year earlier while Richards underwent treatment. Shortly afterward, Pallenberg moved to Sands Point, Long Island, to the estate owned by Mick Taylor. Taylor moved to a smaller home, and Richards paid the lease on the mansion.

By 1981, Taylor returned to touring, first as member of the Alvin Lee Band, then as a member of the reunited John Mayall & the Bluesbreakers, and finally as a solo musician. Taylor soon became a fixture at New York's Lone Star Cafe, a country-western bar at the corner of Fifth Avenue and 13th Street known for its giant sculpture of an iguana on its roof, and at Long Island's legendary club My Father's Place in Roslyn.

Because the Stones were not touring, Richards and Wood decided to go on the road with Ian McLagan and Bobby Keys. The eighteen-date New Barbarians tour included a show at Madison Square Garden on May 7. The set list consisted of rock 'n' roll standards, tracks from Wood's solo work, "Honky Tonk Women," "Before They Make Me Run," and "Jumpin' Jack Flash," as well as the Jagger/Richards composition "Sure the One You Need," which appeared on Wood's 1974 LP *I've Got My Own Album to Do*.

During his various New York escapades, Richards met his future wife, Patti Hansen, on St. Patrick's Day in 1979 at Studio 54 when he was with John Phillips. Though Studio 54 was more Jagger's scene, Richards claims in his autobiography that he was there trying to avoid actress Britt Ekland, who had "the hots" for him. He figured Studio 54 would be the last place she'd look. It happened to be Hansen's twenty-third birthday, and her friend asked Richards to say hello to her (Richards also sent the gorgeous model a bottle of Dom Perignon). In December, Hansen was invited by Jane Rose, Richards's manager, and Jerry Hall, whom she was modeling with, to Richards's thirty-sixth birthday party at Roxy NYC, a Chelsea roller skating nightclub. (This was the party where Richards received his famed skull ring as a gift, a totem that has become a trademark image of the death-defying guitarist.) The two began dating shortly afterward. Hansen, a Staten Island-born supermodel, had been a professional model in Manhattan for nearly a decade before first crossing paths with Richards.

Though much of the rest of 1979 was quiet on the band front, in the fall the Stones still had the follow-up to *Some Girls* to finish. Jagger and Richards did the overdub and mixing sessions at Electric Lady Studios, though the sessions often ended because of disagreements between the pair. The sessions resumed in December and were finally completed in January. In the meantime, Jagger and Hall rang in the new year with celebrities like Robert De Niro, Sylvester Stallone, and Andy Warhol at a party at the East 75th Street Harkness House mansion that was thrown by Woody Allen.

March 1980 was an eventful month for the Stones both professionally and personally. Richards moved into Hansen's Greenwich Village apartment and, like Jagger, began to show his face more around town. On March 18, Jagger jammed with the Jimmy Rogers Blues Band at Trax. On March 26 and 27 the Stones came together for both a photo session and a band meeting, the latter of which fell into anarchy when Richards and Jagger argued over what songs to include on the upcoming album.

Years later, Richards would cite *Emotional Rescue* as the point when cracks began to appear in the Rolling Stones. He recalled,

"When I cleaned up and Emotional Rescue time came around—'Hey, I'm back, I'm clean, I'm ready; I'm back to help and take some of the weight off your shoulders'—immediately I got a sense of resentment. Whereas I felt that he would be happy to unburden himself of some of that shit, he felt that I was horning in and trying to take control. And that's when I first sensed the feeling of discontent, shall we say. It wasn't intended like that from my point of view, but that's when I first got a feeling that he got so used to running the show that there was no way he was going to give it up. That, to him, it was a power struggle."

The next day the band filmed music videos for "Emotional Rescue" and "Where the Boys Go" in New York. Both videos were conceptual, with the band appearing as multi-colored distorted infrared silhouettes, which at the very least hid any visual tension between the band members. The song selection for the videos also reflected Jagger's and Richards's differing opinions on the album's content. "Emotional Rescue" is an obvious, disco-influenced follow-up to "Miss You" with tender lyrics to a hurt woman, while "Where the Boys Go" is an upbeat, punk-like rocker with lyrics that suggest the song is about homosexuals meeting up to dance. One couldn't pick two less similar songs off the album. While "Emotional Rescue" became the album's first single, "Where the Boys Go" wasn't even released as a single.

Jagger and Richards would do the final mixes at Electric Lady Studios in April, and on June 26 the band held a hospital-themed party at the West 37th Street nightclub Danceteria to celebrate the album's June 20 release, though Watts did not attend. After the party, Richards popped into Trax to jam with punk rocker Jim Carroll, who was signed to Rolling Stones Records (in *The Times*, John Rockwell gave Carroll's concert a tepid review—even with Richards's appearance). This was also the night that Bill German, a seventeen-year-old Brooklyn native and the editor of *Beggars Banquet*, the Stones' unofficial fan magazine, briefly met Ronnie Wood and handed him the latest issue. German became an expert on the Stones and tracked their various appearances on New York stages throughout the 1980s. He won the respect of the band, and they offered him exclusive content. The magazine would become the band's official fan club magazine in 1984. Richards even attended the magazine's tenth-anniversary party in New York in 1988.

Emotional Rescue did not receive the glowing reviews of *Some Girls*, and many reviews noted how fatigued the Stones sounded. In his review of *Emotional Rescue*, Steve Morse of the *Boston Globe* remarked that the "insular New York references are getting tiresome." However, unlike the album's predecessor, its lyrics refer to New York only twice. The first track, the funky "Dance (Pt. 1)," opens with Jagger saying, "Hey, what am I doing standing here on the corner of West 8th Street and Sixth Avenue?" That location is in the West Village, just two buildings west of Electric Lady Studios, where Jagger played guitar on Leslie West's "High Roller" in 1974, the Stones recorded with Clapton after the Madison Square Garden gigs in 1975, and, unsurprisingly, where Jagger and Richards mixed most of *Emotional Rescue*, including "Dance (Pt. 1)." That corner is also located in an area well known in the late 1970s (and even today) for its high concentration of gay bars, with one of the city's landmarks, the Stonewall Inn, just two blocks away. The album's second reference comes in "Let Me Go," a sneering rocker in which the singer pleads with his lover to let their relationship end. The lyrics contain a number of signs that indicate the fling is over, and one of the planned escapes that the singer has is to start hanging around some of those West Village establishments by West Eighth Street and Sixth Avenue: "Maybe I'll become a playboy / Hang around in gay bars / And move to the west side of town." It's a curious contrast, since the term "playboy" is often associated with being a womanizer and a gay bar is probably the last place a playboy would find success, but this was coming from the same songwriter who wrote about a masochistic homosexual garbage man, so nothing should really be out of the realm of possibility in New York-inspired Stones lyrics.

Curiously, in an interview with Morse later in the month, an under-the-weather Jagger admitted that he was growing weary of Manhattan. "I think I'm going a little nuts. I think I'm coming to the shaky period. There's just too much to do, too much going on. I've got to get back to Europe for a little while, for a few months this summer. I can't spend the summer here because I'd go nuts.... There's too much TV and everything. It's a nuthouse." Jagger also dismissed the *Emotional Rescue* album, claiming, "It took too long, far too long. We recorded an enormous amount of songs but we just didn't seem to get them finished." Similarly, in an interview with Robert Palmer of *The New York Times* later that month, Richards also remarked about how long it took to finish the album, saying, "I knew it was finished when I said 'It's that or Bellevue,'" a reference to the New York City hospital with a well-known mental institution.

That attitude against their output extended to Jagger's views of rock music as a whole. In an August interview with *Rolling Stone* that was done in his Central Park apartment, Jagger steadfastly insisted, "There *is* no future in rock & roll. It's only recycled past." Later he continued, "Rock & roll is a funny thing. There are two different attitudes, right? One is the English attitude, like when Pete Townshend talks about rock & roll like a religion. And then there are the others, like me, who think it's really a lot of overblown nonsense. *Why bother?* I mean, it's not worth bothering about. As a form of art *or* music." Jagger also denied that *Emotional Rescue* was a New York City album, as the *Boston Globe* had speculated. When asked that question, he responded, "I don't think so. To me New York is like Lou Reed and all those other bands." Naturally, later in the same interview Richards disagreed with Jagger's outlook on the state of rock music, saying rock was "as healthy as ever. We all tend to forget that it's ninety percent crap anyway. But the ten percent is *good*."

In July, the Stones filmed two more music videos in New York—a reshoot of "Emotional Rescue" and a video for the album's second single, "She's So Cold." The "Emotional Rescue" video was a virtual repeat of the *Some Girls* videos—nearly entirely focused on Jagger with shots of the band behind him. The tension between Jagger and Richards appears to have spilled over to the "Emotional Rescue" video session. Richards seems at a loss as to what he should be doing (he didn't play guitar on the studio track and only lent his vocals to the song's closing), unsure of when he was supposed to mock-strum his guitar.

Despite quickly going platinum in the US and hitting number one on Billboard, in comparison to its predecessor *Emotional Rescue* was a flop. The Stones did not tour behind the album, and tensions in the band got to the point that instead of Jagger and Richards writing new songs together to produce a follow-up, producer Chris Kimsey (who had previously engineered *Sticky Fingers*, *Some Girls*, and *Emotional Rescue*) delved into the Stones' vaults to find leftover tracks that could be worked into songs for a new album. The tracks included outtakes from the recent *Emotional Rescue* sessions and stretched all the way back to the 1972 sessions for *Goats Head Soup*—in fact, those tracks featured Mick Taylor on guitar, not Wood. Much of the work in piecing the songs together was done in October and November 1980 in Paris, though the Stones recorded only two songs in their entirety for the album, "Haven" and "Neighbours." By the end of the year the follow-up to *Emotional Rescue* was nearly finished.

The year 1980 ended on a grim note when John Lennon was murdered outside his apartment building in Manhattan. As long-time friends and once-perceived rivals of the Beatles, the Stones were shaken up, especially Jagger, who lived in Lennon's neighborhood. Many expected that Jagger would leave Manhattan, though the following year he denied he would to the *Sunday Times*, saying, "New York's still the place where I mostly want to be." Years later, Jagger remarked,

"I was very sad and surprised. And it was all so horribly ironic. He thought he had found a place to be on his own, have this life, and he was quite taken with the idea that he was no longer in the Beatles, that he didn't have to have a lot of protection, bodyguards. He used to tell me how he would go in a cab in New York—go in a fucking yellow cab. Which, as you know, is probably to be avoided if you've got more than $10. [Laughs] A London cab is one thing, but a New York cab is another. He wanted freedom to walk the block and get in the cab, and he felt in these big cities you can be anonymous."

In early 1981, Richards made two guest appearances in New York—on January 22 he played with Matt "Guitar" Murphy at Trax and then appeared on February 9 with Etta James at the Lone Star Cafe. Richards commented on what he loved about being able to pop in on stages in New York now that he lived there, saying, "To get the most out of New York is not to get stuck in one thing. I've been traveling back and forth to New York for years, but it's not the same as living here. Then you really get a feeling for what it's like to walk out on the streets each day. I have a staggering number of things I could get into. One night it's good blues or reggae, another it's rock and roll. If I wanna go out, it's usually to see someone play. If I know the place they're playing, I'll get someone to call them up and see if I can get in the back door. I don't want to queue up. That's about the only concession I make to all that stardom because I hate pulling rank and all that crap. You can't afford to be paranoid everywhere. Being run by fear is the worst thing anyone can do to themselves. If you're afraid to come out of your house because you're afraid of walking the streets, you're assigning yourself to some kind of purgatory." Unsurprisingly, reading between Richards's lines reveals what must have been some lingering fear about his fame in the wake of Lennon's murder.

Meanwhile, Jagger saw Prince play at The Ritz in March, which influenced Jagger to select Prince to open for some of the shows on the Stones' next tour. Jagger then worked on the next Stones album, which included the Who's Pete Townshend laying down a guitar track for the song "Slave" in New York in early April. Jagger recorded his vocals in Paris while work on the mixing continued at Atlantic Studios in New York. *The New York Times* reported on April 1: "The Rolling Stones' New York office was buzzing with activity last week" and "talk of touring was in the air." The article contained a quote from Richards indicating that a tour was in the works, as well as Jagger's comments about strife within the band. "We're choosing songs and having disagreements, as usual. We disagree a lot when it gets to this stage with an album, but I should imagine most bands do."

Those disagreements also caused a full-blown feud within the band. As work on *Tattoo You* wrapped up, Richards displayed erratic behavior by contacting Ronnie Wood and Bill Wyman and demanding that they come to New York for a band meeting. Richards then left New York for a vacation in Florida with Hansen. When Jagger, Watts, and Wyman met on May 26 to talk about their plans for the album release and a possible tour, Richards and Wood were not present. In fact, Wood didn't arrive in New York until May 29, when the band convened at Jagger's apartment to listen to the album. Richards was still out of the picture.

Luckily, cooler heads prevailed. The Stones finally had a full band meeting in New York at the end of June, and Jagger, Richards, Watts, and Bobby Keys attended a Jimmy Cliff concert together at The Ritz. On June 30 they shot music videos for "Start Me Up," "Hang Fire," and "Worried About You" in New York.

The following day the band shot a video for "Neighbours" at the Taft Hotel at 152 West 51st Street, a historic Times Square hotel. The song itself was inspired by Richards's run-ins with his neighbors at his Greenwich Village apartment and numerous noise complaints. Jagger wrote the lyrics about Richards, and Richards told *Rolling Stone*,

> *"I have a knack of finding a whole building of very cool people, you know, but there'll be one uncool couple—they're always a couple. And my apartment will always be either just above them or next door to them or just below. And they're the kind of people who'll knock you up at six in the morning, while you've just sort of got a little bit of music going. You're trying to be cool, 'cause you're aware of it, you know? By now, I'm aware that I can't blast the sounds. So I'm trying to be cool about it. And these people come up to our door saying, 'We can't even hear Bugs Bunny on our TV, your music's so loud! Turn the kettledrums down!' So, I mean, I'm plagued by that kind of thing. I swear they're the same couple everywhere I go. They just follow me around: 'Let's bug him; he's an asshole, he deserves it.'"*

Finally, on July 2, the band filmed the final music video for *Tattoo You*, for "Waiting on a Friend." In a video that later became an early staple on MTV, a bored-looking Jagger sits on the steps of 96-98 St. Mark's Place, the building that appears on the cover of Led Zeppelin's *Physical Graffiti* album, with several men (one of whom is Peter Tosh). Richards staggers over while smoking a cigarette and when the saxophone solo hits, the pair get up and walk to St. Mark's Bar and Grill at St. Mark's Place and First Avenue, passing posters of the *Tattoo You* album art along the way. They meet Wood, Watts, and Wyman sitting at the bar, and Richards grabs a beer (just when Jagger sings, "I don't need no booze"). The group then finishes playing the song on the bar's small stage, and the jam actually continued after the cameras stopped rolling for the video's lucky extras and the small crowd that gathered on the street outside.

Later that month the band began rehearsing for the upcoming tour at SIR Studios, located on 52nd Street and Eighth Avenue in Manhattan, although the band would soon put the rehearsals on hold before continuing them in August in Massachusetts. At that time, Wood decided to join Jagger and Richards and relocated from Los Angeles to Manhattan, telling *The New York Times*, "Mick and Keith are both in New York most of the time and it's the easiest place for Charlie and Bill, who live in England and France, to commute to. This way I can be closer to the boys, and the move is also a kind of gesture, to let them know that I'm not out there trying to be a solo artist." Despite his words, Wood did in fact have a new solo album, *1234*, which came out a week after *Tattoo You* and featured Charlie Watts on drums on three tracks.

Tattoo You actually ended up in record stores a week sooner than expected when Philadelphia radio station WNMR started playing the album early in its entirety, with rival Philadelphia station WYST following suit. Within days, other stations across the country began doing the same until a New York deejay contacted Atlantic Records and Rolling Stones Records and urged them to push the album out sooner. Reviews were extremely positive, with Robert Palmer of *The New York Times* calling the album "something special" and in particular praising the "crisp, clean, appealingly bright recorded sound that puts the somewhat muddy clutter of previous Stones disks to shame."

While *Tattoo You* was released on August 24 to generally strong reviews, a far more significant development in the music industry happened earlier that month. On August 1, MTV launched and changed the music industry forever. Although MTV wasn't the first time music and television combined with mass audience appeal—after all, as far back as Elvis Presley, musicians' careers were being made by their appearances on television—the visual presentation of a band was becoming increasingly as important as its music. Being the Rolling Stones, the band members were all old hands at creating a media image tied to the Stones' music. Their numerous videos were soon in regular rotation on MTV, especially the "Waiting on a Friend" video. By 1982, Jagger was appearing in the station's famed "I Want

My MTV!" promo campaign. As the New York-based channel grew, it became a firm supporter of the Rolling Stones and later in the decade would feature exclusive Stones content.

Jagger announced the *Tattoo You* tour at a press conference at Philadelphia's John F. Kennedy Stadium on August 26, though the New York City metro area dates were not initially announced and fans were given only November 9 through 13 as a time frame for them. All over the country, tickets to shows sold out, mostly within twenty-four hours. Ian McLagan would again join the touring band on keyboards, with Bobby Keys returning on saxophone along with Ernie Watts, who also played saxophone. The New York dates were not announced until October 13. The dates included three shows at New Jersey's Brendan Byrne Arena on November 4, 6, and 7 and two at Madison Square Garden on November 12 and 13. As with previous tours, fans were offered tickets via a postcard lottery system. More than four million requests were received for just 150,000 seats in the New York area, requiring the US Postal Service to hire 125 part-time employees to handle the increased volume of mail. The band hired an independent auditing firm to the tune of half a million dollars to distribute the tickets. "You never know what to believe," Jagger joked to *The New York Times*. "It may be three grandmothers in Queens sending in tons of ticket requests, for all I know."

Nonetheless, the Stones had grander ideas for the New York leg of their tour that did not end up going according to plan. Though the Roseland Ballroom, a 3,200-capacity theater in Manhattan, was rumored to also be on the itinerary, the show never materialized. The Stones would not play Roseland for another twenty years. Giants Stadium, the New Jersey home of the New York Giants football team, was also considered but would not happen. On October 31, *The New York Times* reported that the band would perform a closed-circuit television special from a New York City nightclub—presumably Roseland—on December 18 to be directed by Hal Ashby, though plans for the special fell through. The Stones ended up broadcasting a concert in Hampton, Virginia, that night on pay-per-view instead. Ashby filmed the November 5 and

6 concerts at Brendan Byrne Arena and a concert in Tempe, Arizona, on December 13, and the footage was combined into a film titled *Let's Spend the Night Together* that was released to theaters in 1983.

Brendan Byrne Arena was built across the highway from Giants Stadium in East Rutherford and had opened earlier that year to serve as the home for the New Jersey Nets basketball team (the sports complex was collectively known as the Meadowlands). It was named after the then governor of the state and opened on July 2, 1981, with a Bruce Springsteen concert. The Nets had started playing there only a few days before the Stones' first concerts. The three dates would be the only ones the Stones ever played at the arena, though throughout its twenty-four-year history it became a popular stop on concert tours for many artists, particularly when its more prestigious (and more expensive to book) counterpart Madison Square Garden was unavailable. While Richards would play there during his 1988 solo tour, all future Stones gigs at the Meadowlands would instead take place at the much larger Giants Stadium. Brendan Byrne Arena, then known as Izod Center, closed in 2015.

The set lists for the five New York-area shows were nearly identical. They included six songs from *Tattoo You*—"Neighbours," "Black Limousine," "Waiting on a Friend," "Little T&A," "Hang Fire," and "Start Me Up"—and two songs from *Emotional Rescue*—"She's So Cold" and "Let Me Go." The rest of the set lists contained a mix of the band's classics, a fair sampling of *Some Girls* tracks, and the Miracles' cover "Going to a Go-Go." The New Jersey shows not only got an extra song ("All Down the Line"), but Tina Turner, who opened the three shows, joined the Stones for "Honky Tonk Women" to sing it as a duet with Jagger. The only other difference was that the November 5 concert featured the boogie-woogie standard "Down the Road Apiece," while the other four concerts replaced it with the Eddie Cochran cover "Twenty Flight Rock." The opener for the New York shows was rhythm and blues legend Screamin' Jay Hawkins, who took the gig on short notice when James Brown canceled the day of the first show because he felt he wasn't being offered enough money.

Stones fans made headlines in between the New Jersey and New York shows when more than one hundred people were arrested at two shows in Hartford, Connecticut, for various crimes, including ticket robberies outside the arena and unruly fans without tickets who refused to take "sold out" as an answer. *The New York Times* wrote about the frenzy over the tickets for the local shows, which originally sold for thirty dollars a pair: "There are advertisements in newspapers in the area placed by ticket scalpers. 'Bids starting $500,' reads one. 'No offer under $400 for pair,' says another." *The Times* also reported that twenty-one people were arrested for "various narcotics infractions" and forty-four received summonses for scalping during the Garden shows. Surprisingly, one of the lawbreakers who was arrested was a twenty-three-year-old off-duty rookie New York cop who robbed a man at gunpoint for a ticket outside the Garden on November 12. If nothing else, the arrests proved the extreme lengths New Yorkers were willing to go for Stones tickets. UPI also reported that Stones fans—those attending and those seeking tickets—jammed up Penn Station, resulting in many complaints from commuters.

The American Tour 1981 grossed $52 million in its fifty shows, setting the record for the highest-grossing concert tour of all time. The Stones also made touring history by accepting $1 million from Jōvan Musk cologne to sponsor the tour, a tactic the Stones and other major bands would fully embrace by the end of the decade. Curiously, Robert Palmer of *The New York Times* wrote an article on the eve of the first New Jersey show about how uneventful the tour was backstage compared to previous tours. There were no arrests, no drug busts, and no notable blowups. In particular, Palmer praised Richards, saying, "He has straightened up dramatically. He looks healthy, he is playing brilliantly, and his backup vocals are often so lusty that they drown out Mr. Jagger, who is working harder to hold up his end of things as a result." In his review of the second Garden show, Palmer praised the sound quality in comparison to the "muddy" sound of the New Jersey shows. Josh Barbanel of *The Times* seemed shocked at the age of the crowd. He wrote, "Most of the fans...were not born when the group was founded more than two decades ago." In her review of the first Garden show, Mary Campbell of the Associated Press wrote that the Stones "are getting better musically and more entertaining and innovative in stagecraft all the time."

Rolling Stone called the tour "the most professional and calmest of the band's career" (quoting Wyman, "They're actually letting us stay in the same hotels as before, but letting us have really nice rooms because we didn't smash 'em up last tour"). In fact, most of the headlines came from the audience instead. There were several audience injuries and even accidental deaths during the tour due to unruly behavior in addition to the hundreds of arrests. But the Stones escaped the tour unscathed, richer, and having schooled the music industry on how to run a tour.

In February, Jagger and Richards worked on the soundtrack for *Let's Spend the Night Together*, the concert film that was shot partially at the first two New Jersey shows, at the Power Station at 441 West 53rd Street. The film wouldn't be released in the US for another year. In March and April, they were joined by Watts and Wood to mix and overdub several songs for a live album, *"Still Life" (American Concert 1981)*, which was rushed for release during the upcoming European tour. While they were mixing the record, the Stones were quite busy on the town. Richards and Hansen attended a party for Wood's girlfriend Jo at Studio 54 on March 18, and famed blues guitarist Stevie Ray Vaughan auditioned for Jagger and Wood for Rolling Stones Records on April 22, though the band didn't sign him (just over a year later, Jagger would be attendance when Vaughan played at The Bottom Line club in Greenwich Village). Four days later, Richards played "Rock Me Baby" with Etta James at The Other End, a famed Greenwich Village nightclub better known as The Bitter End in its 1960s heyday and today. But the Stones soon left town for the two-month European tour, which was another huge financial success.

The Stones reconvened in New York in late October—Wood was spotted playing sitar in the New York restaurant Nirvana on October 25—but the band was soon off to Paris to write and record the follow-up to *Tattoo You*, which took up most of the rest of the year. Wood re-emerged in his new hometown on January 7, 1983, when he was booked to do a lecture at Town Hall. Town Hall—a 1,500-seat concert hall on West 43rd Street—was built in 1921 as a meeting hall for political and social groups and lectures, with occasional concerts. Though billed as a lecture on the music business, Wood's appearance there was a mix between a lecture and a performance, with Wood playing parts from various songs on guitar, bass, and harmonica, as well as taking questions from the audience. Eighteen years later, another Stone would grace the stage when Bill Wyman played there with his solo band, the Rhythm Kings.

On January 18, Jagger, Richards, Watts, and Wood premiered *Let's Spend the Night Together* at Loews Astor Plaza in Times Square, the city's largest cinema at the time. In 2005, the cinema was converted into a 2,100-person capacity concert venue named the Best Buy Theater, making it yet another small New York City venue that the Stones have "played" at. Afterward, the Stones held a party at Tavern on the Green, the famed Central Park restaurant where Jagger had thrown Jerry Hall's twenty-fourth birthday party in 1980.

A headline-grabbing Stones-related press conference occurred in New York on March 16. Earlier in the month, a former member of the Hells Angels known only as "Butch" testified during a Senate Judiciary Committee meeting on the involvement of motorcycle gangs in organized crime that there was an "open contract" for the murder of Mick Jagger, stemming from the gang's disastrous role as security at the 1969 Altamont concert and the band's refusal to defend the gang's actions. Furthermore, "Butch" claimed that two attempts to kill Jagger, both in New York, had failed. The first was when a member planned to murder Jagger in a hotel he was supposedly staying at in the early 1970s (Jagger never arrived), and the second happened during the 1975 tour rehearsals in Montauk when Angels members attempted to bomb the house he was staying in. The Stones were aware of the Montauk plot, and the security team lined the beach outside Warhol's house with barbed wire, preparing for the Hells Angels' Normandy-style assault that never came because the boat the Angels were traveling on sank. On March 16, at a press conference on the Upper East Side, representatives of the organization, including future actor Chuck Zito, denied that there had ever been a contract put out on Jagger. Rumor had it that Jagger's representatives met with Hells Angels representatives earlier at the popular Manhattan nightclub The Ritz just to make sure.

It wasn't until May when the Stones returned to working on the next album, with Jagger and Wood mixing the tracks at The Hit Factory in New York. These sessions ran through June, and a second set of mixing sessions, this time with Jagger and Richards, continued at The Hit Factory in July and August. The Glimmer Twins took a brief sabbatical from the studio to catch David Bowie's July 27 concert together at Madison Square Garden.

The album, now titled *Undercover*, which was nearly finished, would be the band's last for Atlantic Records. In August the band signed a recording contract in New York worth a reported $28 million with CBS Records for four albums and the repackaging rights for all of the band's albums since 1971's *Sticky Fingers*. The CBS offer was nearly double what Atlantic was reportedly offering. The biggest news of the deal was that Jagger signed a side deal with CBS for three solo albums, an action that would again cause a rift between him and Richards. After years of friction, in 1988 Richards told *Rolling Stone* that CBS Records president Walter Yetnikoff had initially signed Jagger to a solo album contract, thinking that Jagger *was* the Stones. Richards said,

"It's understandable that somebody just walking in on the Rolling Stones...it's an obvious thought. Mick is going to be talking to them. He's the frontman. Since then, Walter has certainly changed his mind [laughs]. It's understandable that you would think that, oh, if you've got it together with Mick, then you've got the Stones, because the next person to talk to is myself, and I've been a junkie, unreliable—in business people's minds I'm the dodgy artistic freak. I'm not the one that's going to be up in your office talking business at ten in the morning. So it's an understandable attitude to take. But it certainly didn't help keeping the Stones together at the time."

Nonetheless, with the band's future set it was time to focus on the present, because the new album was set for a November 7 release. Jagger and Richards started doing interviews in New York in late September, and it soon became obvious that the band had no plans to follow the album's release with a tour. On top of that, Jagger seemed more excited for his upcoming solo album instead of *Undercover*.

While the Stones avoided any direct lyrical references to New York on *Tattoo You*, the band returned to them on *Undercover*. The album opener and title track, "Undercover of the Night," is a pounding rocker composed mostly by Jagger and is a rare political song focusing on the political corruption and sexual repression in South America. Being that this was written during the Cold War, Jagger's lyrics reflected how these conflicts reverberated around the globe, including the seemingly throwaway line "The race militia has got itchy fingers / All the way from New York back to Africa." The next song is a more traditional up-tempo Stones rock song, "She Was Hot." The lyrics speak of how a series of dreary days in cities across the United States are improved by an encounter with a "hot" woman, with the opening lines "New York was cold and damp / TV is just a blank / Looks like another dead end Sunday."

The opening track of the second side, "Too Much Blood," also exhibits New York influence. Though the lyrics actually describe an infamous case in which a Japanese man named Issei Sagawa murdered and ate a Dutch woman in Paris in 1981, "Too Much Blood" was heavily influenced by New York's burgeoning hip-hop scene. Though rap was not yet a commercially successful genre, several rap singles, like the Sugarhill Gang's "Rapper's Delight" and Blondie's "Rapture," were gaining popularity in the New York club scene. The Stones (and particularly Jagger) had never been shy about borrowing from music trends—psychedelic for *Their Satanic Majesty's Request*, reggae for *Black and Blue*, and disco and punk for *Some Girls* and *Emotional Rescue*—and hip-hop was no exception. During the recording, Jagger improvised two spoken raps in the song—one about Sagawa and another about the 1974 movie *The Texas Chain Saw Massacre*—though modern listeners wouldn't likely think of Jagger's delivery as rapping. The song was released only as a single in the US, and while it did crack the top forty by hitting number thirty-eight, it was obviously not as successful for the band as their forays into reggae, punk, and disco. The Stones would again experiment with hip-hop trends on the *Bridges to Babylon* album over a decade later, but not to the same degree as with "Too Much Blood."

Undercover was not as successful as *Tattoo You* or *Some Girls*. It was the first Stones album not to hit number one in the US since *Let It Bleed*. While it quickly went platinum, the album didn't have legs. Although "Undercover of the Night" and "She Was Hot" were both top-ten singles, the lack of a tour and the band's general disinterest in promoting the album ensured that *Undercover* soon faded from the public consciousness.

When it was decided the band wasn't going to tour, the various Stones pursued other interests. Jagger began writing songs for his solo album. Watts, Wyman, Wood, and Ian Stewart joined up to tour the US for a series of charity concerts to support Action into Research for Multiple Sclerosis (ARMS) that was spearheaded by Eric Clapton, including shows at Madison Square Garden on December 8 and 9. Afterward, Wood did a stint in rehab. (Wood's addiction problems were later cited by Jagger as one of the main reasons why the band didn't tour in 1983.) Richards, on his fortieth birthday, married Patti Hansen in Mexico with Jagger as his best man.

In early 1984, Jagger and Richards filmed separate interviews in New York for *Friday Night Videos*, a music video program that aired on NBC. Jagger's interview was done at Marylou's, a West Ninth Street restaurant known for its wild after-hours nightclub. It focused on the Stones' history with performance videos, though he did speak at length about how he didn't mind not being on tour. In Richards's interview (billed as his "first network television interview") he mostly reflected on the band's past, the band's relationship with the Beatles, and why he felt the Stones were so successful. On March 2, Jerry Hall gave birth to Jagger's daughter Elizabeth in New York. In terms of the band, however, little was happening publicly, though Jagger, Richards, and Wood were being spotted all over Manhattan at various social functions.

In early April, Jagger was in the Bahamas recording demos for his solo album, and after returning to New York he spent several days in early May at A&R Studios recording vocals for "State of Shock," the first single for the upcoming Jacksons album *Victory*. At the time, Michael Jackson was coming off the massive success of his 1982 album *Thriller* and was inarguably the biggest pop star in the world. When the single was released only weeks later on June 5, it reached number three on the Billboard charts, giving Jagger a solo radio hit before he even started recording his solo album. Several months later Jagger would tell *The New York Times* that he wasn't thrilled with the song, saying that Michael Jackson "had the two of us practice scales for two hours and then we recorded the vocals in two takes. When he sent the finished track to me later I was kind of disappointed in the production and the mix."

With the band members' attention focused elsewhere, there was little celebration when the Rolling Stones became the first rock band to be inducted into Madison Square Garden's Hall of Fame, an honor normally reserved for athletes like Jack Dempsey and Walt Frazier. The induction honored the band's fourteen sellouts out of fifteen shows (only the matinee concert on November 28, 1969, failed to sell out). Despite the honor, the band would not play the Garden again until 1998. In fact, because of the brewing animosity between Jagger and Richards, the Stones wouldn't play together on a New York stage for more than five years. After the Stones had started the decade coming off an album that showed how New York City had revitalized the band and a concert tour that was the highest grossing of all time, by the middle of the decade it seemed like they might finally call it quits.

Oddly, the same manic energy of New York's punk and new wave scenes that had fueled the rise of MTV from its Manhattan studios threatened to leave the Stones on the rock pile of history.

CHAPTER 8

"NEW YORK WAS COLD AND DAMP"

In the fall of 1984, Jagger was hard at work recording and mixing his first solo album at the Power Station. While he took some time away from the studio to meet with Richards, Watts, and Wood on October 2 at the Manhattan office to discuss the band's next moves, it was clear that any serious plans were on hold while he concentrated on his solo album. Another band meeting in November in Amsterdam was even less productive, ending with Watts nearly punching Jagger out of a window while they were both drunk. With nothing happening on the Stones front, Wyman and Watts recorded an album with friends in England, titled *Willie and the Poor Boys*, and Wood prepared for his upcoming wedding to model Jo Karslake in England.

Jagger and Richards met in Paris in early January 1985 to work on song ideas for the next Stones album, and the full band came together at the end of the month to start recording. Unlike for the previous few albums, the sessions were long and arduous. Jagger was absent for many of the sessions because of his commitments to promoting his album, now titled *She's the Boss*. In an interview with *Creem*, Wyman spoke frankly about how Jagger's album drove a wedge in the sessions. "We messed around for weeks because Mick was still buggering around with his solo album instead of working with us. He would fly back to London in the middle of it which, I might add, is a thing that nobody else has ever done, because when it's Stones work, everybody drops solo projects. It kind of caused a bit of resentment in the band."

Indeed, the press was more focused on Jagger's solo album than on the fact that the Stones were working on a new album once the first single, "Just Another Night," was released at the end of January preceding the album's February 19 release. One of the questions Jagger had to keep battling was whether or not his solo album meant that it was the end of the Stones while also fending off probing questions about how angry his bandmates were about his recording a solo album. Though reviews were generally strong and the album eventually went platinum, *She's the Boss* was a commercial disappointment compared to even the lowest-selling Stones albums.

Nonetheless, while *She's the Boss* created some rancor among the Stones, it brought vocalist Bernard Fowler into the fold. New York City native Fowler was in and out of bands throughout the 1970s and 1980s, and had done sessions with Bootsy Collins and Herbie Hancock. He sang background vocals on *She's the Boss*, which would result in an ongoing three-decade association with the Rolling Stones. Fowler would be recruited to perform backing vocals and percussion on all Stones tours from the late 1980s on and, in addition to Jagger's recordings, Fowler has appeared on the solo albums of Richards and Wood, and served as the vocalist of the Charlie Watts Quintet.

The Stones halted their recording sessions at the end of February, and Jagger and Richards returned to New York City, where Patti Hansen gave birth to her and Richards's first child, Theodora, on March 18, the day after Hansen's twenty-ninth birthday. By the time the band reconvened in Paris in April to resume recording sessions, Jagger's album had been rapidly falling down the charts even though "Just Another Night" reached number twelve on the pop charts. The mood amongst the band wasn't any better. When pop musician Bob Geldof asked the Stones to play Live Aid, which would take place in both Philadelphia and London, the band declined. Considering the concert featured reunions of Black Sabbath, the Who, and Led Zeppelin, the media thought the Stones' not appearing was telling. Fueling those rumors was the announcement only weeks later that Jagger would be playing a solo set at Live Aid Philadelphia backed by Hall & Oates and the Temptations' Eddie Kendricks and David Ruffin. Shortly afterward, Bob Dylan announced that his backing band for the Philadelphia Live Aid concert would be Keith Richards and Ronnie Wood. The fact that Jagger and Richards were participating in the landmark concert but as separate entities suggested that the Stones couldn't stand to be on the same stage with one another.

Jagger, Richards, and Wood all returned to New York in early July to prepare for the concert. Jagger began rehearsing with Hall & Oates at SIR Studios, and on July 10, Richards and Wood performed as guests at a Lonnie Mack performance at the Lone Star Cafe that was attended by Jagger, Dylan, and Paul Simon. The next day Dylan, Richards, and Wood rehearsed at Wood's place in Manhattan. Though the concerts raised millions for famine relief and featured dozens of artists, a substantial amount of press coverage mentioned the schism of the Stones. Notably, Jagger's band even played two Stones songs, "Miss You" and "It's Only Rock 'n' Roll," which he performed as a duet with Tina Turner. Live Aid also served as a promotion for Jagger's charity single duet with David Bowie, a cover of the Martha and the Vandellas classic "Dancing in the Street." With a huge promotional push by MTV, the single reached number seven in the US.

With Jagger, Richards, and Wood back home in Manhattan after Live Aid, the Stones held recording sessions for their next album at RPM Studios at 12 East 12th Street, near Union Square. Jimmy Page, fresh off Led Zeppelin's messy performance at Live Aid, was in the studio on July 16 and 17 to record a guitar track on the song "One Hit (to the Body)." There were other guests on the album too, mostly other musicians who happened to be recording in New York at the time. On July 19, Richards played on three tracks for Tom Waits' *Rain Dogs* album at Quadrasonic Studios at 723 Seventh Avenue, and Waits returned the favor by adding backing vocals to the Stones' cover of "Harlem Shuffle," which would eventually be the album's lead single. Likewise, on July 25, Wood recorded with R&B singer Don Covay, who also contributed backing vocals to "One Hit (to the Body)." Bobby Womack visited the studio in early August to contribute backing vocals and guitar to "Back to Zero."

One Stone was absent for much of the sessions, but this time it was not Jagger. Watts would not arrive in New York until August 5, and in the meantime much of the album's drums were recorded by future David Letterman house band drummer Anton Fig (who played on *She's the Boss*) and future Keith Richards collaborators Charley Drayton and Steve Jordan. Wood even played the drums on one track, "Sleep Tonight." Like Richards and Wood in previous years, Watts was struggling with drug addiction and was deemed too unreliable to contribute to the sessions.

On August 9 and 12, the Stones did photo sessions for the album, although it was far from complete. Wyman did the media rounds in New York to promote the *Willie and the Poor Boys* album, appearing on *Late Night With David Letterman* on August 1 and recording an interview with *Friday Night Videos* on August 8. In September and October, Jagger, Richards, and Wood mixed *Dirty Work*. On October 12, the lead singer of U2, Bono, stopped by the studio with E Street Band guitarist Steven Van Zandt, and Bono, Richards, and Wood recorded "Silver and Gold," a track that would be included on Van Zandt's Artists United Against Apartheid benefit album, *Sun City*. Wood played slide guitar on the song using Richards's switchblade, and the entire track was done in only two takes.

By the end of November, Richards, Jagger and Wood were back in New York doing the final mixes for *Dirty Work* at Right Track Studios at 168 West 48th Street, which concluded on December 5. In terms of recording and production time, *Dirty Work* was in production longer than any previous Stones album. *Rolling Stone* would later detail the disjointed proceedings:

"Late in October, in a New York studio at some ridiculous hour of the morning, a typical Stones session was in progress. Well, it was sort of a session. Engineers were carrying out instructions, making minuscule

adjustments in various mixes while Keith Richards and Ron Wood jammed over in a corner. Mick Jagger, not seeming too involved, took a quick tour through the place, then said goodbye to 'the boys.' He was leaving for a holiday in India, and he didn't take any telephone calls after his departure."

The *Rolling Stone* article, published before the release of the album, suggested that *Dirty Work* would be followed by a world tour, with Richards remarking, "Hey, this is our first album for CBS. We've *gotta* tour."

The album's songwriting credits were also telling in terms of the Stones' fractured nature. Of the album's ten tracks, only three are credited to Jagger and Richards. Four are credited to Jagger, Richards, and Wood, and another two to Jagger, Richards, and keyboardist Chuck Leavell (the remaining track, "Harlem Shuffle," is a cover). For the first time, the album featured two lead vocals from Richards. Richards's central role in creating the album is highlighted by the cover art, which features the band in garish DayGlo-colored clothing with Richards pictured in the middle, standing out the most in a pink shirt and red jacket.

Tragedy befell the Stones only a week after *Dirty Work* was completed. Ian Stewart died of a heart attack on December 12 in London. The album is dedicated to his memory. After Stewart's funeral, most of the band went away for the holidays or spent time with their families. Back in New York, Wood and Richards jammed with the members of David Letterman's house band at Wood's home on January 8 and later attended Letterman's show, and on January 12 Jagger visited Wood's home where the two collaborated on a demo that eventually became "Peace for the Wicked" on Jagger's second solo album. On January 23, Richards appeared at the inaugural Rock & Roll Hall of Fame ceremony at the Waldorf hotel to induct Chuck Berry (where he confessed, "I lifted every lick he ever played") and then jammed with Berry, Wood, Jerry Lee Lewis, and others to close out the evening. The Hall of Fame organization was founded by the Stones' former label boss Ahmet Ertegun of Atlantic Records, and Jann Wenner, founder of *Rolling Stone*, was on the board of directors. The ceremony was a success, but the organization had yet to find a permanent home. Though New York was considered, the permanent museum would eventually be established in Cleveland and opened in 1995.

In the weeks leading to the release of *Dirty Work*, the Stones were highly visible around New York—Jagger and Wood attended blues guitarist Johnny Copeland's January 31 show at the Lone Star Cafe, Jagger attended the February 3 opening of Woody Allen's *Hannah and Her Sisters*, and Richards was spotted hanging out at famed tiki bar Trader Vic's, located in the basement of the Plaza hotel.

From February 5 through 7, the Stones filmed the music video for the album's first single, "Harlem Shuffle," in New York. The track was originally released by the R&B duo Bob & Earl in 1963 and became a minor hit in the US, though a 1969 release of the song in the UK hit number seven. The song was a late addition to the album—the Stones did not work on it in Paris and began recording it, appropriately, once they moved the sessions to New York in the summer of 1985. Aside from the title, which references Manhattan's Harlem neighborhood— best known for being the center of African American culture during the 1920s—the lyrics mainly command the listener to do a variety of dance moves. The "Harlem Shuffle" music video features animated sequences that recall cartoons of the 1940s. It was directed by John Kricfalusi, who would later become known for creating the cartoon series *The Ren & Stimpy Show*. The live action sequences were directed by Ralph Bakshi, the famed animation pioneer behind Fritz the Cat. The live action portion takes place in the "Kat Klub," a 1980s neon version of a 1940s or 1950s zoot suit Harlem club, with Jagger dressed in a purple suit and Richards in a fedora looking like a menacing version of Humphrey Bogart. The single, which was released on February 28 and peaked at number five on the Billboard pop charts, also included a 6:35 "New York Mix" that features a pulsating bassline, an added guitar solo, and studio effects.

The following week, Jagger made a brief appearance on *Saturday Night Live* in the opening skit, because the show was hosted by Jerry Hall. The skit featured Jon Lovitz as Tommy Flanagan, his pathological liar character known for his "Yeah, that's the ticket!" catchphrase. Seeing Hall in a bar, he tells her that he's an old friend of Jagger's and claims that he was the true writer of "Satisfaction," that he had convinced Jagger not to go to Vietnam, and that he managed the band. When Jagger arrives, he tells Hall that not only does he know Tommy, but they had gone fishing "last weekend when I didn't come home." When Hall is out of earshot, Jagger thanks Flanagan for covering for him and then shouts the show's longtime opening phrase, "Live from New York, it's *Saturday Night!*"

The musical guest that night was Stevie Ray Vaughan and Double Trouble. Years later, Double Trouble drummer Chris Layton revealed that Jagger had initially wanted to perform with the band, but changed his mind and instead hung out with the band backstage during the show.

Just as the album was about to be released—with positive reviews from *The New York Times*, *Village Voice*, and *Rolling Stone*—stories about the schism between Jagger and Richards gained traction in the press, which seemed particularly focused on whether or not the band would tour. In February, writer Bill Flanagan asked Richards in the Stones' New York office how he would respond if Jagger told him he wanted to go on tour with a solo band instead of the Stones. Richards's response? "I'll slit his throat."

Weeks later Jagger bluntly told Robert Palmer of *The New York Times*, "The fact of the matter is, Keith and I aren't getting on too well. I'd love to be out there playing, and of course the money would be great. But there's no point unless it's going to be fun, and right now things are just too difficult. We are *not* going to tour this year." Richards laid out his case for the tour in an interview with the *Boston Globe*'s Steve Morse in the Stones' New York office.

"I have a selfish reason for feeling the way I do, because I like to play with the Stones. I really enjoy it. Also, I thought it would be a good move for the Stones, because it's been five years since we toured America and four since we played Europe. That's a long time. But hey,

I need two hands to play a guitar. I don't have another hand to hold a gun to anybody's head to say, 'Go onstage.' I can't force anybody to get out there."

Nonetheless, in his belated April 27 review of *Dirty Work*, John Rockwell of *The Times* still speculated that the Stones would in fact tour behind the album that summer.

But Jagger and Richards weren't backing down from their acrimonious stances. In an interview on *The Today Show* that aired April 17 and 18, Richards confirmed that there would be no tour. Jagger was instead thinking about his solo career and had dinner with Dave Stewart of the Eurythmics and Daryl Hall in New York on April 12. A few days later he recorded the title track for the soundtrack for the movie *Ruthless People* with them in New York. Jagger would end up collaborating with Stewart for his next solo album. Aside from filming a music video for "One Hit (to the Body)" in England in early May, the Stones not only were finished with promoting *Dirty Work*, they were finished with all band activities for at least the rest of the year.

In later years several reasons were given for why the Stones didn't tour behind *Dirty Work*. Jagger has insisted that Watts's addictions left him in no condition to tour even though Watts mounted tours with the Charlie Watts Orchestra during the Stones' hiatus. Richards believes that the band was still reeling from the death of Ian Stewart. However, Richards also believes that Jagger was too preoccupied with his solo aspirations to care about moving forward with the Stones at that time, something that Richards would continue to jab Jagger about in the press for the better part of the next two years.

Wood occupied his time by popping up on stages in Manhattan. He performed with Chuck Berry at The Ritz on June 25, made guest appearances during all three Bob Dylan and Tom Petty & the Heartbreakers concerts at the Garden in mid-July, and on July 19 joined blues guitarist Hubert Sumlin onstage at Abilene's. It was something of a "farewell to Manhattan" tour for Wood, who moved back to England permanently on July 30.

Richards likewise kept busy. After shooting the video for "One Hit (to the Body)," Richards and his pregnant wife traveled back to the US on the *Queen Elizabeth 2* cruise ship (their second daughter, Alexandra, would be born on July 28 in New York). In early July, Richards and Wood traveled to Detroit to play on Aretha Franklin's cover of "Jumpin' Jack Flash," which Richards produced and mixed in late July in New York at Electric Lady Studios. Richards then left for an extended vacation in Jamaica on July 31—the same day that Jagger returned to New York after an extended stay in England. Whether inadvertently or not, it made it seem like even New York City wasn't big enough for the two of them at the moment.

Though he wasn't performing, Jagger was spotted all around New York in August and September. With David Bowie he attended the August 1 Prince concert at Madison Square Garden, and a Eurythmics concert in early September at Pier 84 on the Hudson River. Jagger returned to the river when he attended a party on September 11 on *Forbes* magazine publisher Malcolm Forbes's yacht. He was again spotted at Madison Square Garden, attending Elton John's concert on September 14. Jagger then traveled to the Netherlands to begin preliminary work on his second solo album, while Richards turned his attention to his *Hail! Hail! Rock 'n' Roll* concert and documentary to salute Chuck Berry's sixtieth birthday in St. Louis. By the end of October, Jagger's album sessions moved to New York's SIR Studios, before returning to the Netherlands in mid-November.

Charlie Watts was using his downtime to fulfill his boyhood jazz band dreams by touring with his thirty-one-piece Charlie Watts Orchestra, and was in the middle of a US tour to support his *Live at Fulham Town Hall* album. The band booked shows on December 2, 3, and 4 in New York at The Ritz. For Watts, a drummer who had played arenas and stadiums, The Ritz was a small venue, especially with such a large band. The hall's 1,500-person capacity Grand Ballroom dates back to 1886 when it opened as Webster Hall, and for decades it served as more of a catering or meeting hall than a music venue. In the early 1920s, it became known for sordid parties and earned the nickname "The Devil's

Playhouse." It wasn't until the 1950s that Webster Hall became primarily a music hall, and from 1953 to 1968 it was actually owned and operated by RCA Records as a recording studio. Though Webster Hall was used mainly to record soundtracks for Broadway musicals, Elvis Presley recorded "Hound Dog," "Don't Be Cruel," and "Anyway You Want Me" there on July 2, 1956. The day before, Presley had appeared on *The Steve Allen Show* and performed "Hound Dog" in a memorable appearance. Elvis performed the song while singing to an old dog in a top hat (with Allen remarking to Elvis, "You're going to record it tomorrow"), with a screaming crowd long before the song was even a hit for him. Webster Hall was also the site where a young Bob Dylan was first recorded—on February 2, 1962, Dylan laid down a harmonica track for Harry Belafonte's "Midnight Special."

In 1980, Webster Hall was turned into a nightclub concert venue called The Ritz, and it would go on to become perhaps the most storied venue in Rolling Stones history to never have held a Stones concert. Jagger saw Prince perform there in March 1981, and Richards and Patti Hansen saw Steel Pulse there in May. Richards also saw Chuck Berry perform there in June 1981, where famously Berry punched Richards in the eye for touching his guitar backstage when he didn't recognize Richards. Later that month, Jagger, Richards, Watts, and Bobby Keys saw Jimmy Cliff at the The Ritz. However, the first Stone to actually perform at The Ritz was Ronnie Wood, who did it twice as a guest in February 1982—first on February 18 with Bobby Womack, and then on February 21 with Chuck Berry (although Berry accidentally announced Wood as Keith Richards). In April, Wood made another onstage appearance at The Ritz, this time with Toots and the Maytals. Richards saw Tina Turner perform there in January 1983 and August 1984. Jagger saw Frankie Goes to Hollywood there in November 1984, and Wood again guested with Chuck Berry for two shows, both on June 25, 1986. It was finally Richards's turn to perform at The Ritz on November 23, 1986, when he joined Eric Clapton onstage for "Cocaine" and "Layla."

The following year, Mick Taylor would perform at The Ritz on May 29, which included a short reunion of his pre-Stones band John Mayall

& the Bluesbreakers, and Wood would return in November to play a concert alongside Bo Diddley. In 1993, Jagger would play his only concert to support his third solo album at the rechristened and renovated Webster Hall. Webster Hall is therefore the only concert stage in the world that Jagger, Richards, Watts, Wood, and Taylor have all performed as solo musicians at, with Richards being the only one of the five who has yet to play an entire concert there. While the Stones have never played Webster Hall as a group, the venue bears tremendous significance in Stones history, and because of its extensive history in New York City music history, it was designated a New York City landmark in 2008.

Richards was in attendance for Watts's December 4 show, suggesting there was still camaraderie among everyone besides Jagger and Richards. During press for the album and shows in New York, Watts was naturally asked about whether or not the Stones were finished. First he joked, "Don't you think it's about time they did break up?" but then added, "I keep expecting to get a call from Keith one of these days telling me to meet him in the studio next week."

The year 1986 did end with a Stones reunion of sorts in New York. On December 28, Richards joined Mick Taylor onstage at Taylor's second show of the night at the Lone Star Cafe to perform "Key to the Highway" and "Can't You Hear Me Knocking." It was as close as New York was going to get to seeing the Stones together again for over two years.

By the time Richards appeared at the Waldorf Astoria on January 21, 1987, to induct Aretha Franklin into the Rock & Roll Hall of Fame at the second annual ceremony (and later jam with the likes of Chuck Berry, Bo Diddley, Roy Orbison, Bruce Springsteen, and Sting), the scorned-feeling guitarist made a decision—if Jagger was going to take time away from the Stones to record another solo album, why couldn't he? Of the five Stones, Richards was the only one who had never released a solo album. He spent most of February mixing the soundtrack album *Hail! Hail! Rock 'n' Roll* at Giant Sound Studio, and by the end of the month he was regularly meeting with Steve Jordan, the

Bronx-born multi-instrumentalist who had recently left the drumming chair of David Letterman's band. Jordan was one of the drummers who had filled in for Watts on the *Dirty Work* album, and he had again worked with Richards on Aretha Franklin's cover of "Jumpin' Jack Flash" and *Hail! Hail! Rock 'n' Roll* the previous year. Richards decided to continue their collaboration and began writing with Jordan at Studio 900, located at 900 Broadway just west of Gramercy Park ("a cute little pink room where people wouldn't bother us," according to Jordan). Jordan would later recall,

> *"The first time we went in there, we played twelve hours straight. Keith didn't even go out and take a piss! It was unbelievable. It was just sheer love of music that bound us. But it was clearly liberating for him. He had so many ideas he wanted to get out. And he certainly wasn't upset, or, at least when it came to writing, wearing his heart on his sleeve. Much of the music was very specific. It was about his old partner."*

Mick Taylor visited Richards in the studio on March 6, and Taylor would eventually contribute guitar to the track "I Could Have Stood You Up" later in the year.

At the same time that Richards was working on ideas for his solo album, Jagger returned to New York to continue recording his second solo album at Right Track Studios. Only twenty-eight Manhattan blocks separated the Glimmer Twins, though most of their communication was being done through the British press. In an interview with the *Daily Mirror*, Jagger remarked, "I love Keith, I admire him...but I don't feel we can really work together anymore." Richards responded in an interview in the *Sun* the next day that Jagger "should stop trying to be like Peter Pan and grow up." Richards followed up his remark when asked if the Stones were going to stop "bitching" at each other, responding, "You'd better ask the bitch."

Richards flew out to Los Angeles to do more mixing on the *Hail! Hail! Rock 'n' Roll* soundtrack. While Richards was across the country, Jagger made an announcement that infuriated him nearly to the breaking point: After he finished his second solo album, Jagger planned to go on his first solo tour. In England, *Music Box* asked Wyman if the Stones were through, and he responded, "It looks that way. I think the time comes when, you know, all good things must pass.... It's a pity we didn't go out with a big bang but instead...with a bit of a whimper. [Jagger is] the guilty one, really. He's decided he wanted to do his own thing...be famous in his own right." A spokesperson for Wyman later claimed he was misquoted, although *Music Box* aired the footage unedited. As it were, it wasn't just the media that suspected that the Stones were through—the other band members were convinced of it.

At the end of March, Richards and Jordan began demoing songs at Studio 900, coming up with about forty ideas for songs, while Jagger finished the mixes for his album, now titled *Primitive Cool*, at Right Track. During the mixing, Jagger also produced two songs for the New York-based hard rock band Living Colour, a popular club act in Manhattan that consisted of all African American musicians. Jagger also contributed harmonica to one track and backing vocals. The songs would end up on the band's most successful album, 1988's *Vivid*. Jagger also helped promote the band by appearing at its May 27 gig at the Lone Star Cafe.

During the first week of June, Jagger turned in *Primitive Cool* to CBS Records and held several listening parties for the album. Meanwhile, Richards continued mixing *Hail! Hail! Rock 'n' Roll*—now at Electric Lady Studios—this time with Chuck Berry stopping in on June 10 to listen to the results.

Watts returned with his orchestra—this time a thirty-three-piece band—to do a US tour during the second half of June. The tour included one New York show as part of the JVC Jazz Festival at Avery Fisher Hall, part of the Upper West Side's famed Lincoln Center for the Performing Arts. Opened in 1962 (the same year the Stones were established) and named after the Brooklyn-born electronics magnate who donated the money for its construction, the 2,738-seat hall was a considerable step up from The Ritz, where they had played the previous year. It was also more befitting in terms of jazz—Avery Fisher Hall is home to the New York Philharmonic, and classical and jazz concerts make up much of the performance schedule. In fact, JVC Jazz Festival officials who had attended Watts's Ritz performance the year before were sufficiently impressed to invite the Stone and his jazz orchestra to be showcase performers at the 1987 festival. Both Richards and Mick Taylor attended the performance.

After finally finishing the mixes for *Hail! Hail! Rock 'n' Roll*, Richards publicly announced on July 13 what band insiders had known for months: He had signed a solo recording contract. However, unlike the Stones and Jagger, who were signed to CBS Records, Richards signed with Virgin Records, followed by an after-party in Richard Branson's Manhattan hotel room. It marked something of a declaration of independence for Richards from the Stones bubble, and was followed by Richards's also being the only Stone to miss Jagger's forty-fourth birthday party in London on July 26.

Meanwhile, Jagger was hard at work beginning to promote the September release of *Primitive Cool*. In July he filmed a video for "Let's Work" in New York. The video is perhaps the most dated Stones-related music video. It was shot via blue screen and shows Jagger, children, butchers, doctors, construction workers, clowns, and all kinds of other people who appear to be rejects from the Village People superimposed on a highway that they're supposedly running down as Jagger sings the upbeat song about taking pride in the work that one does for a living. In addition, Jagger also gave defiant interviews in the press about not living in the past with the Stones and being forced to work with people whom he didn't get along with. But Jagger's solo tour plans deflated when he was forced to postpone the European leg of his tour when guitarist Jeff Beck, who had played on much of *Primitive Cool*, announced he could not tour due to an "inability to commit himself to a tour of that length"—though Beck later admitted, "I quit because he offered me peanuts." Plans for a Jagger European solo tour were eventually scrapped altogether.

Part of the problem with Jagger's touring plans for *Primitive Cool* was that the album was a commercial disappointment. Though the first two singles, "Let's Work" and "Throwaway," both reached number seven on Billboard's mainstream rock charts, only "Let's Work" cracked the top forty on the pop charts, peaking at thirty-nine. The third single, "Say You Will," failed to make the Billboard Hot 100 at all, and *Primitive Cool* failed to become a gold record. If *She's the Boss* was a disappointment, *Primitive Cool* could only be considered a commercial failure. Critics were not impressed either. In his lukewarm review of the album, *New York Times* critic Robert Palmer wrote, "With his new album, Mr. Jagger persuades us to take him seriously as solo artist. But he doesn't persuade us to forget about his former band, not by a long shot."

While Jagger was promoting *Primitive Cool* in Europe, Richards was attending the New York and Los Angeles premieres of *Hail! Hail! Rock 'n' Roll*, with the New York premiere being at Avery Fisher Hall. In October, Richards played guitar on a Ziggy Marley track at Sigma Sound Studios and on Mick Taylor's cover of Bob Dylan's "Blind Willie McTell" at Electric Lady Studios before continuing work on his solo album.

Sometime in the fall, Wood decided to follow Richards's lead from his project with Chuck Berry and agreed to do a tour with another founding father, Bo Diddley. The duo began rehearsing at Top Cat Studio in New York on 28th Street on November 2 and 3 for The Gunslingers Tour. Wood and Diddley played at The Sundance, a small theater in Bay Shore on Long Island on November 14. The pair then looped back to play The Ritz in New York on November 25, a performance that was professionally filmed and broadcast live on Westwood One radio and included Wood, without Diddley, covering one Stones song, "Honky Tonk Women." Earlier that day, Wood also taped an appearance on *Late Night With David Letterman* to promote his recently released autobiography.

On November 14, Jagger was originally scheduled to appear on *Saturday Night Live*, but the appearance was canceled. In fact, Jagger ended up doing very little promotion for *Primitive Cool* in the US. He appeared on the New York-based radio show *Rockline*, but other than a few international interviews, it appeared that Jagger was done promoting until a scheduled tour of Japan in March 1988.

Richards was still hard at work on his solo album, and instead of his usual island retreat for the holidays, he stayed close to New York by renting a home in Connecticut, where Ronnie Wood joined him for Christmas. Within the next few years, Richards would eventually settle in Connecticut. He did spend several days in Antigua after the new year, and upon his return went to work mixing his solo album. In the ensuing months he would receive visits in the studio from Tom Waits and Bono. Richards would also mix parts of the album in Bermuda and back in New York at The Hit Factory and Atlantic Studios, finally finishing the album in May.

Jagger re-emerged to appear at the third annual Rock & Roll Hall of Fame induction ceremony at the Waldorf Astoria on January 20. Following in Richards's footsteps, he served as an inductor, this time for the Beatles, and ended the night singing "Satisfaction" with an all-star band. Six days later, Jagger appeared onstage at The Bottom Line with Long Island-born guitar virtuoso Joe Satriani to perform Jimi Hendrix's "Red House," which served as an unofficial announcement that Satriani would be joining Jagger's solo touring band. Jagger and Satriani auditioned musicians at SIR Studios throughout the month of February and rehearsed for the Japanese tour. Tour rehearsals continued during the first week of March at Silvercup Studios in Astoria, Queens, with a lineup of Jagger, Satriani, Jimmy Rip (guitar), Phil Ashley (keyboards), Richard Cottle (keyboard and sax), Doug Wimbish (bass), and Simon Phillips (drums), all of whom except Satriani had played on the album. Among the backing vocalists were Bernard Fowler and Lisa Fischer, two singers who would later become perennial members of the Rolling Stones touring band.

Wood and Diddley continued their Gunslingers Tour by touring Japan in early March, and Jagger followed suit by launching his-first ever solo tour on March 15 in Osaka. Jagger's set list for the tour was heavy on Rolling Stones songs. They comprised sixteen of the twenty-five songs played on opening night. Six others came from *Primitive Cool* and three from *She's the Boss*. In his autobiography, Richards criticizes

Jagger, writing, "The way he expressed himself was to go on tour with another band singing Rolling Stones songs."

The Japanese tour ended on March 28, and Jagger returned to New York. As Richards prepared for the October 3 release of *Talk Is Cheap*, he and Jagger finally met face-to-face for the first time in months in the office of Richards's manager, Jane Rose. Richards actually played his solo album for Jagger and claimed he caught Jagger dancing to it when he didn't think Richards was looking. However, Richards admits, "I don't know what he really thinks about it, because it's all tied up with what happened with his solo stuff."

Regardless of whether or not Jagger liked *Talk Is Cheap*, the meeting was the first step in the thawing process between Jagger and Richards that would soon bring about the return of the Rolling Stones, with the machine more than twice the size it ever was, and led to the group's playing one of the most hallowed venues in the history of rock and roll.

CHAPTER 9

"I SEE IT AS
THE ROLLING STONES IN 1989"

In late October 1988, it was announced by the Rock & Roll Hall of Fame that the Rolling Stones would be inducted at the fourth annual ceremony at the Waldorf Astoria in New York on January 18, 1989. The honor could not have come at a more discordant time for the band. Jagger was finishing his tour for *Primitive Cool*, which consisted of dates in only Australia, Indonesia, and New Zealand. Neither Jagger nor concert promoters sensed much interest in bringing a solo tour to the United States or the United Kingdom based on the album's disappointing commercial performance. In fact, Jagger's set for the second leg of the tour consisted of even more Stones songs than the already Stones-heavy set of the Japanese leg, suggesting that Jagger himself wasn't confident in how his solo songs were accepted by live audiences. In contrast, Richards released his first solo album, *Talk Is Cheap*, in October and was about to embark on what would be a well-received fifteen-date US tour with the X-Pensive Winos, in which all eleven songs from the album were played along with a dash of Stones favorites.

It helped that reviews of *Talk Is Cheap* were overwhelmingly positive. Jon Pareles of *The New York Times* praised the album, saying *Talk Is Cheap* "sounds loose, sloppy, thrown-together, unfinished. That's why I like it—it's a relief to hear a musician open the lid on canned music," and adding, "After two decades of experience, Mr. Richards knows exactly what he's up to when he makes records, and he has chosen to let listeners hear what he hears as a musician at work—continually testing nuances, making decisions, listening to the band, fooling around." *Rolling Stone* reviewer David Fricke even took a shot at Jagger's recent solo album in his review, writing, "Mick Jagger's recent solo may be high on style and sass, but it's tough to beat *Talk Is Cheap* for real primitive cool. Indeed, Richards's first solo album is a masterpiece of underachievement."

Richards's tour included a November 29 show at New York's Beacon Theatre and ended with a December 17 show at Brendan Byrne Arena in New Jersey. Pareles's album review was echoed in his praise in *The Times* for Richards's November 29 Beacon Theatre show. He called the performance "raucous, scruffy, unkempt and often out-of-tune," but added, "It was also inspired rock and roll," and praised it as "gleeful, pretentious-free rock with irresistible momentum." Similarly, *Rolling Stone* called the concert "spontaneous and loose, but never out of control" and concluded that Keith's performance "[left] little doubt about who constituted the backbone of what was once called the Greatest Rock & Roll Band in the World. Mick is put on notice: Keith's got live—and then some—if you want it." If either Glimmer Twin was keeping score, there was no doubt that Richards was on the winning side in the court of public opinion.

The lavish Beacon Theatre has held a significant place in the city's rock 'n' roll history. It opened in December 1929 as a movie palace owned by Warner Bros. after a several-year delay. The original plan for the theater was to make it an Upper West Side version of the nearly six-thousand-seat Roxy Theatre in Times Square, though when it finally opened it had less than half of the seats. The Beacon was converted into a music venue in 1974, and it hosted notable rock acts including Steve

151

Miller Band, Rush, KISS, Chicago, The Kinks, Fleetwood Mac, Queen, and the Grateful Dead throughout the 1970s. In 1982 it was added to the National Register of Historic Places. That designation actually saved the venue from being converted into a nightclub in the mid-1980s when a judge denied the work permits because it would damage the landmark's architecture.

The first Stone to play the Beacon was Mick Taylor, who played the venue with the reunited John Mayall & the Bluesbreakers on June 19, 1982. Jagger was the first Stone to attend a show there when he saw Stevie Ray Vaughan perform on December 28, 1983. Wood took the stage on October 18, 1985, to perform with Bobby Womack, and Richards attended a James Brown concert on October 16, 1987. Wood also jammed with David Bowie, Iggy Pop, and Steve Winwood during a Bowie gig at the China Club on November 19, 1985. At the time, the China Club was a popular nightclub located on the ground floor of the Beacon Theatre that Jagger was occasionally spotted at during his days living in New York. The venue would make even more Stones history over the next two decades.

Perhaps inflated by his solo success, Richards didn't let up on Jagger in the press. In October, Richards told Stephen Holden of *The Times*,

> *"Mick has a Peter Pan complex. He worries that the Rolling Stones are old-fashioned and thinks he can do better on his own making high-tech records. I've reminded him that the Rolling Stones are in a unique position. We've been on top for 25 years and don't have to worry about suddenly coming to the end of the road. But Mick keeps looking back over his shoulder at Michael Jackson, Prince and George Michael. I've told him it's ludicrous to try to pretend you're 20 when you're 45."*

Nonetheless, Richards ended the interview on a hopeful note about a Stones reunion, adding, "Barring any really big problems over the next few months, I think you'll find a new record by the Stones and a tour next year. Mick is now on a solo tour of Australia. But before he left, he called me and said, 'Let's put it back together.'" In a November interview with Hillel Italie of the Associated Press in Richards's Manhattan office, Richards laid it on further. "I tell him he's blowing 20-odd years of integrity of the Stones because he's got a problem. I ask him, 'What's your problem? What's so tough about being Mick Jagger?' Suddenly you got to compete and be fashionable. The Stones don't need that. I love the guy and I love to work with him but I don't understand this star trip he's on." Again, the article concluded with Richards's insistence that the Stones could put aside differences and get the Rolling Stones machine back in service. In fact, nearly every interview with Richards during that period consists of Richards's ripping on his longtime collaborator's solo work but ends with reassurances that the Stones would return sooner rather than later.

The Hall of Fame induction appeared to give Jagger and Richards an excuse to do that. In the days preceding the ceremony, Jagger and Richards met in Barbados to discuss the future of the Stones and to start developing ideas for the next album and tour.

Though Wyman and Watts couldn't make the January 18 ceremony (Wyman would later say in his autobiography that he thought it was hypocritical that the Stones were accepting an award from the establishment), the most important news was that Jagger, Richards, and Wood—along with Mick Taylor, who was inducted along with the deceased Brian Jones and Ian Stewart—stood onstage together and participated in the end-of-ceremony jam, playing "Satisfaction," "Honky Tonk Women," and "Start Me Up" alongside Tina Turner, Bruce Springsteen, Little Richard, Stevie Wonder, Pete Townshend, the Temptations, and many other honored guests on the overcrowded stage. It was the first time that Jagger and Richards had worked together publicly since filming the video for "One Hit (to the Body)" in May 1986. Though the pair sat at separate tables during the ceremony, Jagger concluded his acceptance speech with an eye on putting the Stones back together, saying, "Jean Cocteau said that Americans are funny people. First you shock them, and then they put you in a museum. But we're not ready to hang up the number yet, so on behalf of the Stones, I'd like to thank you very much."

The following day, Jagger, Richards, Wood, and Watts (who finally made it to New York) had a band meeting to discuss the band's future and how a Stones reunion would mark a new era for the band. Up-and-coming Canadian promoter Michael Cohl pitched a touring model that would sell the Stones as a musical product in a way no pop band had ever embraced before. The Stones' partnership with Cohl marked the end of their nearly two-decade run with Bill Graham. Later Jagger recalled the meeting's going very smoothly despite the months of animosity. He said,

> *"What actually happened was, we had a meeting to plan the tour, and as far as I was concerned, it was very easy. At the time, everyone was asking [whispers], 'Wow, what was it like? What happened? How did it all work?' It was a non-event. What could have been a lot of name-calling, wasn't. I think everyone just decided that we'd done all that. Of course, we had to work out what the modus vivendi was for everybody, because we were planning a very different kind of tour. Everyone had to realize that they were in a new kind of world. We had to invent new rules. It was bigger business, more efficient than previous tours, than the '70s drug tours. We were all gonna be on time at the shows. Everyone realized they had to pull their weight, and everyone had a role to play, and they were all up for doing it."*

Aside from two more commitments Richards had to his solo career—he shot a video for "Make No Mistake" at the North River Bar in Manhattan on February 9 and had a one-off performance with the X-Pensive Winos on May 31 at the 69th Regiment Armory for US TV's International Rock Awards when he was given the Living Legend Award—the table was set for the Rolling Stones' comeback.

After spending April through June recording *Steel Wheels* in Montserrat, in the Caribbean, the Stones gathered in New York City for the July 11 publicity stunt and press conference that would announce their long-speculated return.

The July 11 event was one day before the twenty-seventh anniversary of the Stones' first performance. Fans and over three hundred members of the international media were gathered in a cordoned-off area of Grand Central Terminal in Midtown, and the Stones arrived via an antique train caboose (left over from the 1984 Francis Ford Coppola film *The Cotton Club*) from the Harlem-125th Street Metro North train station. During the fifteen-minute press conference, Jagger—who had stripped down to his undershirt by the end of the event—was quick to point out that the tour was not a farewell tour, as the media had been speculating. He said, "I know you're dying to ask questions like 'Will this be the last tour you ever do?' That's a good one. Or, 'How much money are you going to earn on this tour?' But I won't preempt you completely." When the "last tour" question did come up, Jagger remarked that they had been getting that question since 1966. As for whether they were only in it for the money, Wood answered, "No, that's the Who." (The Who had recently embarked on a controversial twenty-fifth-anniversary tour featuring an expanded lineup after claiming that their 1982 tour would be their last.) As for the "final tour" questions, Jagger later clarified, "This tour is not a historical tour as such. It's more of a 1989 tour. I mean, I don't see it as a sort of retrospective or farewell or anything like that. I see it as the Rolling Stones in 1989."

One of the early questions came from New York's *Howard Stern Show* producer Gary Dell'Abate, who asked if Jagger and Richards had ended their feud. Jagger embraced Richards, and Richards said, "Well, the answer to that is that we both gave up masochism," with Jagger adding, "We don't have fights, just disagreements." After a few more questions with equally noncommittal answers, the conference ended with Jagger playing a ten-second snippet of the next single, "Mixed Emotions," on a boom box, remarking, "It's got a nice beat to it."

The substantial information about the tour dates, opening act (Jagger's pet project Living Colour would serve as the opener for most of the tour), and ticket prices—$28.50 and not the rumored $35—had been released to the press shortly before the conference. Per the Stones, the event was not without controversy. The group offered little more than what had already been announced via press release, resulting in several unhappy members of the media. Deborah Wilker, writing for the

Fort Lauderdale Sun Sentinel, called the spectacle a "sorry affair," adding, "Everything was played for a cheap laugh. The band's faked arrival via an old-fashioned caboose was as hokey as a stale vaudeville act." Steve Morse of the *Boston Globe* called it "a staged, made-for-TV farce" and complained that the Stones were an hour late. Wood must have thought the disappointment stemmed from the lack of spectacle, because he wrote in his autobiography, "Everyone thought we were going to play something live right there, or blow the train up." But for the assembled fans, the first Rolling Stones album and tour in years made those gripes moot. MTV provided extensive coverage of the event as part of its promotional sponsorship of the tour. The cable channel would heavily promote the tour, including recording interviews with the band members for its *This Week in Rock* program on August 22 at the Garden City Hotel in Garden City, Long Island, during tour rehearsals.

When *Steel Wheels* was finally released on August 29, New York critics generally hailed it as a back-to-basics, return-to-form album, though stopped short of acclaiming it as one of the band's best. Jon Pareles of *The New York Times* complimented the riffs and the scaled-back production but complained about the generic lyrics, concluding that *Steel Wheels* was "a safe, enjoyable, hollow album." In contrast, Anthony DeCurtis of *Rolling Stone* praised the album, remarking, "Against all odds, and at this late date, the Stones have once again generated an album that will have the world dancing to deeply troubling, unresolved emotions."

Inevitably, questions about the Stones' aims came up. The Steel Wheels Tour—originally set to begin on September 1 in Buffalo, New York, but later canceled in favor of a two-night stand at Philadelphia's Veterans Stadium on August 31 and September 1—would be the group's most massive undertaking to date in terms of length, venue size, and scope of production. Many questioned the possibility of the tour's succeeding in the face of the Stones' ages in the music video era and recent infighting.

In particular, one key piece of information was missing from the announcements surrounding the July 11 press conference: Though dates were announced for twenty-seven US and Canadian cities, no dates in New York City were included. The Stones booked Nassau Coliseum—thirty miles east of Manhattan on Long Island—for two weeks in mid-August for rehearsals, but the eighteen-thousand-seat arena was much too small for a New York concert. The Coliseum rehearsals, however, did mark the return of saxophonist Bobby Keys to the touring band after a multi-year hiatus due to differences with Jagger. Richards was able to "smuggle" Keys back into the band when he arranged for him to play the sax solo for "Brown Sugar" while the band rehearsed the song, unbeknownst to Jagger. Jagger accepted Keys back into the band, but the Coliseum still wasn't big enough to hold the Stones on this tour. A venue much more historical in nature was necessary for the return of "The World's Greatest Rock 'n' Roll Band."

* * * * *

Some venues are built to be great halls for music, such as Carnegie Hall and Town Hall. Others have greatness thrust upon them. Shea Stadium, located in the borough of Queens near LaGuardia Airport and the USTA National Tennis Center, was not built with the expectation that it would become one of the most hallowed venues in rock 'n' roll history. Shea Stadium was built to serve as the home for the New York Mets baseball team and the New York Jets football team. Prior to the completion of the construction of Shea, both teams had played home games at the Polo Grounds in northern Manhattan, an inadequate relic of the late nineteenth century that was older than the parents of most of the fans who attended games at the stadium.

After the Brooklyn Dodgers and the New York Giants baseball teams left New York for California after the 1957 baseball season, New York City was left with only one professional baseball team, the famed New York Yankees of the American League. New York lawyer William A. Shea was appointed the head of a committee that was responsible for bringing a new National League baseball team to New York. One of the league's conditions for adding a team was that New York needed to build a stadium to replace the aging Polo Grounds. Construction on the new stadium broke ground in October 1961 ten miles southeast of the Polo Grounds in Flushing, and shortly before opening it was named in honor of William A. Shea. Shea Stadium opened to great fanfare just five days before the opening of the 1964–1965 New York World's Fair across the street. The then state-of-the-art Shea was in that sense an unofficial exhibition of the exposition.

Rock music—or to be more accurate, amplifier technology—was not quite ready for stadium concerts when the Beatles played at Shea before fifty-five thousand fans on August 15, 1965, and shattered attendance and box office records for a pop music concert with the $304,000 gross. Famously, the screams of the crowd were so loud that fans could not even hear what the band was playing—and neither could the Beatles. The Beatles returned to Shea on August 23, 1966, with New York natives the Ronettes opening, with little improvement to the sound. Rock concerts did not become a staple of Shea Stadium, although there were several over the next two decades, including the 1970 Festival for Peace (featuring Big Brother & the Holding Company, Paul Simon, Creedence Clearwater Revival, and Miles Davis), Grand Funk Railroad in 1971, Stevie Wonder in 1973, Jethro Tull in 1976, the Who in 1982, and the Police in 1983. Yet the Beatles' first performance there in 1965 already firmly entrenched Shea Stadium in rock legend. When Jagger and Richards attended that first Beatles concert, it's unlikely that they imagined themselves playing a multi-night stand at the stadium almost a quarter of a century later. Prior to the Stones, the Who was the only group to play Shea for consecutive shows (October 12 and 13, 1982).

Of course, the Stones had already played stadiums before. During their last American tour in 1981, they had performed at over a dozen stadiums, including the Carrier Dome in upstate Syracuse, New York (which they played again on the Steel Wheels Tour—twice). While booking both the 1981 and 1989 tours, the Stones inquired about playing at the seventy-seven-thousand-seat Giants Stadium in East Rutherford, New Jersey, but were rejected by the Giants because the stadium's football practice schedule could not accommodate the concerts and their multi-day load-in and load-out times. Shea Stadium was available because the late-October dates would be after the baseball postseason concluded and the New York Jets, which had previously used Shea in the late fall, no longer played there (the Jets had moved to Giants Stadium in 1984).

The Stones officially announced the first two concerts at Shea— October 26 and 28—in mid-August, though the initial four dates (October 25, 26, 28, and 29) were correctly reported by *New York Newsday* in mid-July. By that time the tour had already broken box office records. Considering that prior to the announcement, the Stones were already scheduled to play two shows at Philadelphia's Veterans Stadium and two shows at Syracuse's Carrier Dome, two shows at Shea seemed to be more than enough based on likely demand. (The Stones also played a secret warm-up gig at the seven-hundred-person-capacity rock club Toad's Place in New Haven, Connecticut, on August 12, located about seventy miles northeast of Manhattan. Of course, tickets were hard to come by for a show so intimate.) However, by the time the tickets for Shea went on sale on August 19, the Stones had added shows on October 25 and 29 and sold nearly 250,000 tickets for the four shows in just six hours. That still wasn't enough to meet demand. Once the New York Mets were eliminated from playoff contention in late September, the Stones added two additional dates before their four-night series on October 10 and 11, for a total of six shows at the sixty-thousand-person-capacity stadium. In 1965 it seemed incredible that a rock 'n' roll band could gross $304,000 at just a single show in a stadium of that size, yet almost twenty-five years later another band from the same era sold over 350,000 tickets for six shows, for a gross of $12 million.

Besides the record-breaking box office, what separated the Steel Wheels Tour from previous tours was the sheer magnitude of the stage. On October 5, *The New York Times* published a feature on the tour's massive set, calling it "a towering amalgam of chutes, pipes, chain mail balustrades, and other steely portents of urban decay" and "the manifestation of an approach to rock-concert design that began in 1965 when the Beatles played their first concert at Shea Stadium." The extra time that was made possible by the Mets' elimination from the playoffs was necessary because the stage took three to five days to construct. Because of that, the band toured with two versions of the set, which enabled them to play four shows at the Los Angeles Memorial Coliseum in the gap between the October 11 and October 25 Shea Stadium shows without deconstructing the stage in Queens and shipping it across the country only to reconstruct it a few days later back in Queens.

The night before the first Shea Stadium concert, the Stones held a party in New York to celebrate the twenty-fifth anniversary of Charlie and Shirley Watts. Though the tour had been running for over a month and early reviews were overwhelmingly positive, the party provided the band with a brief respite from the ensuing media circus that would surround the New York and Los Angeles gigs.

Media concerns about the fortysomething Stones (and the nearly fifty-three-year-old Bill Wyman) being able to draw thousands from the MTV generation to their concerts turned out to be completely unfounded. The day after the first Shea show, *The Times* published a profile on young Stones fans and parents with their teenage children who had attended the previous night's concert. In fact, a thirty-six-year-old fan joked about the audience's skewing toward younger fans, pointing out, "It's a little inundating when you're our age and you go to a show and you feel like a babysitter."

The first two Shea concerts included special guest Eric Clapton, who played "Little Red Rooster" with the band. There were few variations in the set list across the six shows at Shea, as the lighting and production effects prevented the band from spontaneous changes. Appropriate for New York City, "Harlem Shuffle" was played on October 10, 11, 26, and 29, while "One Hit (to the Body)" was played instead on October 24 and 28. Richards sang "Before They Make Me Run" at the first two shows, but sang his *Steel Wheels* track "Can't Be Seen" at the last four. "Angie" and "Little Red Rooster" were played on October 10, 25, and

28, while "Play With Fire" and "Dead Flowers" were played on October 11, 26, and 29. "Little Red Rooster" was also played on October 11, making that the only night at Shea on which twenty-six songs were played instead of twenty-five. Interestingly, "Shattered" was rehearsed by the band for the tour but played only at the first show, on August 31 at Veterans Stadium in Philadelphia. However, during the performance the sound system died and the Stones were forced to leave the stage while the issue was resolved. The song was subsequently dropped from the set list for the remainder of the tour. Jon Bream, the famed music journalist of the *Minneapolis Star Tribune*, was backstage before one of the Shea shows and overheard a member of the road crew tell Richards an hour before showtime that Jagger wanted to do the band's "Fun City" tribute "Shattered" that night. Richards responded pugnaciously, "If he does, you tell him to meet me in the rehearsal room." Needless to say, "Shattered" wasn't played at any of the Shea concerts.

The Times gave the first show at Shea positive marks, with reviewer Peter Watrous noting, "The members played their standards beautifully, reminding their listeners what a great dance band they are. On tune after tune, after raw and granitelike guitar introductions by the guitarists Keith Richards and Ron Wood, the band moved directly into a hard, greased dance rhythm, underscoring how precise, yet effortless-sounding, the rhythm section can be." However, praise for the return of the Stones was not unanimous in the New York media. While David Browne of the *Daily News* said the shows were "awesome," he bemoaned, "There was no getting around that the concert was like watching a petrified forest that moved. It seemed as though Mick Jagger didn't believe a word he sang, and his aging-marionette dance steps and vocal slurs are often embarrassing."

When the Stones returned to New York after the third Los Angeles concert on October 22, they spent time in Manhattan. Wyman celebrated his fifty-third birthday with Charlie Watts, Eric Clapton, and Sting on October 24. ("The band gave me a pool table and shipped it back to London," he later revealed.) That same night, Wood's East Village nightclub Woody's In The Village opened its doors, succeeding his Florida nightclub, Woody's on the Beach, which was closed due to repeated noise complaints. On the band's one night off between the fourth and fifth Shea concerts, Richards saw classical guitarist Carlos Montoya in concert and Jagger saw the Red Hot Chili Peppers perform at The Ritz. The last four Shea concerts went as planned, and the Steel Wheels Tour continued, wrapping up its North American leg with three concerts at the Convention Center in Atlantic City, New Jersey. The 14,700-seat Convention Center was much smaller than the other stops on the tour, but it was specifically picked because the second night was broadcast live as a pay-per-view special that featured Eric Clapton, John Lee Hooker, and Axl Rose and Izzy Stradlin of Guns N' Roses as guests. Being a frequently used venue for televised boxing events, the Convention Center was already equipped to air the concert.

The tour would continue in February 1990 for a ten-night stand at the Tokyo Dome, and then would resume for a final leg from May to August in Europe rebilled as the Urban Jungle Tour with a new stage. Eight years earlier, the fifty-date Rolling Stones American Tour 1981 had grossed $52 million. The 115-date Steel Wheels Tour grossed $260 million worldwide—and ticket sales accounted for only about forty percent of that gross. The Stones themselves pocketed $70 million in guaranteed money from promoter Michael Cohl and millions more from other revenue streams. The Stones also marketed the Steel Wheels Tour in ways that no other band had done before and made immense profits. The tour was sponsored by Anheuser-Busch to the tune of $6 million, which let the brewing empire plaster the Budweiser logo all over promotional materials. Tour merchandise was sold not just at concerts but also at major department stores like JCPenney and Macy's.

Jagger would later reflect on how the Steel Wheels Tour changed the industry and how it turned the Stones from a rock band to a world-class entertainment venture. "It took us twenty years of doing shows before we actually put on these big stadium concerts. It will be interesting to see if any of these bands today ever do the kind of shows we're doing. I don't think they will, because they don't seem to be that interested in it. You have to be really interested in showbiz to do this; you have to be interested in theater, otherwise there's no point doing it. It's only interesting if you're in control of it. And to be in control of it, you have to initiate it. I wonder if there's anybody that's going to do that."

Even considering its enormous success, the Steel Wheels Tour served as only a prototype for the even more colossal and record-breaking tours to come for the band. The Rolling Stones were now a cultural product. The rock 'n' roll hell raisers had become an institution. Much like the *Some Girls* song anticipated, the Stones had become "Respectable."

* * * * *

The Stones weren't the only once decried institution that was becoming respectable at that time.

The Manhattan that the Stones had explored in the music of 1978's *Some Girls* was becoming a very different place, beginning not long after the Steel Wheels Tour rolled into Shea Stadium. The seediness of the 1970s was giving way to the capitalism of the 1980s on the streets of New York. Many of the city's celebrated public parks had become dangerous in the 1970s, and under Koch's administration they saw significant restoration. Central Park, suffering from mismanagement and poor maintenance in the 1960s and 1970s, was considered off-limits by sane New Yorkers after dark, and its once magnificent Great Lawn was covered with patches of dead grass and parched dust. In 1980, the Central Park Conservancy began addressing the landscape, architecture, and refuse problems plaguing the park, and over the next thirty years restored Central Park as one of the top tourist destinations in the city. In 1988, Bryant Park in Midtown was closed for a multi-year renovation to complete its rehabilitation from the drug-infested and homeless-filled grounds that it had become during the 1970s. Most dramatic were the events in Tompkins Square Park, an East Village public space that had become a haven for the homeless, heroin users, and all-night punk rock parties. In August 1988, the City announced that the park would close after dark in order to clear it of the homeless. Close to midnight on August 6, over four hundred police officers in riot gear attempted to clear the park, which resulted in rioting by hundreds of protestors who saw Koch's efforts as the first steps toward gentrifying an area that had traditionally been a home to artists. The police were accused of using excessive force, and Koch backed off his plan. Koch's successor, Mayor David Dinkins, however, closed the park in June 1991 for a yearlong restoration that finally cleared the park of the homeless squatters.

But cleaning up the parks did little to improve the quality of life for most New Yorkers. The cover of the September 17, 1990, issue of *TIME* magazine featured an ominous drawing of New York City, with the city's glorious landmarks casting a shadow over the crime-ridden outskirts. The cover featured the familiar "I Love New York" logo, but the heart was broken. Underneath, the headline read "THE ROTTING OF THE BIG APPLE."

Inside the magazine, author Joelle Attinger's article "The Decline of New York" looked at the chasm-like dichotomy of New York—a center of finance, politics, and culture yet also plagued by social ills. Attinger wrote, "Only about 1 of every 100 New Yorkers is homeless, but that adds up to 90,000 people huddling in shelters or eking out a life of not-so-quiet desperation on the street. A mere 1 in 300 New Yorkers may be a victim of AIDS, but that totals 27,000 people, a staggering 19 percent of all confirmed cases in the US." In particular, Attinger focused on the escalating murder rate, highlighting the details of several recent grisly murders. Her message to the nation was that New York, for all its glitz and glamour, was still a crime-ridden city:

> *"Outside the city it confirmed what most Americans already believed: New York is an exciting but dangerous place. Among New Yorkers it reinforced the spreading conviction that the city has spun out of control. A growing sense of vulnerability has been deepened by the belief that deadly violence, once mostly confined to crime-ridden*

ghetto neighborhoods that the police wrote off as free-fire zones, is now lashing out randomly at anyone, anytime, even in areas once considered relatively safe."

Attinger blamed the city's social ills on "decades of benign neglect, misplaced priorities and outright incompetence at every level of government."

To provide an example, Attinger rattled off a list of how city services had declined: "Even with the addition of 1,058 new police officers in October, the force will still be 14 percent smaller than its 1975 level of 31,683. Meanwhile crime, fueled by the drug epidemic, has jumped 25 percent. Since 1987, the number of street sweepers has been slashed from 1,400 to 300, trash collections in midtown Manhattan have been reduced by a third, and what used to be daily rounds in the outer boroughs have been reduced to twice a week. Epidemics of AIDS, tuberculosis and syphilis have pushed the health-care system to the breaking point. As many New Yorkers are waiting for public housing as there are existing units, leading occupants to double or triple up in a frantic bid for shelter."

Attinger gave the new mayor in office—David Dinkins, the city's first African American mayor, who was elected in November 1989—little praise for the direction in which he was taking New York. As a whole, her gloom-and-doom outlook on the future of the city made it seem like New York's comeback would be even less likelier than the Rolling Stones' had been. As it turned out, New York's return to prominence took a page or two out of the Stones' own playbook.

CHAPTER 10

"WE WALK THE HIGHWIRE"

As if the Steel Wheels Tour wasn't already one of the biggest tours in rock 'n' roll history and a game changer for the touring industry, the Stones found a few more ways to squeeze additional revenue out of the tour over the next two years. The pay-per-view broadcast of the Atlantic City shows was edited for a network TV broadcast and aired on May 30, 1990, in 3-D. The Stones partnered with 7-Eleven to distribute the glasses. Almost a year later, the Stones compiled recordings from throughout the tour for a live collection titled *Flashpoint*, which was released in April 1991. The album contained two new studio tracks, including "Highwire," which was released as a single. The video was recorded in March near the Brooklyn Bridge at Pier 3, on the Brooklyn side of the East River. Absent from the shoot was Bill Wyman, whose contributions to the two new tracks ended up being his last recordings as a member of the band. A combination of Wyman's dislike of traveling (particularly of flying) and his troubled personal life meant that the group's bassist had no desire to remain part of the Stones' record-breaking world-tour era.

Shortly after the release of *Flashpoint*, the Stones turned their individual attentions to solo projects. Jagger began auditioning musicians in New York for his next album, and in June, Watts celebrated his fiftieth birthday with two Charlie Watts Quintet shows at Blue Note jazz club in Greenwich Village on June 3 (with Richards in attendance) and a live performance with the Quintet on *Good Morning America* at ABC Studios. Blue Note opened in the Village in 1981 and quickly became the most prestigious and popular jazz club in New York. Watts played there again in 1992 and 2001.

Taking his cue from his bandmates, Richards turned to working on songs for his second album and selecting tracks for a live album of his 1988 tour. It wasn't until November when another Stones-related project appeared, and it was yet another release from the Steel Wheels Tour. *Rolling Stones: Live at the Max* was another concert film from the 1989–1990 tour culled from several shows on the Urban Jungle European Tour that were filmed in IMAX format. Yet again, the Stones were trailblazers. They were the first band to release a concert film in the large format, which had previously been used exclusively for science and nature programs for museums. There were few IMAX theaters that would screen the film. The management of the IMAX theater at the Museum of Natural History in Manhattan—the only IMAX screen in New York City at the time—refused to screen the film because it was already committed to showing a documentary called *Beavers*. ("Let them keep the beavers if they want," Richards quipped.)

Instead, the concert film had an extended run at the Beacon Theatre, which had to be converted into an IMAX theater. Janet Maslin of *The New York Times* gave the film a strong review, remarking, "At such close range, the rough edges of a performance might be expected to show up, but in the Stones' case the opposite is true. The big revelation here is the utter professionalism with which a Stones performance is staged." *Rolling Stones: Live at the Max* played in large-format theaters for several years thereafter and ended up helping make IMAX a popular format for non-nature films. Other groups, like U2 and Metallica, would follow the Stones' lead and release IMAX concert films, and the Stones would explore the format further. Almost twenty years later, they recorded a show at the Beacon Theatre for a second IMAX release.

The year 1992 marked the thirtieth anniversary of the band's formation, but the Stones did not mark it with any celebration. Richards made an appearance as a Rock & Roll Hall of Fame inductor at the Waldorf Astoria in January when he did the honors for Leo Fender, but otherwise he was working on his solo album tracks at several New York City studios, including The Hit Factory and Master Sound Astoria. Watts continued his solo work with another tour of the Charlie Watts Quintet titled "A Tribute to Charlie Parker" to promote his recent album of the same name. The tour was highlighted by Watts's performing twelve concerts in six nights at Blue Note in July.

During the lengthy stand, Watts's band engaged in a feud with the house band of *Late Night With David Letterman* when the Charlie Watts Quintet was scheduled to play on the late-night program. According to Watts, when his band arrived at NBC's Studio 6A at 30 Rockefeller Plaza, he was told by producers that his band's performance would be accompanied by Letterman's band, Paul Shaffer and the World's Most Dangerous Band. Watts balked at the idea of his band's having to share the stage and canceled his appearance only minutes before the taping of the episode. Though Watts would eventually play Letterman's CBS show several years later, the feud made minor headlines in the New York press.

The following month, it was Wood's turn to do promotion in New York for his fifth solo album, *Slide on This*, which was to be released in September. On August 4, Wood appeared with vocalist Bernard Fowler on the New York radio institution *The Howard Stern Show*. The duo performed the Temptations' classic "(I Know) I'm Losing You" and the Faces' "Stay With Me." (Incidentally, Fowler scored a hat trick in 1992 by appearing on the solo albums of Watts, Wood, and Richards all in the same year.) Wood appeared on the syndicated New York radio show *Rockline* the following week, and in October took part in the 30th Anniversary Concert Celebration for Bob Dylan at Madison Square Garden. Wood performed Dylan's "Seven Days" and participated in the ensemble version of "Knockin' on Heaven's Door" at the end of the concert. The following week, Wood and Fowler—joined by Wood's Faces bandmate Ian McLagan—rehearsed for Wood's upcoming solo tour at SIR Studios.

However, the Stones weren't done with 1992 just yet. There was one more solo album to come, this time from Richards, and, just a month before the scheduled release, Richards was still tinkering with the songs at The Hit Factory. Richards appeared on *Rockline* on October 19, the day before *Main Offender* was released. He spent the day of the release signing copies at New York's Tower Records at East 4th Street and Broadway. He then rehearsed with the X-Pensive Winos for his upcoming tour.

Wood dropped in on Richards's rehearsals, and he didn't leave town until after he performed "Stay With Me" on *Late Night With David Letterman* on October 28, which he followed with a warm-up performance at Toad's Place in New Haven, Connecticut (the same small venue where the Stones had done a warm-up show for the Steel Wheels Tour in 1989). Wood kicked off his tour with a Halloween show at The Ritz, which had moved uptown in April 1989 to the space formerly occupied by Studio 54.

Main Offender was promoted with a lengthy profile of Richards in the October 18 edition of *The New York Times*, written by Karen Schoemer; it focused on Richards's peculiar recording methods—in particular, Richards's habit of recording vocals without having the words memorized or even written down. The opening of the piece is a slice of noirish New York midnight literature. "It's somewhere past midnight in a recording studio on lower Broadway, and Keith Richards is smoking. All around him the lights have been lowered for atmosphere. Every time he takes a drag, the tip of his cigarette glows red like a beacon."

The interview touched on the still unconfirmed rumors that Bill Wyman had left the Stones. Richards remarked, "When we're ready to work, I'm hoping he'll be there. I've spoke to some of his old girlfriends that know him *really* well who've said he'll probably be there." On December 3, Jagger announced on MTV Europe that Wyman had left the band and that the Stones were in the process of finding a new bassist—the first time the group had to look for a new member since Wood joined in 1975.

After three months of promotion and rehearsals, Richards and the X-Pensive Winos played a New Year's Eve concert at the Academy on West 43rd Street featuring guest appearances by bluesman Robert Cray and members of Pearl Jam on the blues standard "Goin' Down." Part of the concert was broadcast on CBS as the *Hard Rock Cafe New Year's Special*. The Academy, a former Broadway theater built in 1903 that had served as a concert venue since earlier that year, ended up closing as a live performance venue in 1996 and was combined with the closed theater next door to create the Broadway theater now known as the Lyric Theatre.

Other than Wyman's departure, when 1993 dawned there was little news on what the Stones would be doing as a group. Richards followed the New Year's Eve show with more tour rehearsals, and Jagger prepared to promote his third solo album, *Wandering Spirit*, which was set for a February 8 release. Jagger based nearly all of his promotion for the album in New York City, in contrast to his promotion for *Primitive Cool*, during which he barely visited the United States. First, Jagger appeared on the February 4 episode of *Late Night With David Letterman*, becoming the second Stone after Wood to appear on the show. Two days later, Jagger appeared as the musical guest on *Saturday Night Live* and performed two songs, "Sweet Thing" and "Don't Tear Me Up." More notably, he appeared in a "Weekend Update" skit as Keith Richards—dressed in a torn shirt, smoking a cigarette, and lounging about—with cast member Mike Myers playing Jagger. The pair discussed rap artist Ice-T, who had recently been dropped by Warner Bros. Records over the controversial song "Cop Killer." "Mick" argues that Ice-T was just trying to express himself, while "Keith" takes the side of the cops, calling them "the backbone of our bloody society" and referring to "Mick" as an "ignorant slut." Eventually, the argument by "Keith" turns into mumbles, and somehow the two end up collaborating on Richards's mumbles to come up with a song. The skit was one of the most memorable moments of the series in the 1990s because of Jagger's dead-on impersonation of his longtime collaborator.

While Watts and Wood toured for their latest solo albums and Richards himself was in the beginnings of a tour, Jagger—perhaps to avoid the embarrassment of his uncelebrated *Primitive Cool* tour—performed only one concert on February 9 at Webster Hall, which had reverted to its original name when The Ritz moved uptown. Unlike with previous Jagger shows, much of the set list was not devoted to Stones songs. Only the final three songs were by the Stones, and all three hadn't been performed live since the 1960s or 1970s—"Rip This Joint," "Live With Me," and "Have You Seen Your Mother, Baby, Standing in the Shadow?" The rest of the set was made up of eleven of the album's fourteen tracks. The concert was broadcast via closed-circuit television. *Village Voice* writer Deborah Frost blasted the performance in her mostly negative review of *Wandering Spirit* and the concert, remarking,

> *"Jagger ran through highly stylized versions of all his familiar moves, desperately trying to remind us of the object of desire he was at 20; what he looked like stagefront, next to his teleprompter, was less the pansexual nymph of old than the CEO of a shaky conglomerate staunchly determined to restore investor faith. Primping and posing in order that we might forgive Michael Bolton and desperately miss David Johansen, Jagger suddenly seemed a man very much out of time—his narcissism no longer pretty, his chauvinism intolerable, his hedonism hardly liberating, and his 'I'm as hard as a brick/Hope I never go limp!' confessions better saved for the prostate man."*

She also admonished Jagger for not playing more Stones songs in the set.

Ten days later, Richards concluded his tour with a five-night stand at the Beacon Theatre. Writing for *The New York Times*, Jon Pareles reviewed the first gig, and in praising Richards he took a shot at Jagger's show earlier in the month, which he said had come "dangerously close to self-parody." In contrast, Pareles said Richards "thrives on

171

understatement and concentrated guitar playing, radiating a consummate rock 'n' roll cool." Again, Richards came out on top in the New York press, though Jagger's album sold better in the US this time around.

Curiously, in *The Times* the day before, Karen Schoemer—who had written the October 18 profile of Richards—wrote a profile on Jagger in the February 21 edition. When asked about his upcoming fiftieth birthday, Jagger played coy. "I don't think I'd even think of it very much if it wasn't for journalists. Because these *things*, these great milestones, they sort of come and go. The next day it's all over. It doesn't last very long." He also jokingly recalled how the drug culture had changed. "In the '60s it was a minority. It was still, like, artists only. In the '70s, it was, like, *everyone*. The secretary at the fashion company went to Studio 54. Quaaludes and all that. Women loved Quaaludes. For men—you couldn't perform on Quaaludes, so to speak, and I don't mean the tours." On the 1980s, he was less reminiscent, saying, "It was very greedy, wasn't it? And everyone seemed to have a reaction against taking Quaaludes at Studio 54. Suddenly they wanted to be bankers and traders."

* * * * *

Jagger was far from the only person to notice these changes in New York. In November 1993, Rudy Giuliani was elected mayor; he took office on January 1, 1994. Giuliani had gained nationwide fame as the US attorney for the Southern District of New York during the mid-1980s when he successfully prosecuted mafia leaders and insider traders in highly publicized trials. His efforts gave him the reputation of being tough on crime. He unsuccessfully ran for mayor as a Republican against David Dinkins in 1989, though it was the closest election loss in New York City history. That put Giuliani in a strong position for a rematch against Dinkins in 1993. As before, Giuliani touted his ability to cut crime and subscribed to the so-called broken windows theory of policing—that is, if a police force takes seemingly petty crimes seriously, the actions would promote lawfulness and, in turn, reduce more significant crime. In actuality, crime had already been dropping at the end of Koch's time in office and more dramatically during Dinkins's term as a result of Dinkins's similar Safe Streets, Safe Cities program and a 25 percent increase in the size of the police force. Giuliani's message, however, resonated with New Yorkers, especially in light of several well-publicized issues that had arisen during Dinkins's term, including his handling of the racially charged Crown Heights riots in 1991 and the continuing crack epidemic that was plaguing the black community.

Shortly after Giuliani took office and appointed Bill Bratton as police commissioner, the New York City Police Department announced, in March 1994, that it would begin more strictly policing "quality of life" offenses, such as public urination, public consumption of alcohol, and perhaps most famously, the proliferation of "squeegee men," who would wash the windows of cars stopped in traffic and demand money for the "service." Though the crackdown on squeegee men actually began during Dinkins's administration under Police Commissioner Ray Kelly, Giuliani's "war on the squeegee men" became symbolic of his quality-of-life-offenses crackdown. Under Giuliani's leadership, crime rates in New York continued to decline.

Giuliani also continued the revitalization of tourist attractions that had begun under Koch and Dinkins, and nowhere were the changes in Manhattan better evidenced than in Times Square. What had once been the entertainment showcase of New York City in the early to mid-twentieth century had become a crime-ridden area filled with porn theaters and peep shows not far removed from the urban decay suggested by the Stones' massive Steel Wheels Tour stage.

In 1990, a not-for-profit organization called The New 42nd Street was created to redevelop the area, particularly the former Broadway theaters that were sitting vacant in disrepair or had been converted to movie theaters. Over the next two years, the City of New York seized seven of the theaters and converted them into legitimate Broadway theaters or other tourist attractions. In less than a decade, Times Square was reclaimed and recast as a center of family tourism. In a

2002 interview with *Fortune*, Steel Wheels Tour director Michael Cohl explained how the Stones similarly upped the spectacle and value of the rock 'n' roll stadium show and turned stadiums like Shea into theaters of their own: "When you look at what a stadium show was pre-*Steel Wheels*, it was a bit of a scrim, and a big, wide, flat piece of lumber, and that was it. The band turned a stadium into a theater. It all started with Mick. He simply said, 'We have to fill the end space.' It was complicated to the third power and expensive to the fifth. But it worked."

Like the Stones, New York recognized the immense financial rewards that could be gained from economic development, corporate branding, and, most importantly, improving entertainment facilities to increase tourism. While the rehabilitation was largely welcomed and championed by public officials, critics of the changes have argued that the rehabilitation made the pendulum swing too far in the opposite direction. What had been a vice-ridden eyesore was turned into the equivalent of a glitzy outdoor shopping mall.

Symbolic of these changes was the role Disney took in the transformation of Times Square when the company entered the Broadway business, starting with signing a ninety-nine-year lease on the newly restored New Amsterdam Theatre on 42nd Street in 1993 and shortly afterward producing a series of stage adaptations of the company's catalog of family films. But much like the Stones' own corporate facelift that started in 1989, the "Disneyfication" of Times Square in the 1990s resulted in millions of dollars in new revenue, both for the area and for the corporations that invested in the once sordid streets of Midtown. This transformation included the Giuliani administration's forcing the closure of dozens of adult entertainment businesses, like strip clubs and video stores, in tourist areas. Those who missed the sleazy days of *Some Girls*—in the case of both New York City and the Rolling Stones—would see both institutions only continue to change in pursuit of the almighty dollar.

CHAPTER 11

"LOVE IS STRONG"

With both Jagger and Richards in New York in February 1993, they met to discuss the next Rolling Stones album. In early June, Richards attended the New York ceremony that inducted him and Jagger into the Songwriters Hall of Fame. For Richards, this was a distinctive honor, perhaps even his proudest, because the plaque "was signed by Sammy Cahn on his deathbed." New York City-born Cahn was one of America's most prolific songwriters during the first half of the twentieth century and wrote famous songs such as "Come Fly With Me," "Love and Marriage," and "High Hopes." As Cahn was the president of the institution before his death in January 1993, Jagger and Richards were in the last class selected during his tenure.

By the end of the month, the Glimmer Twins, Watts, and Wood reconvened at SIR Studios for bass player auditions and to find a producer for the upcoming album. They would settle on Don Was of Was (Not Was). Was later recalled,

> *"I knew Mick a bit but I'd never met Keith before. I went to an audition in New York, where they were trying out bass players. My interview for the job was listening to Keith tell me why he doesn't need a*

producer. (I)t was shocking to me to contrast the Saturday Night Live parody image...with this vibrant, really intelligent, lucid, mind-racing character. He's the exact opposite of what you picture. The man is as creative as anyone I've encountered in my whole life. Whether he's doing a handwritten fax or playing guitar riffs, he's always inspired. It's a remarkable thing."

Among the many bassists who auditioned was Darryl Jones, who previously had played with Sting, Eric Clapton, Miles Davis, and Herbie Hancock. It was his jazz background that connected with Watts, who had final say over who would be supporting the Stones as their new sideman. Years later, Richards would remark to the *New York Daily News*, "They just fit. There's something instinctive between them, probably because of the jazz angle. Jazz bass players and drummers have a history of making great rock 'n' roll, back to cats like Earl Palmer. They understand what I always try to tell people: It's not the rock that's important. It's the roll."

After cementing their rhythm section, the Stones went to work on the album through much of the fall of 1993 and early 1994, recording in Ireland, with the final mixes of the song "I Go Wild" done in April 1994 at Right Track Studios in New York. Watts spent a short bit of downtime in October 1993 back in New York to promote his third Charlie Watts Quintet album, *Warm & Tender*, with a press party show at the Oak Room in the Algonquin Hotel. Watts also did press rounds with appearances on NBC's *Later* and VH-1's *Music Talks*, and live performances on *Live With Regis and Kathie Lee* and *Late Night With Conan O'Brien*, but by November he was back in Ireland with the Stones. During another break, Richards was thrown a surprise party for his fiftieth birthday and tenth wedding anniversary on December 18 in New York, which included friends like Eric Clapton, Bobby Keys, and new Stones bassist, Darryl Jones.

Jagger, Watts, and Wood joined Richards in New York at the end of April, where the band prepared to announce the new album and upcoming tour. The last time the Stones had announced a tour in New

York, they arrived at Grand Central station in an antique railway car. This time the Stones held their press conference at Pier 60 (now the site of the Chelsea Piers Sports and Entertainment Complex) on May 4. As the ranks of press waited on the pier, the Stones arrived via a huge yacht to announce the *Voodoo Lounge* album and tour. Among the announcements, the Stones said they would play two shows at Giants Stadium in August, and shortly afterward they added a third show when the first two sold out (a fourth was eventually added as well). They also announced the addition of Darryl Jones on bass, though the official lineup would remain Jagger, Richards, Watts, and Wood.

The next month the Stones were in Toronto rehearsing for the tour. They also filmed their parts for the video for the first single, "Love Is Strong," which were combined with footage of New York City. The video features giant versions of the Stones walking through the streets of Manhattan along with several giant young folks waking up all over the city and aimlessly meandering bout.

Jon Pareles in *The New York Times* focused more on the Stones' advancing ages than their material in both his July 10 review of *Voodoo Lounge* and his August 3 review of the tour opener in Washington. It was a criticism the Stones were used to hearing at this point. On August 7, Pareles even devoted a third column to trying to discover what it was that kept the Stones going. Of course, the band members had their own opinions. In a pre-tour interview in the Stones' Manhattan office with *Rolling Stone*, Richards remarked on the band's longevity:

> *"It's like one of those old maps where there are dragons, and it says End of The World. Where is it? You don't know. You're supposed to fall off here. We have no road maps, no way of knowing how to deal with this. But everyone wanted to do it. 'We can still show 'em a trick or two. And learn a trick or two in the process.' I'm very proud of the career, as long as it's gone. Still, it's the old story—who's gonna get off of this bus while you're still feeling good about it?"*

Other articles that appeared in *The Times* were more positive. A profile on the Stones' lighting crew appeared on August 17, and a reflection on the Stones' longevity by Michiko Kakutani on September 4 celebrated their decades-long connection to their audience. In November, *The Times* marveled at the Stones' becoming the first major rock band to broadcast a concert live on the internet when they broadcast twenty minutes of their Dallas concert.

* * * * *

With twenty thousand more seats than Shea Stadium, Giants Stadium was the venue that the Stones had wanted to play at during the Steel Wheels Tour. However, with those shows being in October, the football stadium had been unable to accommodate them. Giants Stadium was the only venue to host two NFL teams—the New York Giants and New York Jets—and was in constant use during the NFL season. With the Voodoo Lounge Tour hitting the area in mid-August, the Stones were able to schedule their concerts during an NFL pre-season week when both teams were out of town.

During the Giants Stadium concerts, the Stones played at least six songs from the new album on each night: "You Got Me Rocking," "Sparks Will Fly," "Out of Tears," "I Go Wild," "The Worst," and "Love Is Strong." Though they usually covered The Temptations' "I Can't Get Next to You" during the tour, on August 15 they ditched it in favor of a seventh track from the new album, "Brand New Car," and on August 17 they didn't play that either and shortened the otherwise twenty-four-song set by one song. One of the shows was drenched in rain in the aftermath of a tropical storm. Richards would later tell *Rolling Stone* that it was one of the best shows of the entire tour. "You realize you're gonna get soaked and say, 'Fuck it,' and have a great time. I'm wet, and I love it."

Less than a month later, the Stones were back in New York on September 8 to receive a Lifetime Achievement Award presented by Jann Wenner at the MTV Awards at Radio City Music Hall, where the band also played "Love Is Strong" and "Start Me Up." During the performance of "Love Is Strong," Jagger wore a long dress coat covered with trinkets and a top hat, looking like a stylish voodoo priest. It was the first time the Stones had ever played the legendary venue.

The Stones were barely able to squeeze the appearance into their schedule—they had performed in Raleigh, North Carolina, the night before and would perform in East Lansing, Michigan, the following day—yet they still attended a post-show party thrown in their honor by Virgin Records at the Four Seasons Hotel. It was all par for the course for the Stones' hectic tour schedule, though—earlier in the year Richards had confessed in an interview with Rich Cohen of *Rolling Stone*, "I'm all messed up when a tour ends. Eight o'clock rolls around, and I'm looking for the gig. And what I really miss is the police motorcade. Even better than a platinum record is going through a Manhattan rush hour in 20 minutes."

After wrapping up the US and Canadian dates in mid-December, the Stones played Mexico, South America, and South Africa in January and February; Japan and Australia in March and April; and finally Europe from May through August. Only months into the 124-date Voodoo Lounge Tour, it became the highest-grossing concert tour of all time, accumulating an incredible $320 million, more than triple the take of the 115-date Steel Wheels Tour just five years earlier.

Yet the Stones weren't through with *Voodoo Lounge* yet. As was becoming common, they issued a live album, *Stripped*, on November 13, 1995. It included recordings from smaller venues played on the European leg and a few live-in-the-studio unplugged tunes recorded in Tokyo and Portugal. Although at the time it was fashionable for bands to do unplugged sets for MTV at the channel's New York studio, the Stones instead chose to do their own live version of the concept. In an interview with Jann Wenner in *Rolling Stone* later that year, Jagger explained why they hadn't collaborated with MTV. "Because everyone has done it, and I didn't want to particularly come to New York and do *Unplugged* in the middle of the European tour. And I felt that we would take the best element from *Unplugged*, the intimate thing of it, without actually doing it completely unplugged." Of course, it also meant that the Stones didn't have to share the profits with MTV.

In November, both Jagger and Richards were in New York to promote *Stripped*, and Richards also took some time to add some guitar to a few tracks by Bo Diddley in a New York studio. That fall, Jagger was spotted throughout the city, with the *Daily News* revealing his new favorite hangout—a Greene Street lounge named Spy (located at 17 West 19th Street)—and writing about his visits until a presumably fed-up Jagger stopped going in early 1996.

Besides the live album, the other big news of the fall of 1995 was one that divided fans. To launch its new operating system, Windows 95, computer software giant Microsoft paid the Stones millions of dollars to use "Start Me Up" in the commercials. Though the band was far from the first pop group to license a song for commercial use, the multi-million-dollar marketing campaign was one of the first to utilize a rock song in such a significant way, because it was central to the almost unavoidable ad blitz to promote the product. Whereas some fans saw it as "selling out," others reacted to it as yet another step in the Stones' marketing their music and image as a product. While Jagger would later claim he was against the deal and wouldn't make a similar one in the future, the Stones repeated the stunt by allowing Apple to use "She's a Rainbow" in a similar multi-million-dollar advertising campaign to launch the company's iMac computer in August 1998.

* * * * *

At the same time as the Stones were once again shattering box office and music licensing records, New York City—particularly Times Square—was undergoing an economic boom under Mayor Rudy Giuliani.

However, while tourism and the economy were revitalizing the city, Giuliani's quality-of-life initiatives reached farther than those of either of his most recent predecessors, Koch and Dinkins. In Giuliani's second term, which began in 1998, his administration targeted adult businesses even outside of known tourist areas, such as Billy's Topless, an old-fashioned topless bar located at the corner of Sixth Avenue and 24th Street in Chelsea, that had been open since 1970. To avoid being branded an "adult establishment," Billy's removed the apostrophe on the sign and became Billy Stopless, a bikini bar. The rebranding was unpopular with patrons, and by 2001 Billy's had closed and become another of hundreds of bagel shops. *The New York Times* reported that twenty-three topless bars closed across New York between August and October 1998. Despite what Jagger sang in "Shattered," dirty dreams were no longer surviving on the street. "Fun City" was officially over.

While strict policing of adult entertainment happened in part because of the broken windows philosophy, an important aspect of "cleaning up" New York City's image was to bolster its reputation among tourists. Annual visitors increased by over 20 percent from 1990 to 2000, while spending by tourists increased by over 60 percent. By the end of the 1990s, tourists were spending more than $15 billion per year in New York City, an increase of more than 50 percent from the previous decade. The "brand" of New York was regaining the international luster it had lost during the 1970s and 1980s. There was obviously bigger money in a cleaner, family-friendly Manhattan. By the same logic, there was more money in the Rolling Stones' becoming a slick stadium act funded by corporate sponsors rather than being a gritty, drug-fueled party band grinding out shows in arenas.

No matter how much fame Richards had gained as a rock 'n' roll survivor, there wasn't much money left in being an outlaw in the 1990s. As always, the Stones rolled with the times.

CHAPTER 12

"ANYBODY SEEN MY BABY?"

After the massive Voodoo Lounge Tour, each of the Stones took a long break by working on personal projects for the first half of 1996. Jagger was the only one spotted around Manhattan during that time. On February 13, Jagger and Jerry Hall were in attendance when Jagger's younger brother Chris's band Atcha performed at The Bottom Line (the *New York Daily News* reported that the elder Jagger did not take his brother up on a request to duet onstage).

In July, the Charlie Watts Quintet went on a North American tour to support the group's new album, *Long Ago & Far Away*. The tour marked the end of Watts's feud with the David Letterman house band. This time, producers of Letterman's current show, *The Late Show With David Letterman*, insisted that the 1992 walk-off had been "an unfortunate miscommunication." Watts remarked, "It was nothing to do with David Letterman. It was the producers, or whoever, that said I had to play with the house band, not my own. I found it ridiculous and insulting, because the whole reason I was there in the first place was to play with my group. If it happened again, I'd walk out again."

Since 1992, Letterman had changed not only networks but also studios. His show was now recorded at the historic Ed Sullivan Theater at 1697 Broadway, where the Stones had played five times in the 1960s when it was the location for *The Ed Sullivan Show* and known as CBS-TV Studio 50. The Charlie Watts Quintet played Letterman's show without incident, performing the standard "What's New?" The following day, Watts played New York's Supper Club with Richards in attendance. That same month, Richards put his East Village apartment that he had owned since 1983 on sale for $2.25 million, intent on making his move to Connecticut permanent. Richards ended up selling the place in the fall of 1998 to Def Jam executive Russell Simmons, but kept his foot in New York by buying an Upper East Side condo overlooking Central Park at 923 Fifth Avenue.

It wasn't until October that Jagger, Richards, and Wood got together to discuss future plans for the Stones. The decision was made to release an album and launch another tour by the end of the following year. In addition, the band finally decided to release *The Rolling Stones Rock and Roll Circus*, a performance filmed in 1968 for the BBC that the Stones had never released because of their admittedly substandard performance (they had filmed their part at five in the morning because of technical problems). The film screened at the New York Film Festival, with Richards attending a screening on October 12, and was released on video and CD later that week. It would be the first of two times a Stones-related archival project premiered at the New York Film Festival, the city's most prestigious film festival, which has run at Lincoln Center annually since 1963.

The following month, Jagger and Richards began writing songs and recording demos at both Dangerous Music Studios in New York's East Village and Richards's home studio in Connecticut. Richards later remarked that he liked the sound of his studio, saying, "I wanted to cut the whole album there, it was sounding so good, but it was a bit too small for everybody." In December, Jagger and Richards continued their sessions but now in London, and then returned to Dangerous Music for two weeks with Watts to flesh out the demos for the album. While there, Jagger invited producers Michael Simpson and John King, the duo known as the Dust Brothers, who produced New York hip-hop trio the Beastie Boys' acclaimed *Paul's Boutique* album, to the studio to discuss a collaboration. The Dust Brothers ended up working on three of the album's tracks, "Saint of Me," "Might as Well Get Juiced," and "Anybody Seen My Baby?" Richards disliked their production style, which featured sampling. In fact, Richards didn't even play on "Saint of Me." Months later, the *Daily News* reported that Richards had nixed a collaboration between Jagger and R&B producer Babyface for the album, quoting a "well-placed spy" who said Richards said to the young producer, "So you're Babyface. Well, you don't look like Babyface to me. You look like Fuckface." (Naturally, the quote was denied by Stones reps.)

In fact, many of the recording sessions for the album, eventually titled *Bridges to Babylon*, were done piecemeal. While the Stones recorded the album primarily in Los Angeles from March through July, the album's credits include a longer-than-normal list of non-Stones contributors, including X-Pensive Wino Waddy Wachtel, who played guitar on many of the album's tracks. Richards ended up working extensively with producer Rob Fraboni on his own tracks. In his autobiography, Richards revealed that he and the other producers had such significant disagreements over the song "Thief in the Night" that was sung by Richards that he mixed the track in New York unbeknownst to the Los Angeles production team. He revealed,

> *"Eventually Rob and I had to steal the two-inch master tapes of the half mixes of 'Thief in the Night' from Ocean Way studios in LA, where we'd record it, and fly them to the East Coast where I had now returned homewards to Connecticut. Pierre [du Beauport, "Thief in the Night" co-writer] found a studio on the north shore of Long Island where we remixed it to my liking for two days and two nights, with my vocal.... This was near to the deadline, so the quickest way to get the tapes back to LA was to take them by speedboat from Port Jefferson, Long Island, to Westport, the nearest harbor to my house on the Connecticut coast. We did this at midnight, under a very nice moon, roaring across the Long Island Sound, successfully avoiding the lobster pots with a swerve here and a shout there. Next day Rob got them to New York*

and they were flown back to LA to the mastering studio to be inserted into the album."

On August 18, the Stones revealed the *Bridges to Babylon* album and tour with a press conference at the Brooklyn Bridge, which was broadcast live on VH-1. The announcement continued the Stones' trend of arriving at their tour announcement press conferences in a unique fashion. In his autobiography, Wood recalls, "We staged the announcement of our tour under the Brooklyn Bridge, on the Brooklyn side, with Manhattan as our backdrop.... There was a huge screen set up next to the stage, and the 300 waiting journalists and photographers suddenly saw a helicopter view of a red 1955 Cadillac convertible coming across the bridge, with a police escort. Mick was driving and Keith was sitting next to him. Charlie and I were in the back seat, throwing CDs to the crowds lining the streets." The band announced that the tour was going to visit Giants Stadium on October 16, though a second date on October 17 was eventually added as well.

Naturally, the question of whether or not this would be the band's last tour came up, which caused Richards to quip, "Yeah, this and the next five." Jagger also remarked that they had chosen the setting for the press conference because "it is said that New York is Babylon on Hudson." It probably helped that the spot offered views of three iconic New York City bridges to tie into the album's title. Like the previous press conferences from the Stones, this one was short. *Times* columnist Neil Strauss pointed out, "Band members hardly stuck around for any questions before leaving, because they knew that all the news media needed to fit the band into its own formula was one good image and one quotation." Strauss also predicted that the Stones' press conference for the next tour would involve the Stones' arriving at Central Park via hot-air balloon—a prediction that turned out not to be far off when the Stones announced their 2002 world tour.

The following day the Stones shot a music video for the album's first single, "Anybody Seen My Baby?" in New York. The three-day shoot featured up-and-coming twenty-two-year-old actress Angelina

Jolie as a stripper wandering the streets of New York (naturally, Jolie and Jagger were linked as an item in the press). Shot in cool tones, the video features the Stones holding court in a New York burlesque club called the Sleazeball Lounge—the type of joint Giuliani would have run out of town—with Wood as the club's sleazy master of ceremonies. Jagger becomes transfixed by Jolie and follows her out into the streets after she leaves the club, passing various New Yorkers who appear to be struggling with their own emotional anguish. The video premiered on September 15 on MTV, and the single was released a week later.

The song itself, which is about a man searching for his lost love, has two lyrical references to New York—first, "I was flippin' magazines / In that place on Mercer Street." Mercer Street runs south from East 8th Street to Canal Street, through the campus of New York University. The Bottom Line, a venue where the members of the Stones made several appearances over the years, was located on West 4th Street between Mercer Street and Greene Street. The second is the rap over the song's bridge, which is performed by New Jersey native Biz Markie and which namechecks all five New York City boroughs as well as New Jersey and Long Island.

After finishing the video shoot, the Stones were off to Toronto to rehearse for the tour, which kicked off on September 23 in Chicago after warm-up club dates in Toronto and Chicago. The *Daily News* was critical of the Stones' huge touring machine, with writer Jim Farber declaring, "The stage, marked by humongous gold-plated statues meant to depict ancient Babylon, looked like something Donald Trump might have dreamt up for Atlantic City." Farber also gave the *Bridges to Babylon* album a negative review, remarking, "These days the Stones put out albums less as meaningful works than as aural links in a merchandising campaign for the tour." The *Times*' John Pareles was only slightly more complimentary, stating, "Of the album's 13 songs, less than half may linger."

It was announced that the Stones would play a gig at a New York City-area club that would be broadcast live on MTV on October 14 to kick off the channel's *Live From the Ten Spot* series of live performances, but the Stones were forced to postpone because Jagger had a sore throat. David Bowie was selected to replace the Stones, and the Stones rescheduled their performance for October 25. The gig was to take place at the Capitol Theatre in Port Chester, New York, just twenty miles north of Manhattan. The 1,800-person-capacity venue has had a long history as a concert venue since the 1970s, after previously operating as a vaudeville and movie theater since its opening in 1926. Most famously, Janis Joplin debuted her song "Mercedes Benz" at the venue on August 8 after writing it at a local bar, and the venue hosted many Grateful Dead concerts in the 1970s. Though the venue closed to music performances not long after the Bowie and Stones concerts, it reopened to concerts in 2012 after extensive renovations.

Jagger was back in singing shape in time for the Stones' two concerts at Giants Stadium on October 16 and 17. The Stones played nearly the exact same set on both nights, which included three songs from *Bridges to Babylon*: "Flip the Switch," "Out of Control," and "Anybody Seen My Baby?" On the first night, the Stones played "Factory Girl" as the night's "web choice" song (they had allowed fans to vote on a song choice via the internet) and "The Last Time," while on the second night those songs were replaced with "Star Star" as the web choice song and "You Got Me Rocking." Both the *Daily News* and *The Times* praised the shows. *The Times* also profiled the computer systems that kept the massive stage set operating night after night.

After gigs in Foxboro, Massachusetts, on October 21 and Washington, DC, on October 23, the Stones returned to New York on October 24 to perform two songs—"Anybody Seen My Baby?" and "Out of Control"—at Madison Square Garden's Paramount Theater for the VH-1 Fashion Awards, which aired on October 28. It was the first time the band had performed on the Garden premises since being inducted into the Madison Square Garden Hall of Fame in 1984. The 5,600-seat Paramount Theater opened as a smaller concert venue underneath the arena when the current Garden opened in 1968. It was originally named the Felt Forum, after the then president of the Madison Square Garden Corporation, Irving M. Felt, and the venue was renovated in 1991 and renamed the Paramount Theater (it is now known as Hulu Theater at Madison Square Garden). There isn't much Stones history associated with the theater—Jagger attended Lou Reed's October 9, 1974, concert there, and Richards again attended the Fashion Awards (then renamed the *Vogue* Fashion Awards, sponsored by the famed Manhattan-based fashion magazine) there on October 20, 2000, and spent much of the night shooting pool with Paul McCartney. Not surprisingly, much of the Stones' history with the Garden occurred upstairs in the "main room." During the awards, the band performed on a side stage—though naturally Jagger made liberal use of the catwalk—that would have been dwarfed by the massive Bridges to Babylon Tour stadium set, but it prepared the group for the next night's rescheduled *Live at the Ten Spot* in Port Chester. At the Capitol Theatre that night, the Stones performed an abbreviated seventy-five-minute version of their *Bridges to Babylon* set, with "Tumbling Dice," "Sister Morphine," "Out of Control," "Gimme Shelter," and "Anybody Seen My Baby?" broadcast live on MTV. Pro tennis legend John McEnroe and New York State governor George Pataki were both in attendance.

Before the year was even over, the Stones tour easily won the title "highest-grossing tour of 1997" even though it did not even start until the end of September. However, the Bridges to Babylon Tour was scheduled to continue well into 1998. A long-rumored December 19, 1997, date at Madison Square Garden was later nixed by the Garden to accommodate a Naseem Hamed boxing match, and in November the Stones rescheduled two concerts at the Garden on January 14 and 16, 1998. (A third date was eventually added on January 17.) These would be the band's first shows at the Garden since 1981 (and the first since being inducted into the Garden's Hall of Fame), and Joel Peresman, the vice president of concerts and entertainment at the Garden, was adamant that the Stones would return to his venue after a long hiatus. He told the *Daily News*, "I can't tell you how many people I meet who can tell me exactly which Stones show they saw here. They remember everything about it. It's a benchmark in their lives. This is the kind of show that generates excitement for weeks ahead of time and a buzz for weeks after. It's awareness for the Garden, awareness for the city. This is the biggest rock band in the world. There's nothing like it." Some in the media criticized the Stones for selling tickets for the Garden shows as high as three hundred dollars, but Jagger shot back, "Let me put it in perspective—people pay much, much more to watch the Knicks here every week." Curiously, the Spice Girls, a new English pop sensation girl group, were premiering their movie *Spice World* in New York on the same night as the Stones' first show, leading the press to dub it "The Battle of the British Bands." In terms of sheer drawing power, it wasn't exactly a contest.

On the first night, Jagger joked at the size of the Garden compared to the stadiums the Stones had played on the first leg, saying, "It's a real intimate venue for us." The bonus of that was that the Stones were able to play with the set more than usual, since they were not beholden to the effects of the stadium stage. The sets for the three Garden shows not only differed from one another, but they differed significantly from the 1997 *Bridges to Babylon* shows in New Jersey. Though each show began with the same four songs—"Satisfaction," "Let's Spend the Night Together," "Flip the Switch," and "Gimme Shelter"—and ended with the same eight songs—"Like a Rolling Stone" (as a nod to Bob Dylan, who was playing the downstairs Paramount Theater on the same nights), "Sympathy for the Devil," "Tumbling Dice," "Honky Tonk Women," "Start Me Up," "Jumpin' Jack Flash," "You Can't Always Get What You Want," and "Brown Sugar"—the middle section of all three show featured an assortment of classics along with new cuts from *Bridges to Babylon*. The January 14 show featured "Low Down," "Saint of Me," "Out of Control," and "How Can I Stop" from the new album. (This remains the only live performance of "How Can I Stop.") The older classics that rounded out the set were "Bitch," "Miss You," "Wanna Hold You," "It's Only Rock 'n' Roll," "Little Red Rooster" and, for the first time ever being performed in New York, "Memory Motel." The January 16 show retained "Bitch," "Saint of Me," "Out of Control," and "Miss You," but the group added "Already Over Me" and "All About You" from *Bridges to Babylon* as well as "Respectable," "You

Don't Have to Mean It," "Little Queenie," and "Let It Bleed." On the final night they kept "Saint of Me," "Out of Control," "Miss You," "You Don't Have to Mean It," and "Little Queenie" from the previous night and added "Might as Well Get Juiced" and "Thief in the Night" from the new album and "When the Whip Comes Down," "All Down the Line," and "I Just Wanna Make Love to You." The varied set lists amounted to the Stones' playing thirty-three different songs over the course of the three concerts, a rare treat for New York Stones fans. Dylan was supposed to make it upstairs to play "Like a Rolling Stone" with the group on one of the nights (he was listed on the set list), but the collaboration did not end up happening. However, Dylan joined the Stones to perform the song three months later during the South American tour when he served as the Stones' opening act.

The Stones remained on tour through September, with the tour including the group's first-ever performances in Moscow. The Bridges to Babylon Tour grossed $274 million, with $6.4 million from the three sold-out Madison Square Garden nights alone. The tour had to settle for second place on the all-time list behind the Voodoo Lounge Tour. Of course, the Stones played sixteen fewer gigs on this tour, which accounts for much of the difference. Yet they played even more dates when they launched a shorter US tour of arena-size venues for 1999, called the No Security Tour, to support the band's live album from the Bridges to Babylon Tour, *No Security*. The follow-up tour did not feature any New York City-area dates despite rumors of additional Garden dates. (In November 1998, Richards said to the *Daily News*, "I can't imagine we wouldn't play New York.") However, on an off day, Richards and Hansen attended the controversial Evander Holyfield versus Lennox Lewis heavyweight title fight at Madison Square Garden on March 13. (Richards quipped, not entirely truthfully, "It's the first time I've been in Madison Square Garden that I'm not working.") Richards was seated next to US senator—and future presidential candidate— John McCain. In late 1998 it was rumored in the press that the Stones would play Madison Square Garden on New Year's Eve 1999, though the Stones ended up not performing any concerts to mark the new year, and New York native Billy Joel performed on the historic night at the Garden instead. Word in the *Daily News* was that Watts was the one who had nixed the plan.

As far as the end of 1998, though, Richards marked it by appearing at Ronnie Spector's Christmas party at Life, a nightclub on Bleecker Street, to perform "Run, Rudolph, Run." Though the Stones would spend the first half of 1999 on the No Security Tour, Richards's appearance with Spector marked the beginning of another quiet period for the Stones. After the two-shot blitz of *Voodoo Lounge* and *Bridges to Babylon* in the mid-1990s, the Stones went on another extended break before emerging to celebrate the band's fortieth anniversary.

CHAPTER 13

"YOU DON'T FUCK WITH NEW YORK, OKAY?"

The disjoined production of the *Bridges to Babylon* sessions appeared to sour the Stones' desire to get back into the studio together once the No Security Tour ended. Richards spent much of 2000 and 2001 appearing at movie premieres and popping up on stages and in recording studios all over New York. During that time, it appeared that Jagger and Richards were again engaged in one of their famous feuds. Richards wasn't shy about complaining about Jagger's decision to donate money to his former grammar school to open an arts center named after him as well as his pursuing yet another solo album. Richards appeared at the Waldorf Astoria on March 19, 2001, to induct pioneer sidemen Johnnie Johnson and James Burton into the Rock & Roll Hall of Fame. An interviewer asked Richards what he would do differently if he had to do it all over. He said, "I'd shoot the lead singer."

For most of 2001, Jagger worked on songs for his fourth solo album. In January, he worked with Matchbox Twenty frontman Rob Thomas in New York, and in July he returned to New York to record with Wyclef Jean of the Fugees at The Hit Factory. Jagger enlisted numerous big names to assist him with his album in a deliberate attempt to emulate the success of Carlos Santana's 1999 guest star-laden *Supernatural*, which sold more than thirty million copies worldwide. Thomas co-wrote and sang that album's biggest hit, "Smooth." Jagger even tried to enlist the help of hip-hop producer and New York native Sean Combs to produce a track, something that would undoubtedly have infuriated Richards even more if it had come to pass. Richards's accusations regarding Jagger's attempt to trend-hop from the mid-1980s would have seemed just as valid. Nonetheless, Jagger and Richards did meet in New York in early April 2001 in order to discuss plans for the Stones' fortieth anniversary. That month was a busy one for Richards in New York. On April 26 he attended his first-ever Knicks game at Madison Square Garden (he told the *Daily News*, "Usually when I come here, I only have two questions: Where is the dressing room, and what time am I on?"). Four days later, he appeared at Sheryl Crow's star-studded gig at the SoHo club Shine, where he played on four songs, including "Not Fade Away." Kid Rock also performed with Crow and Richards on the Dobie Gray hit "Drift Away" (the *Daily News* said that Richards appeared annoyed by Rock's initial struggles with singing the song). Richards had previously appeared onstage with Crow in New York on September 14, 1999, at her massive concert in Central Park. Richards performed "Happy" and "Sweet Little Rock 'n Roller" with Crow and then Bob Dylan's "Tombstone Blues" with an all-star lineup that included Eric Clapton.

In July, *Post* gossip columnist Neal Travis published an item from an "industry insider" suggesting that the Stones would be unable to tour in 2002 because of the slumping economy and concerns that they would be unable to draw younger crowds to fill stadium seats. It was undeniable that the pop world was changing and drifting away from rock music—even Richards must have recognized that, as he, Hansen, and their two daughters were spotted in the front row of a concert by boyband *NSYNC at Madison Square Garden the previous July—but the *Post's* concerns that thousands of Stones fans had dried up since the end of the No Security Tour would prove to be unfounded. Unfortunately, the gossip column legend and admitted Stones fan would not live to see the tour—he died on August 15, 2002, two weeks before the band's fortieth-anniversary tour launched in Boston.

On August 10, 2001, Bill Wyman played his first—and so far only—solo New York gig at Town Hall, where Wood had held his 1983 lecture. After leaving the Stones, Wyman formed Bill Wyman's Rhythm Kings, a blues-rock band that played early rock 'n' roll songs like "Hit the Road Jack" and "Good Golly Miss Molly." In an interview with the *Daily News*, Wyman said he preferred playing the smaller shows as opposed to the massive stadiums he had played on the Steel Wheels Tour. "With the Stones now, you're a speck on a stage. As a fan, if I wanted to see Dylan or Elvis in the early days, I'd want to be close enough to see the sweat. With this band, you can be 6 feet away." He also compared his first-ever Rhythm Kings American tour to the Stones' first American tour, adding, "In a way, this is like when the Stones first came over. Nobody knows what to expect. People assumed the Stones were another band riding the Beatles' hype, when of course we were nothing of the sort. We were throwing Chicago blues at them."

* * * * *

The terrorist attacks on the morning of September 11 that destroyed the Twin Towers of the World Trade Center profoundly affected New Yorkers, many of whom lost friends and family in the attacks.

On September 11, Jagger was in France. Just five days earlier he had presented the Video of the Year award alongside Kid Rock at the MTV Video Music Awards at the Metropolitan Opera House in Lincoln Center in New York. When the terrorist attacks happened, Richards was recording an as-yet-unreleased song titled "Love Affair" with Ronnie Spector at his home studio. Jagger and Richards felt the emotional impact of the attacks. Speaking to *Rolling Stone*, Jagger reflected on how the attacks affected him. He said, "Being a long way away, you take a slightly different view of it. If I'd been in New York, I'm sure I would have felt a lot differently: 'Wow, I just escaped it.' But I felt this awful shock, where you don't know what you're thinking."

Being that Jagger felt this strongly about the attacks—not to mention that he was also gearing up to promote his solo album coming out on November 19—when Paul McCartney began putting together a benefit concert to be held on October 20 at Madison Square Garden to raise money for the families who had lost loved ones in the attacks, Jagger was one of the first musicians to agree to participate, though as a solo artist. It appeared that the importance of the Concert for New York City was the impetus for Jagger and Richards to put their resurrected feud to bed once again, as Richards agreed on very short notice to join Jagger for the two-song performance. While Richards still wasn't thrilled with Jagger's doing a guest-filled solo album, the pair appeared to be on the same page once again—or, at the very least, in the same book.

Though Watts had been quiet during the immediate post-No Security Tour period, in mid-2001 he expanded his quintet into a decuplet and launched a lengthy residency at Ronnie Scott's in London, followed by a shorter residency at Blue Note in Tokyo in late October and early November. Those dates led right into another residency at Blue Note, but this time in the original location in New York, from November 6 through November 11 with two shows per night. (Richards attended the first night—*The Times* reported that when Watts introduced bassist Dave Green as "my childhood friend," Richards shot back from the audience, "You have one?")

To promote the November 19 release of *Goddess in the Doorway* as well as to promote the upcoming US release of the World War II film *Enigma*, which Jagger produced with Lorne Michaels (which ultimately was not released in the US until 2002, more than six months after its UK release), Jagger appeared as the musical guest on the December 8 episode of *Saturday Night Live*. In addition to performing "God Gave Me Everything" and "Visions of Paradise" from the album, Jagger appeared in two skits—"Mick Jagger's Dressing Room," in which he spoke to himself in the mirror about his stage moves (Jagger's reflection was played by Jimmy Fallon), and a skit parodying Donatella Versace (played by Maya Rudolph) with Jagger playing German fashion designer Karl

Lagerfeld. The *Saturday Night Live* performance was one of only three live performances Jagger did in the US to support the album. The other two were a half-hour gig at the El Rey Theatre in Los Angeles (which Jagger dubbed "the world tour for this album") and a performance of "God Gave Me Everything" with co-writer Lenny Kravitz at the VH-1 Music Awards (also in Los Angeles). The crux of the album's promotion rested on the hour-long documentary *Being Mick* that aired on ABC in the US on November 22, which was Thanksgiving. The documentary included footage of Jagger recording "Hideaway" with Wyclef Jean at The Hit Factory in New York. *New York Times* television reviewer Caryn James called the documentary well made but an obvious puff piece, noting, "There is Mick the Dad, in a recording studio with two of his daughters singing backup. There is Mick the Concerned Citizen, going to a poll in London to cast his vote. Most important, there is Mick the Guy With a New Solo Album and Mick the Producer of a New Film. Like many slick celebrity profiles, it is completely vapid but knows how to work its surface glamour and behind-the-scenes allure."

If the reviews of *Being Mick* were considered bad, the reviews of *Goddess in the Doorway* were a disaster. Jim Farber of the *Daily News* dismissed the album, writing, "From the musicianship and production to the performance and the lyrics, everything sounds cold and corporate. It doesn't even sound like a contemporary version of corporate. It's more like an '80s version of it," adding that "here, everything sounds stitched together by studio clock-punchers." The general critical consensus among New York newspapers was the same—there was nothing on *Goddess in the Doorway* that was particularly impressive. Richards agreed with that assessment, calling the album "Dogshit in the Doorway" in just about any media outlet that would listen.

Despite heavy promotion by Virgin—including getting the "God Gave Me Everything" video played on MTV's hit teen music show *Total Request Live*—*Goddess in the Doorway* debuted at number thirty-nine on the Billboard charts (its peak position), selling just 67,839 copies in its first week in the US and less than one thousand in the UK, sales figures that the *New York Post* called "laughably low." The album dropped out of the Billboard top two hundred after only eight weeks, and "God Gave Me Everything" never even made the main pop charts. In March 2002, the *New York Post* reported that *Goddess in the Doorway* had sold only 294,000 copies in the United States since its November release, substantially lower than any of Jagger's previous solo albums.

Perhaps the most notable story was Jann Wenner's review in *Rolling Stone* that inexplicably awarded the album five stars, a rare honor for anyone in the twenty-first century not named Bruce Springsteen or Bob Dylan. The review is completely absurd, praising Jagger for utilizing "some outstanding guests" and for generic lyrics like "I'm gonna fly away / And no one's gonna find me" while comparing some of the songs to Stones classics like "Wild Horses," "Moonlight Mile," and "Street Fighting Man." Jagger was also named one of the People of the Year by *Rolling Stone* at the end of 2001. Naturally, Wenner's longstanding friendship with Jagger calls the review into question, especially since by 2001 Wenner was rarely writing reviews. It's worth noting that only one of the magazine's three dozen critics put the album on a Top Albums of 2001 list, and despite its five-star rating, *Goddess in the Doorway* did not make *Rolling Stone*'s list of the one hundred best albums of the 2000s that was published in December 2009, while many albums that were awarded fewer stars did.

The second single, "Vision of Paradise," was released in early 2002 and similarly flopped despite heavy promotion in Europe. Because of the obvious commercial failure of the album, Jagger quickly put the album behind him, especially since the Stones were already working on plans to mark their fortieth anniversary. In the meantime, while doing promotional work in Paris, Jagger met six-foot-three-inch fashion designer L'Wren Scott. The two became an off-and-on couple, and Scott designed many of Jagger's onstage clothes. They were often spotted together in New York later in the decade once Scott relocated to Manhattan.

In March 2002, Jagger and Richards worked on demos in Jamaica for a handful of new songs. Aside from Jagger's appearance at the New York premiere of *Enigma* at the Upper East Side movie house the

Beekman Theatre on April 11, 2002—the original location was at 1254 Second Avenue, which was demolished in late 2005, and the Beekman Theatre name was then transferred to the smaller movie theater across the street—the Stones were ready to celebrate with their most distinctively configured tour yet, and New York would get the best of it.

* * * * *

In part because of the support of Giuliani, and the success of his message that his vast business experience was evidence that he was the right man to ensure economic growth in a post-9/11 New York, billionaire Mike Bloomberg was elected mayor in 2001, taking office in 2002. Bloomberg had made his fortune with Bloomberg L.P., a financial data corporation that created a computerized stock market system that was eventually used throughout the industry. Over his twelve years as mayor, Bloomberg continued many of Giuliani's quality-of-life policies and pushed to restore the tourism and retail industries in New York, both of which suffered after 9/11.

Many of Bloomberg's policies were controversial. Skyrocketing rents led to many decades-old small businesses' shuttering and being replaced by retail, food, and banking chains. Times Square continued its path to becoming a glitzy outdoor shopping mall, culminating in Broadway's being closed to vehicle traffic on Broadway from 42nd Street to 47th Street on Memorial Day 2009, a change that was made permanent in February 2010. The initiative confronted the problem of increasing throngs of pedestrian traffic in Times Square that made passing through the area in a car increasingly more difficult as tourism boomed.

Another controversial neighborhood-changing plan spearheaded by the Bloomberg administration was the creation of the High Line, a pedestrian walkway created on abandoned elevated train tracks on the west side of Manhattan, the first phase of which opened in 2009. While wildly popular with tourists and many New Yorkers, longtime businesses were driven out by escalating rents as the High Line became an attraction, changing the character of the neighborhood. The West Side area known as the Meatpacking District, which had gradually become a nightclub and fashion boutique hot spot since the early 1970s and had become a home to many gay bars in the 1980s, was now one of the trendiest areas in the city, and the industrial meatpacking businesses that had given the area its name had almost completely vanished. While few would complain about the effect the High Line had on lowering crime in Chelsea, the High Line transformed a once gritty, industrial neighborhood into a gentrified area of commerce and tourism.

It was almost as if New York City was following the lead set by "Rolling Stone, Inc.," as the band was dubbed by *Fortune* magazine writer Andy Serwer in his in-depth profile on the band's business operations. Starting with the 1989 Steel Wheels Tour, the Stones completely revolutionized the way bands executed concert tours by marketing them as cultural events, mainly because they realized after their unfortunate deals with Allen Klein in the late 1960s that the music business is just that, a business. On the Stones' continued blockbuster success, Serwer wrote, "Unlike some other groups, the Stones carry no Woodstock-esque, antibusiness baggage. The group has tendrils deep in American business, cutting sponsorship and rights deals with stalwarts like Anheuser-Busch, Microsoft, and Sprint.... [I]f the Stones were a traditional company, they would be the cash cow."

Likewise, New York sought economic revitalization by embracing corporate branding and sponsorship.

CHAPTER 14

"WE'LL PROBABLY DO A SUBMARINE NEXT TIME"

To announce their 2002 fortieth-anniversary tour—later dubbed the Licks Tour after the upcoming compilation album *Forty Licks*—the Stones arrived at Van Cortlandt Park in the Bronx for their May 7 press conference and boarded a yellow blimp emblazoned with the band's tongue logo. The blimp spent about twenty minutes soaring above the park before landing for a typically short press conference.

For the first time since the band's stadium tour era had started, the Stones announced that they would play venues of various sizes in select cities to give fans different live experiences. Richards would later call it "the Fruit of the Loom tour—small, medium and large," and at the press conference he explained why playing small venues appealed to the band: "We can play stuff that doesn't work in stadiums." For New York, the Stones set September 26 at Madison Square Garden, September 28 at Giants Stadium and, for the first time, September 30 at the Roseland Ballroom, a 3,200-person-capacity hall on West 52nd Street. Only one block from the Ed Sullivan Theater, Roseland opened at its 52nd Street location in 1956; the place had previously housed ice skating and roller skating rinks. Though Roseland had a long tradition of hosting concerts, it wasn't until the late 1980s that it became a popular venue for up-and-coming rock bands while also being an intimate venue for established bands. Roseland closed in April 2014 after a short residency by pop sensation Lady Gaga.

On the surface, playing shows in theaters (and even arenas) appeared to go against the Stones' economic model. After all, it was simple math: Playing in a stadium meant more people, and more people meant more tickets sold. While the Stones projected that the Licks Tour would gross less money than the two previous tours, they would save money by having minimal stage effects (making the ever-changing set list the true "special effect" of the show) and a simpler production. As Joe Rascoff, the band's business manager, told *Fortune* in 2002, "Doing fewer stadiums this time cuts costs because in previous tours we had to have three stages and three crews. This tour we have one stadium stage with one crew." Even when the Stones were doing smaller shows, they figured out how to do it while making more money off the bigger ones.

Rumor had it that the Stones would also return to the Garden on January 15 and 16, 2003, though the band did not confirm that (the dates ended up being January 16 and 18 instead). During the press conference, the band joked about why they were going out on tour again. Jagger said, "Either we stay at home and become pillars of the community, or we go out and tour. We couldn't find any communities that still needed pillars." When asked why tickets for the Stones concerts were more expensive than tickets to see Paul McCartney, Richards responded, "There's more of us." Wood joked that the next time the band had a tour to announce, "We'll probably do a submarine next time."

Though most of the New York media outlets covering the return of the Stones were overwhelmingly welcoming, *The New York Times* published a dissenting voice. Writer Neal Pollack wrote an editorial published on the eve of the tour's Boston kickoff that criticized the Stones for still touring when he thought they were already over the hill. He had been thoroughly disappointed by the concert he had seen on the Steel Wheels Tour. Pollack called the band "boring" and a "Vegas headliner show" in a piece that essentially amounts to self-criticism for ever having had the audacity to actually like the Rolling Stones in comparison to hipper bands of the day. Letters to the editor about the article over the next three weeks were highly critical. A more glowing evaluation of the Stones' appeal by Jim Farber had appeared in the *Daily News* the previous month, with Farber remarking, "However corporate the Stones' sponsorship, domesticated their fans, and predictable their repertoire, the essence of the band still thrives whenever Keith Richards flicks his riffs, Charlie Watts slaps the snare drum, and Mick Jagger swaggers through the blues." Three days after Pollack's editorial was published, Jon Pareles's review of the opening show of the tour in *The Times* praised the band and particularly marveled at how deep the Stones went into their catalog compared to previous tours. Because the Stones were using a much smaller, less gimmicky stage, it made varying the set list easier. The stadium and arena setup also contained a central "B-stage" where the Stones would go mid-show to play mainly deep cuts from their catalog.

Indeed, when the Stones arrived at Madison Square Garden on September 26, the set list contained songs that had infrequently been played live since the Steel Wheels Tour: "Wild Horses," "Loving Cup," "Rocks Off," "Rip This Joint," "Thru and Thru," and, during the B-stage segment, "Mannish Boy" and "Shattered." The band even threw in a cover of the O'Jays' "Love Train" and also played a new single, "Don't Stop." The *New York Post* called the O'Jays cover a stumble, but said that any missteps in the concert "made the show seem like it was crafted for New York rather than a high-polish choreographed concert that plays like a carbon copy at every tour stop." Likewise, the *Daily News* concluded, "The Rolling Stones do something rare among pop culture icons. They live up to the legend."

Once again, Stones mania erupted throughout the city. The night before the Garden concert, Wood did a private show of his paintings at Pop International Galleries in SoHo on West Broadway. The *Daily News* reported that not only were tickets being scalped for as high as $5,400 for the Garden show, but Virgin Records had to turn down roughly 75 percent of ticket requests from industry figures. Nonetheless, spotted at the Garden were Jack Nicholson, Lenny Kravitz, John McEnroe, Jackson Browne, Peter Gabriel, Clive Davis, Lorne Michaels, Jann Wenner, and Barry Diller. However, the tour's sponsor, the online brokerage firm E*Trade, managed to snag premium tickets for all of its executives. Perhaps to quell the insane ticket prices on the secondary market, a week before the Garden show HBO announced that the band's January 18 Madison Square Garden concert would be televised live on the premium channel.

While the Giants Stadium concert was predictably more of a "greatest hits" show, the band still played a few surprises, including "Angie," "Monkey Man," and a cover of Otis Redding's "I Can't Turn You Loose."

As promised, the Roseland show saw the Stones digging deep into their catalog, with renditions of "All Down the Line," "Hand of Fate," "Sweet Virginia," "Neighbours," "Dance Pt. 1," "Everybody Needs Somebody to Love," "That's How Strong My Love Is," "Going to a Go-Go," "Ain't Too Proud to Beg," and "You Don't Have to Mean It," while guitarist Jonny Lang joined the band for "Rock Me Baby." However, the highlight of the evening for many longtime fans was "She Smiled Sweetly," a ballad that had appeared on the 1967 album *Between the Buttons* and on the soundtrack of the 2001 Manhattan-set film *The Royal Tenenbaums*. It was the first—and so far only—time the song was performed live. "For 3,000 Rolling Stones fans," wrote Isaac Guzmán in the *Daily News*, "last night's concert at the Roseland Ballroom was a dream come true." However, Dan Aquilante of the *New York Post* thought the middle section of rarities made the show drag, called the show the "smaller-isn't-necessarily better concert," and lamented that "it should have been a great show. It could have been a great show. But the Stones may have gotten so big, they've forgotten how to be small and intimate. Or maybe the greatest rock 'n' roll band in the world just had a bad night."

The *Forty Licks* compilation was released on October 1, containing thirty-six tracks that spanned the group's entire history (a first for a

Stones compilation because of a license agreement with ABKCO) as well as four new songs. The New York media largely praised the song selection, with Dan Aquilante of the *New York Post* saying that the biggest surprise of the album is "that the new songs are so strong." *Rolling Stone* agreed, calling the new songs "their toughest rock in years, especially 'Don't Stop,' a plea for emotional rescue, and Keith Richards's piano ballad 'Losing My Touch,' which he isn't." The only complaint was nitpicking over overlooked classics that could have been included, though adding more would've obviously ruined the "forty" concept.

The Licks Tour continued across the United States along with two shows in Toronto. The first leg of the tour ended on November 30 in Las Vegas. The tour picked up again in the new year on January 8 in Montreal, with the band playing arenas only until the end of the second US leg on February 8, which was also in Las Vegas. On January 16, the Stones returned to Madison Square Garden for their first of two return engagement performances, with that first concert being something of a dress rehearsal for the second night's live HBO broadcast. Because of that, the set lists for the two shows were almost identical. January 16 had an extra song ("Live With Me") and Richards's solo songs were different—"Slipping Away" and "Before They Make Me Run" on January 16, "Thru and Thru" and "Happy" on January 18. The concerts also had different guests. Seventy-one-year-old bluesman Hubert Sumlin played guitar with the band on "Let It Bleed" the first night, while Sheryl Crow performed "Honky Tonk Women" as a duet with Jagger on the HBO broadcast. During the broadcast, Jagger said to the roars of the crowd, "I read in the paper today that this is probably our last show at the Garden. I don't think so!" Jagger was right—the Stones would return to the Garden less than three years later.

Once the tour wrapped, the Stones turned to the as-expected releases to commemorate the tour. First up was *Four Flicks*, a DVD set containing four shows recorded on the tour. One of the shows was the January 18 Madison Square Garden concert that had aired on HBO. The band faced considerable backlash for signing a deal to sell *Four Flicks* exclusively at Best Buy stores in the US and Future Shop stores in Canada through March 2004 (some Canadian retailers actually went as far as removing all Stones products from their shelves in protest). Regardless, the DVD set still hit number one on the Billboard chart the week of its release in early November.

On October 29, Best Buy threw the band a release party at the Capitale, a lavish nightclub venue on the Bowery, with guests including Steven Van Zandt, Tom Jones, and Ryan Adams. The band was introduced by Whoopi Goldberg, though they stayed for barely two minutes. The band members were soon off to Hong Kong to perform their final two shows of the Licks Tour.

The year 2003 ended for the Stones with Mick Jagger's being knighted by Prince Charles at Buckingham Palace on December 12, despite Richards's objections to Jagger's accepting the honor. But the animosity seemed to be all under the bridge, because the band met in March 2004 to discuss their next moves. Prior to that, Wood had been in New York, appearing at Rod Stewart's February 26 concert at Madison Square Garden and performing "Stay With Me" onstage with his former Faces bandmate. Wood also had another exhibition of his work at the Pop International Galleries that week—this time his portraits were of musicians including Chuck Berry, Bo Diddley, Jerry Lee Lewis, Ray Charles, Jimi Hendrix, and Bob Dylan—where he sat for a half-hour interview. The show was attended by Patti Hansen and her and Richards's daughter, Alexandra.

Two weeks later, Jagger was in town. He was spotted at several clubs with his daughter Elizabeth celebrating her birthday. On Sunday, March 14, he was at the Upper East Side celebrity hangout Elaine's with Bruce Springsteen, Don Henley, John Mellencamp, and many others. The next day he inducted Jann Wenner into the Rock & Roll Hall of Fame, in its Lifetime Achievement category, at the Waldorf Astoria. The induction was something of a formality, as Wenner had been sitting on the Hall of Fame's board since the organization was founded. In fact, the party at Elaine's the night before was thrown in Wenner's honor by Ahmet Ertegun, who was one of the organization's founders. Though Jagger's induction speech was full of jokes, he neglected to mention Wenner's five-star review for *Goddess in the Doorway*. More substantial was Richards, who also appeared at the ceremony to induct ZZ Top. Richards also participated in the traditional end-of-the-night jam. It was the fifth time that Richards had inducted an artist into the Hall of Fame, and only the second induction by Jagger.

In June, Watts was diagnosed with throat cancer, putting any plans to tour on hold. Jagger and Richards convened at Jagger's house in France to write and record demos for an upcoming Stones album. While Watts was undergoing radiation treatment (which ultimately proved successful), Jagger and Richards moved to St. Vincent, in the Caribbean, to continue working on the songs. Meanwhile, Wood had been popping up on stages all over Europe, playing with friends and former bandmates, and did the same when he appeared with Rod Stewart at the Condé Nast Fashion Rocks award show on September 8 at Radio City Music Hall to perform "Maggie May" and "Stay With Me." Later that month, Jagger was in New York to do the press rounds for the movie *Alfie*, a remake of the 1966 Michael Caine film, for which Jagger and frequent collaborator Dave Stewart had recorded the soundtrack. On the heels of that came the November 1 release of *Live Licks*, a live album from the Licks Tour, which included ten songs from the January 18, 2003, Garden show (the same one broadcast on HBO and featured on the *Four Flicks* DVD set). Other than Jagger's attending Lorne Michaels's sixtieth-birthday party in Manhattan, none of the Stones appeared in New York for the rest of 2004 because they spent the time recording their next album in France with a rejuvenated Watts. Though the band was away from New York for several months, New York would once again be central to their plans for launching the Rolling Stones' first album of the twenty-first century.

CHAPTER 15

"THANK YOU, JUILLIARD!"

In 1969, the renowned New York performance arts institution, the Juilliard School, moved from Morningside Heights to the Lincoln Center complex on the Upper West Side. Juilliard is the premier music, dance, and theater institution in the United States. It was founded in 1905 downtown as the Institute of Music, and in 1926 it merged with the Juilliard Graduate School, which was named after Augustus D. Juilliard, a businessman who established the school in his will. Juilliard is distinguished by its expert faculty in classical music, dance, and drama, and the list of graduates reads like a who's who of classical music performers and composers of the twentieth century. Less than 10 percent of those who apply for the school's prestigious programs are granted admission, and the applicant pool is made up of highly advanced musicians and performers.

Though some New Yorkers would argue the classical background of the World's Greatest Rock 'n' Roll Band, the Stones would join the many elite musical talents to leave their stamp on Juilliard.

After rehearsing at SIR Studios in New York, the Stones broke from their transportation tradition to perform a three-song set at Juilliard on May 10, 2003. There they announced a new album and supporting world tour. The band appeared before the press on a stage built on the balcony that overlooks the 65th Street walkway connecting Juilliard to Lincoln Center, and performed "Start Me Up," a track called "Oh No, Not You Again" from the unnamed upcoming album, and "Brown Sugar"—the same song the Stones had played on a flatbed driving down Fifth Avenue when announcing their 1975 tour. After the performance, Jagger shouted, "Thank you, Juilliard!"—a sentence that likely nobody had thought would ever come out of the mouth of a Rolling Stone. Adding to the humor, the band made a rare mistake during the new song, and afterward Jagger joked, "I think the examiners at Juilliard would have us come back and retake that one."

The Stones announced that the new tour would begin in Boston. Only one New York-area date—September 15 at Giants Stadium—was announced. The coverage in the New York newspapers was full of jokes. The *New York Post* headline was "STONES AGAIN ROLL OUT THAT ROCK OF AGES," while the *Daily News* report was titled "THAT'S 242 YEARS OF THE ROLLING BONES!" and included a list of a songs the Stones should perform, like "Limpin' Jack Flash" and "Let's Take a Nap Together."

But the New York papers couldn't limit themselves to jokes. Later that week, the *Post* detailed Jagger's exercise regimen, because he appeared to be in especially toned shape for the press conference, while *The Times* used the Stones as an example of the increasing number of senior citizens who remain active in their old age and defended the Stones' continued touring as "their just doing what they know how to do," like millions of other seniors with hobbies (though none of those hobbies are likely as lucrative as playing in "The World's Greatest Rock 'n' Roll Band," of course). In the *Daily News*, columnist David Hinckley—who had written the "Rolling Bones" article just a few days earlier—wrote about how the Stones always played with their tongues firmly in cheek and going out on tour yet again was no joke.

Though it was announced at the press conference that the Stones would follow their previous tour and play a mixture of stadiums, arenas, and theaters, they avoided theaters this time except for the traditional nightclub pre-tour "secret show," this time in Toronto, and three special performances in New York later in the tour. In addition to the September 15 date at Giants Stadium, the Stones added a September 13 performance at Madison Square Garden. The name of the album, *A Bigger Bang*, was soon revealed, and the tour was dubbed the same.

The Times, *Post*, and *Daily News* all included coverage of the tour opener in Boston's Fenway Park—home of Major League Baseball's Boston Red Sox, the archrivals of the New York Yankees—on August 21. All three papers largely praised the show, although Dan Aquilante in the *Post* criticized Richards's singing. The *Daily News* was wowed by the band's new stage, which included two four-level balconies "where several hundred fortunate and affluent fans can stand and look down on the show from almost directly above." There were some last-minute changes to the tour in Boston. The gossip column in the *Daily News* reported that a troupe of twenty-five "gorgeous professional female dancers" from New York were paid to come to Fenway to dance behind the band during "Honky Tonk Women," but Richards nixed the idea after the sound check. The girls were on a bus back to New York before the concert even started.

A Bigger Bang—the group's longest album since *Exile on Main St.*—was released on September 6 to rave reviews in the New York media. The *Post*'s Aquilante gave the album three and a half stars, saying the Glimmer Twins "have rediscovered their mojo and delivered a terrific, if completely derivative, album." In *The New York Times*, Jon Pareles called it the best Stones album in two decades. Similarly, in the *Daily News*, Jim Farber wrote, "It has more hot tracks than *Steel Wheels*, the group's last pretty-good album from sixteen years ago, not to mention as many trim and spunky cuts as their last quite-good album, *Tattoo You*, released nearly a quarter century back." The four-and-a-half-star review in *Rolling Stone* called it "a straight-up, damn fine Rolling Stones album, with no qualifiers or apologies necessary for the first time in a few decades." Even Ben Greenman in *The New Yorker* gave props to the album, saying "While there's nothing that will make fans forget 'Paint It, Black' or 'Shattered' (or even 'Dirty Work'), there's plenty here, especially on the fast ones, that will make you remember them, and that's something." Curiously enough, the album features more musical contributions from Jagger than any previous Stones album—Jagger played harmonica, guitar, and keyboard, and even performed bass on four tracks. On the other hand, Wood missed several of the sessions and appeared on only ten of the album's sixteen tracks. In an interview with the *Daily News*, Richards was complimentary of Jagger's guitar-work, saying, "He's been working on his electric guitar since we've been off the road. He's always been a great acoustic player, but the electric always seemed to run out of his hands. Now, I think he finally tamed the beast."

In pre-show press for the New York dates, Jagger told Aquilante of the *Post* that the Garden was a special venue for them. He said, "We're obviously looking forward to playing the Garden—it's always a cauldron." He later added, "We're just doing this one show at the Garden, so I would imagine it's going to have an opening-night feel. I expected there's going to be excitement, and this is an audience that wants to be at an event. Playing New York is always the most exciting show because the city is so full of energy. I look forward to the rush of playing the Garden—I guarantee we won't be flat."

Though the order was different each night, both the September 13 Garden show—the band's twentieth at the hallowed venue—and the September 15 Giants Stadium show featured "Start Me Up," "She's So Cold," "You Got Me Rocking," "Tumbling Dice," "The Worst," "Miss You," "Satisfaction," "Honky Tonk Women," "Sympathy for the Devil," "It's Only Rock 'n' Roll," "Jumpin' Jack Flash," "You Can't Always Get What You Want," "Brown Sugar," and, from the new album, "Rough Justice," "Oh No, Not You Again," and "Infamy." At the Garden, the band also played "Back of My Hand" from the new album as well as "19th Nervous Breakdown," "Bitch," "All Down the Line," and a cover of Bob Marley's "Get Up Stand Up." Giants Stadium got "Shattered," "Ruby Tuesday," "Heartbreaker," "Out of Control," and a cover of Ray Charles's "Night Time Is the Right Time."

As usual, the reviews of the Garden show in the New York press were overwhelmingly positive. Jim Farber of the *Daily News* began his review with: "The Rolling Stones spat in the eye of age at Madison Square Garden last night." In the *Post*, Aquilante wrote that the Stones made the Garden feel like an intimate venue, writing, "It takes the greatest rock band in the world to shrink a Madison Square Garden gig to the point that it feels like an intimate affair." Ben Ratliff was less complimentary in his *Times* review, calling the executions of "Start Me Up," "Infamy," and "19th Nervous Breakdown" missteps and giving full credit to Jagger for smoothing over the rough spots. *The Times* also reported that celebrities in the crowd included Ahmet Ertegun, Jann Wenner, Bette Midler, and Kate Moss, who came with Richards's daughters Theodora and Alexandra.

The Stones continued touring through a December 3 concert in Memphis, resuming the tour after the new year on January 10 in Montreal. In the meantime, they signed deals to get their music to new audiences. The music video for "Streets of Love," a track on *A Bigger Bang*, premiered on the NBC soap opera *Days of Our Lives* in October, while the band also agreed to perform at the halftime show for the February 2006 Super Bowl; each year, the halftime show has the largest television audience in the United States. The Stones also announced they would return to Madison Square Garden on January 18 and January 20 and wrap up the North American leg of the tour with a private show on March 14 at Radio City Music Hall, their first full gig at the historic venue. It wasn't all business though during the holiday break—according to the *Daily News*, Richards spent a drunken New Year's Eve 2005 with Rod Stewart at the River Café in Brooklyn under the Brooklyn Bridge.

The Stones were more adventurous with the set lists for the January 18 and January 20 Garden shows than they had been the previous fall. The band played "Jumpin' Jack Flash," "Let's Spend the Night Together," "Tumbling Dice," "Gimme Shelter," "Happy," "Miss You," "Get Off of My Cloud," "Honky Tonk Women," "Sympathy for the Devil," "Start Me Up," "Brown Sugar," "You Can't Always Get What You Want," "Satisfaction," and, from the new album, "Oh No, Not You Again," "Rain Fall Down," and "This Place is Empty." On January 18, the Stones also played "Love Is Strong," "Rocks Off," "Worried About You," "Midnight Rambler," and "Rough Justice." On January 20, the band played "It's Only Rock 'n' Roll," "Sway," "As Tears Go By," "Ain't Too Proud to Beg," and "Paint It, Black" instead. During the first concert, Jagger joked that during the band's upcoming Super Bowl performance, he was "going to show both my tits," a reference to the 2004 Super Bowl halftime performance in which an infamous "wardrobe malfunction" exposed singer Janet Jackson's right breast on live television. In the *Post*, Dan Aquilante called the January 18 concert a "near perfect gig that showcased all their strengths."

The Stones stuck around New York before departing for their Chicago concerts on January 23 and 25, with Jagger visiting the Whitney Museum of American Art at its original location on the Upper East Side. Following this, the band did more dates in the US, including their first-ever show in Puerto Rico. They also did the largest concert in the history of the Rolling Stones—estimates for the free concert at Copacabana Beach in Rio de Janeiro, Brazil, vary between one and two million. After two dates each in Argentina and Mexico and a handful of US dates, the Stones returned to New York City for a March 14 charity concert at Radio City Music Hall to end this portion of the North and South American tours.

The neon marquee of Sixth Avenue's Radio City Music Hall is one of the most recognizable sights in all of Manhattan. The landmark theater opened in 1932 as part of the Rockefeller Center complex and was originally intended to be a live-entertainment venue for variety shows. However, within a month the venue was converted into a movie theater (at the time the largest in the world) that also featured stage entertainment as part of its daily program. The hybrid programming format would last through the end of the 1970s. Though there were initial plans to close Radio City and turn it into an office building, the Art Deco interior was given landmark status by the city in 1978 and underwent extensive renovation to return the theater to its original intended use as a live-entertainment venue. Radio City is most famous for its *Christmas Spectacular*, an annual holiday stage show that has been performed in various forms since 1933 starring the theater's iconic leggy dance troupe, the Rockettes.

Since reopening in 1980 after the renovation, Radio City has become a popular venue for concerts because of its six-thousand-seat capacity. It has also hosted a number of awards shows, including the Grammy Awards, the Tony Awards, and MTV's Video Music Awards. The Stones played Radio City to benefit the Robin Hood Foundation, a charity founded in 1988 by billionaire Paul Tudor Jones to address poverty issues in New York City and also to fund relief efforts from disasters that have struck New York. The Robin Hood Fund was one of the charities that benefited from 2001's Concert for New York City. The Stones' performance raised $11.5 million for the organization. Unsurprisingly, the nineteen-song set list of the Radio City show concentrated on the hits. Only "Oh No, Not You Again" and "This Place Is Empty" were played from *A Bigger Bang*. The only out-of-the-box selection was "Worried About You."

One might have thought the Stones would be done with New York in terms of this tour, but they weren't even close. While the band turned its attention to touring the Pacific, including the group's first-ever performance in China, from March to April and then touring Europe from July to September, it was announced that Jagger would appear in a New York-set television series titled *Let's Rob Mick Jagger* about a group of bumbling thieves who plan to rob Jagger's Manhattan penthouse. Jagger filmed a cameo for the pilot episode while in Australia, and though the series later premiered in January 2007 under the title *The Knights of Prosperity*, it was quickly canceled due to low ratings. The reason for the band's three-month break between the Pacific and European legs of the tour was that Richards sustained a serious head injury in Fiji when he fell out of a tree, requiring brain surgery. Though Richards made a full recovery, the injury required the rescheduling of dates to give him more time to heal.

Once he was in the clear, it was announced that the Stones would once again play the New York metro area on September 27 at Giants Stadium, as well as two special performances at the Beacon Theatre on

October 29 and October 31 (which was later pushed to November 1, while a performance at Atlantic City's Boardwalk Hall, originally scheduled for October 27, was postponed to November 17).

The night before the Giants Stadium return, Jagger and Wood attended the New York premiere of director Martin Scorsese's film *The Departed* at the Ziegfeld Theatre, where *Let's Spend the Night Together* had premiered. The visit wasn't just about entertainment. Scorsese had agreed to film the band's upcoming shows at the Beacon Theatre for a concert film.

While the Stones had worked with acclaimed directors before, they had not worked with anyone close to Scorsese's caliber. Regarded as one of the greatest American filmmakers, Scorsese is a native New Yorker whose acclaim began after the release of two gritty New York-set crime dramas he directed starring Robert De Niro, 1973's *Mean Streets* and 1976's *Taxi Driver*. His fame increased with subsequent projects, many of which displayed his affinity for the Stones' music. He used "Jumpin' Jack Flash" and "Tell Me" in *Mean Streets*, "Monkey Man" and "Memo From Turner" in 1990's *Goodfellas*, "Long Long While," "Satisfaction," "Heart of Stone," "Sweet Virginia," and "Can't You Hear Me Knocking" in 1995's *Casino*, "Let It Loose" in *The Departed* and, most significantly, "Gimme Shelter" in *Goodfellas*, *Casino*, and *The Departed*. When his Stones documentary finally premiered, Scorsese explained why the band had meant so much to him, revealing, "At different times in my life, the Rolling Stones' music dealt with different aspects of my life that I was trying to make sense of. Their music has stayed with me and been a very important part of my life over the years."

Scorsese had also received acclaim as a pop music documentary filmmaker. His 1978 film *The Last Waltz* chronicles the farewell concert of the Band on November 25, 1976, in San Francisco, which featured an appearance by Wood. In 2003 he served as the producer of a film series titled *The Blues*, which chronicles the history of blues music, and in 2005 he released *No Direction Home*, a documentary about Bob Dylan's New York years from 1961 to 1966. Scorsese was the perfect choice to film the intimate concerts the band was to perform at the Beacon.

Jagger initially wanted to hire Scorsese to shoot the massive record-breaking gig in Rio, but Scorsese was uninterested. He would later say, "I went to see the show again and I'm sitting there, and the band is this small on the screen; they've got 50 cameras already—what am I going to bring to that? So then I thought, what if I can convince them to play on a smaller stage, the Beacon Theatre in New York, with the best cameramen in the world?" The Rio show was eventually released by the band anyway in a DVD set titled *The Biggest Bang* that chronicled the Bigger Bang Tour.

But before that, the Stones had Giants Stadium to play on September 27. Surprisingly for a stadium concert, the Stones dug a bit deeper into the catalog than normal. They played "Live With Me," "Monkey Man," "Sway," "Far Away Eyes," "Just My Imagination," "You Got the Silver," "Little T & A," "Under My Thumb," and "Streets of Love," and "Rough Justice" from the new album, then ended the set with the expected greatest hits.

While the Stones had nine other concerts to do before the return to New York at the end of October, arrangements were being made for the Beacon Theatre gig. Approximately 2,100 of the tickets for the October 29 gig at the 2,800-seat Beacon were set aside for the Clinton Foundation to celebrate former US president Bill Clinton's sixtieth birthday (though Clinton's actual birthday is in late August). Packages started at the low, low price of a $60,000 donation to the Clinton Foundation. Though celebrities like Michael J. Fox, Sheryl Crow, Matt Lauer, Michael Stipe, and Elvis Costello and scores of politicians (like former Czech president Václav Havel) and millionaires were able to get tickets, fans were mostly left out in the cold. The Beacon was set up with seventeen cameras to capture the onstage action.

Curiously, the set list for the first night did not contain any songs from *A Bigger Bang*. In fact, the set list didn't include any song released after 1983. It had "Start Me Up," "Shattered," "She Was Hot," "All Down the Line," "Loving Cup" (featuring White Stripes singer-guitarist Jack White), "As Tears Go By," "I'm Free" (which the Stones had not performed live since 1969), "Undercover of the Night," "Just

My Imagination," "Shine a Light," a cover of the Muddy Waters song "Champagne & Reefer" (featuring Buddy Guy), "Tumbling Dice," "You Got the Silver," "Little T & A," "Sympathy for the Devil," "Live With Me" (featuring pop singer Christina Aguilera), "Paint It, Black," "Jumpin' Jack Flash," and "Satisfaction." As a nod to President John F. Kennedy's forty-fifth birthday celebration on May 19, 1962, downtown at Madison Square Garden, Jagger joked onstage, "President Kennedy had Marilyn Monroe at his birthday party. I thought about wearing a dress. But then I thought, 'I'd better not.'" Coincidentally, Kennedy's nephew, Bobby Kennedy Jr., was in attendance. Notably, Jagger didn't sing the "Who killed the Kennedys?" line in "Sympathy for the Devil," as he had generally dropped that line for most performances since it returned to the set list several years after Altamont.

Though the first concert was filmed, most of the footage in Scorsese's final film came from the second concert, which also featured a deep set list. Jagger later explained at the premiere that he viewed the first concert as something of a dress rehearsal. He said, "Shooting this movie was quite nerve-racking. The first night we played was more of a rehearsal, and by the second night we got adjusted to playing a small theater again." Again, there were no songs from *A Bigger Bang*, and no songs released after 1983 were played. Instead of "Undercover of the Night," "Shine a Light," "Little T & A," and "Paint It, Black," the band played "Some Girls," "Far Away Eyes," "Connection" (the first time since 1995, and sung by Richards), "Honky Tonk Women," and "Brown Sugar." The three guests from the previous night, Jack White, Buddy Guy, and Christina Aguilera, all returned.

Though the Beacon Theatre shows were a celebration of the Stones' enduring popularity, the band was affected by tragic circumstances surrounding the concerts. Immediately after the first Beacon show, Wood flew to England to visit his older brother Art, who was hospitalized due to being in the final stages of prostate cancer. The elder Wood was also a musician and had actually played with Charlie Watts back in the early 1960s when they both collaborated with Blues Incorporated. Art Wood passed away on November 3. Just over a week later, Jagger's father, Joe

Jagger, passed away. Finally, backstage before the first Beacon concert, Ahmet Ertegun suffered a fall and was hospitalized, eventually passing away on December 14 from the head injury he sustained. In comments to *Rolling Stone* after his passing, Richards remembered, "I was with Ahmet at the Beacon, ten minutes before he went to the john. He asked me how my head was, after the bang. I said, 'Have a feel.' Because I have a big dent on the left side, front lobe. He was rubbing it, and we were laughing our heads off. By the time I got offstage, I'd heard what happened. It's almost as if I cursed him. So nobody else can rub my head anymore." He also added, "He was one of the Stones' father figures. I looked up to Ahmet the way I did Muddy Waters. Until the day he died, his whole thing was to be involved with musicians. His love of the music, his joy from it, stayed with him. Otherwise, he wouldn't have been backstage at the Beacon a couple of weeks ago. It was full circle. And that touches me."

The timing of the Beacon shows also caused some headaches for their New York and New Jersey fans. The Stones were supposed to play Atlantic City on October 27, but the concert was canceled just four hours before the scheduled start; the claim was that Jagger had a sore throat. The concert was rescheduled for November 17, but Brooklyn Stones fan Rosalie Druyan filed a $51-million class action lawsuit for the late cancelation because she had been unable to cancel her Atlantic City hotel reservations on such short notice. Also, the second Beacon show was originally scheduled for October 31, but the band again had to postpone it because of Jagger's sore throat. And there was a significant issue with the tickets for both Beacon shows, because the tickets were tied to the names of the ticket purchaser, to prevent scalping. Fans who had bought tickets to either show from a reseller discovered they were denied entry, especially for the security-tight October 29 concert. In *The New Yorker*, journalist Shauna Lyon even reported issues with the show, revealing that the film crew had hired attractive Stones fans to attend the concert for seventy-five dollars and that, during the second show, which made up the bulk of the documentary, the production team had issued a set of rules to the "workers:"

You should be dressed trendy, sexy, hip. Do not come looking sloppy or disheveled. Women really glam it up, but not trashy. You can wear Rolling Stones shirts or other band shirts but please do NOT wear the following: no fan club shirts, no logos (Nike, Coca-Cola), nothing too over the top and outrageous (wigs, crazy hats, etc.) and do not wear WHITE.... You will not be allowed to purchase alcohol. Again, you are not just attending a concert, you are working.

MOST IMPORTANT NOTE: You guys will be in the very front of the stage and will be the only people on camera for the documentary. We really need high energy. Dance, sing along, cheer on the band. They need your energy to play a really amazing show.

According to the magazine, production assistants selected the smallest, most attractive women and put them closest to the stage, and the article even claimed, "Some of the statuesque seventy-five-dollar women looked bored, some walked out." In his review of the film for the *Post*, Kyle Smith noted the girls closest the stage: "The front row has been salted with a vaguely baffled-looking candy box of blond sweeties—nice to see hot girls catching a break for once—clapping slightly out of time. One of them is unaware that the rock experience does not allow for snapping one's fingers."

Interestingly enough, the crowd interaction in the final film is occasionally puzzling. During the first chorus of the subdued "Far Away Eyes," Richards accidentally sings the wrong lyric. A female in the audience heckles him, which causes Richards to say, "Shut up!" and laugh. A visibly annoyed Jagger walks between Richards and the catcaller, and Richards backs away. He initially skips out on singing the background vocals for the second chorus until Jagger comes up to him with the microphone, and they finish the chorus together while a smiling Richards places his arm around Jagger. However, Richards again screws up the lyrics when he approaches his microphone to finish the chorus. It's a sloppy rendition of the tune, but it perhaps highlights best why Scorsese was the right filmmaker for the job. This was not meant to be a slickly produced concert film; this was the Stones at their most intimate and raw. However, Stones fans would not get to see the final results until the film's release in April 2008 as *Shine a Light*.

After playing eight shows in the New York City metro area from September 2005 to November 2006, the Stones took an extended break before returning to Europe in summer 2007 to finish the tour, including a three-night stand at London's O2 Arena. At the time of its completion, the 141-date tour became not only the highest-grossing Rolling Stones tour ever, but also the highest-grossing tour of all time with a record-shattering $558-million gross—the first rock concert tour to ever gross more than half a billion dollars. The previous record holder, U2 (which broke the Stones' record for the Voodoo Lounge Tour), had earned a total gross of $389 million with 131 shows on the 2005–2006 Vertigo Tour. The fact that the Stones grossed over $150 million more than that proved just how well-oiled the Stones marketing and touring machine had become since the Steel Wheels Tour had started rolling in 1989.

Because they were busy touring from June to August 2007, the Stones made relatively few appearances in New York throughout 2007. Richards returned to the Waldorf Astoria on March 12 to induct New York natives the Ronettes into the Rock & Roll Hall of Fame, and on April 17, Jagger spoke at a memorial for Ahmet Ertegun at Lincoln Center and earned raves for his speech, which recalled many humorous times he had spent with the mogul. After the tour, Jagger, Wood, and Richards all recorded sessions at One East Recording for their touring band saxophonist Tim Ries' album *Stones World: The Rolling Stones Project II*, which features covers of Rolling Stones songs, while Richards also recorded the Merle Haggard track "Sing Me Back Home" at the same studio with Marianne Faithfull for her 2008 album, *Easy Come Easy Go*. Richards ended the year by attending the December 3 premiere of the film *Sweeney Todd: The Demon Barber of Fleet Street* at the Ziegfeld Theatre to support his friend and *Pirates of the Caribbean* co-star Johnny Depp, who stars in the movie. Around that time, Richards's wife, Patti Hansen, began undergoing treatment for bladder cancer in New York. She eventually made a recovery.

At the end of March 2008, the Stones reconvened in New York to promote *Shine a Light*, as well as the film's soundtrack album. On March 28, Jagger and Richards appeared on *The Today Show*. Two days later the Stones and Scorsese did a press conference at the Palace Hotel on Madison Avenue to discuss the film's release, which was followed by the premiere at the Ziegfeld later that night.

While most reviews in the New York press for *Shine a Light* were very positive, Camille Dodero's review in the *Village Voice* was negative, focusing more on Jagger's midriff on the poster than the actual film itself. Dodero called the film "not only a vanity project for everyone involved, it's a total tongue bath," and said it chronicled "a fairly decent, mostly unsurprising Stones concert." In *The New Yorker*, Anthony Lane was more upbeat but still wondered why Scorsese hadn't had anything better to do than film a Stones concert.

In July 2008, the Stones made news again by switching their record label from EMI (which had acquired Virgin Records in 1992) to Universal Music Group, a change that netted the band not only a reported $15-million advance but a tremendous advantage: access to the band's entire catalog. Universal already owned the distribution rights to ABKCO Records, meaning that the label now had the rights to distribute every single Stones song. This gave the Stones a renewed opportunity to look backward, as they had done in 2002 with the fortieth-anniversary tour. Despite strong reviews and a hugely successful tour, *A Bigger Bang* was not a strong seller for the Stones. Though it went platinum for shipping a million units, the album ultimately sold about half as many copies as *Bridges to Babylon*. As the set lists for the Beacon Theatre shows demonstrated, there was a deep market for the Stones to dig into their past. Fans who had been waiting for the Stones to open the vaults as they approached their fiftieth anniversary were finally getting their wish.

CHAPTER 16

"I NEED A YELLOW CAB"

After all the events surrounding the Bigger Bang Tour and the release of *Shine a Light*, 2009 was one of the quietest years in the history of the Rolling Stones. In May, Universal began releasing remastered versions of the band's albums from the 1970s on. Later that month, Richards was spotted in the audience at Bernard Fowler's gig at the Knitting Factory. But there was very little activity on the Stones front in New York until September, when the band was working on outtakes for the remastered version of *Exile on Main St*. At Universal's request, Jagger and Richards revisited some of tracks they had recorded for the album but hadn't finished or had to cut from the already lengthy double album. One of them, "Following the River," was worked on by Jagger with Don Was in New York. Jagger told *Rolling Stone*, "I just started from nothing on that. The core tape of it was the piano and the drums, bass, and guitar. There was no top line or lyric. I started from scratch—I mean, that's what I do, and I've done it many times before. And it's daunting in the beginning, but after a while you get into it." Of the ten extra tracks, "Following the River" was one that needed completely new lyrics and vocals from Jagger. Other tracks required some additional tinkering from Richards and, recording with the Stones for the first time in decades, Mick Taylor.

After the recordings, Jagger was back in New York on October 30 and appeared at a special concert to celebrate the twenty-fifth anniversary of the Rock & Roll Hall of Fame. He performed alongside U2 and Black Eyed Peas singer Fergie on "Gimme Shelter" and then performed "Stuck in a Moment You Can't Get Out Of" with U2. Incidentally, Jagger had originally recorded background vocals for U2's studio version of that song with his daughter Elizabeth in 2000, but neither vocal was used on the original track.

Though Jagger was spotted socializing around New York in early 2010, it wasn't until May that the Stones gathered together to promote the May 18 release of the *Exile on Main St.* reissue (minus Wood, who had not yet been a Stone when *Exile* was originally released and was undergoing another stint of trying to stay sober anyway). Promotion started on May 3, with Jagger in attendance at the Costume Institute Gala Benefit at the Metropolitan Museum of Art, and later that week he hosted a benefit for the victims of the recent Haiti earthquake at the GreenHouse - Scholastic Cafeteria in SoHo. On May 11, Jagger, Richards, and Watts walked the red carpet at the premiere of *Stones in Exile*, a documentary about the making of *Exile on Main St.*, at the Museum of Modern Art. The trio also did an interview on *Late Night With Jimmy Fallon* on May 11, and on May 17 Jagger and Richards appeared on *The Today Show*.

Richards capped his month in New York by going to Bernard Fowler's May 27 gig at the Canal Room—a Tribeca nightclub known for its popular cover band nights—where his daughter Alexandra was opening as a deejay. The *Daily News* reported that Richards's attempt to sneak in via the back entrance failed, and he had to be hustled to the VIP section before he could be mobbed.

There was another flurry of Stones activity in New York in September. On September 15, Jagger was a guest at the premiere of Martin Scorsese's HBO television series *Boardwalk Empire* and also participated in Fashion Week events. On September 24, it was Wood's turn to appear on *Late Night With Jimmy Fallon*, to promote his latest solo album, *I Feel Like Playing*, which was released that day. The *Post* reported that the following day, Ronnie Wood was spotted playing piano in the West 49th Street restaurant Da Marino accompanying *Sex and the City* actor Chris Noth, who sung several 1970s songs. Richards then launched into the promotion of his autobiography, *Life*, which was released on October 26. Richards did most of the press for the book in New York, and the tabloids had a field day with Richards's accusation in the book that Jagger had a "tiny todger" (speaking on the authority of Marianne Faithfull) and other swipes he took at his longtime collaborator and friend. *Life* earned rave reviews from *The New Yorker* and *The Times*, stayed on *The New York Times* Bestsellers list for months, and even earned an unlikely glowing endorsement from *Times* columnist Maureen Dowd. To demonstrate the fact that in some ways the Stones' hell-raising reputation has never changed with some people, a lengthy interview with Richards in *The Times* was followed by a letter to the editor that asked, "Did you have to subject readers to such a wholly degenerate character? The Rolling Stones to us are a terrible stain on our civilization, and for *The Times* to devote such space and photos to any of those creeps is a real travesty." It was almost as if *The Times* had unearthed a letter from 1964 following the band's first appearance on *The Ed Sullivan Show*.

Richards's media appearances also included an interview on *CBS Sunday Morning* (at his home in Connecticut), an interview on NPR, a multi-part interview with Steven Van Zandt on Sirius satellite radio, and an interview on *The Today Show*. On October 29, Richards appeared at the New York Public Library's main branch on Fifth Avenue to talk about his book to a jam-packed audience of five hundred (tickets had sold out in forty-three seconds). On the fact that he was being interviewed in unlikely territory, Richards quipped, "I love libraries. They're places where you want to obey the laws—even the ones about silence. I still owe fines on overdue books from 50 years ago." However, Richards did make one faux pas when he was at the New York Public Library. The *Post* reported that before taking the stage, Richards smoked a cigarette in the office of the library's Cullman Center deputy director Marie d'Origny and used the clay saucer of her flowerpot, which contained an orchid, as an ashtray. Because Richards left the window open, the orchid ended up dying a few days later. However, Richards autographed the makeshift ashtray, leaving d'Origny a unique piece of memorabilia that if she sold it could net her enough money to buy plenty of replacement orchids.

Jagger received his own profile in the December 5 edition of the *New York Times* magazine, and was asked about Richards's criticisms of him in *Life*. Jagger's terse response was:

"Personally, I think it's really quite tedious raking over the past. Mostly, people only do it for the money." Jagger later told *Rolling Stone* magazine that the following year he refused to participate in the band's fiftieth-anniversary tour until Richards apologized for his shots at him in *Life*, which Richards did. However, Richards later walked back on the apology, telling the magazine, "I'd say anything to get the band together, you know? I'd lie to my mother."

That apology came in April 2011, when Jagger and Richards met in New York to discuss the band's next moves. Over the previous several months, the Stones had all been pursuing outside projects, and Jagger and Richards made several appearances in New York. Richards appeared on *Late Night With Jimmy Fallon* on May 11 to promote the latest *Pirates of the Caribbean* movie, where he admitted that the Stones had no plans for the future at the moment. ("I'm trying to nail them down," he quipped, "but I don't want to crucify them!") While in Los Angeles for the premiere, Richards was asked by *USA Today* about U2's recently eclipsing the Stones' record for the highest-grossing concert tour with the band's U2 360° Tour. Richards shrugged it off and took a swipe at Bono and the Edge's Broadway musical *Spider-Man: Turn Off the Dark*, the infamous multi-million-dollar musical that was mired in bad press: "So what? U2 made a few mill more, or maybe not by the time the gross is done and you look at the net. Meanwhile, *Spider-Man* is going down the tubes."

However, even with no tour in the cards, there were two big Stones-related projects on the horizon. The Stones decided to give *Some Girls* the same treatment that the recent *Exile on Main St.* reissue had gotten, and would put the album out with twelve outtakes at the end of the year. Meanwhile, Jagger would release an album with an eclectic "supergroup" dubbed SuperHeavy, with Dave Stewart, soul singer Joss Stone, Indian musician A. R. Rahman, and reggae artist Damian Marley (youngest son of Bob Marley). Jagger and Stewart had been working on the initial tracks since 2008 but formed the band in 2009, recording the album in bits and pieces over the next two years. In the meantime, Richards took part in a charity dinner with former US president Bill Clinton at Craft, a restaurant near Grammercy Park. He told the *New York Post*, "We talked about saxophones."

Jagger did promotional work for SuperHeavy, though very little of it was done in New York except for the music's being featured during L'Wren Scott's September 15 fashion show during Fashion Week, which Jagger attended. The group's album, also called *SuperHeavy*, was released the next day. Reviews in the New York press—outside of *Rolling Stone*, naturally, which gave the album four stars—were terrible. Jim Farber in the *Daily News* gave the album one star, calling it "a history-making mess," while in *The Times* Ben Ratliff said, "An almost total lack of good songs constitutes the album's basic problem.... It is a credible soundtrack for someone's gold-plated midwinter Caribbean vacation—someone who doesn't really listen to music per se—and it could be a pretty heavy comedy album if its intent were moved a few inches." Neither review was kind to Jagger, with both suggesting that he had reached a new level of self-parody. On September 21, Jagger appeared on *Good Morning America* and also held a small album release party at the Double Seven nightclub in the Meatpacking District. Along with A. R. Rahman and Dave Stewart, Lorne Michaels, Tommy Hilfiger, and comedian Steve Martin were in attendance. Though the album performed well internationally, *SuperHeavy* peaked at number twenty-six in the US, and its released single, "Miracle Worker," failed to make the main pop charts.

Surprisingly, despite all of his accusations in *Life* about Jagger's being too concerned with mingling with celebrities, Richards marked the fall of 2011 by rubbing elbows with the rich and famous. When Sirius satellite radio did a "one night only" Studio 54 party at the club's original location on October 18, 2011, it was Richards, not Jagger, who attended alongside his wife, Patti Hansen, and dozens of celebrities. Of course, since it was the place where Richards and Hansen had first met, it was appropriate. A week later Richards was in attendance at the premiere of his friend Johnny Depp's film *The Rum Diary* at the Museum of Modern Art, then celebrated the occasion at the Playboy-sponsored after-party at the Hiro Ballroom inside the 16th Street Maritime Hotel. At the end of the night, Richards and Depp joined the house band for a rendition of "Key to the Highway." Finally, on November 8, Richards again was in the presence of Bill Clinton when the former president awarded him the Norman Mailer Award for Distinguished Biography for *Life* at the Mandarin Oriental hotel. By that time, sales of *Life* had exceeded one million copies. In his speech, Clinton recalled how excited his mother-in-law had been to meet Richards at the Stones' 2006 Beacon Theatre gig to celebrate Clinton's birthday, saying, "Do you have any idea of what it's like to have a 92-year-old groupie living in your house?" In the audience were literary icons Gay Talese, Elie Wiesel, and Tina Brown.

Later that month, on November 21, the Stones released the expanded edition of *Some Girls*. As with the *Exile on Main St.* reissue, Jagger and Richards had done some work to finish the vintage tracks from the late 1970s. Jagger did his overdubs at his home studio in France in August 2011, while Richards did his in two days at Electric Lady Studios in New York in September 2011. In the same spirit as that of the original New York-based album, two of the songs on the *Some Girls* reissue feature lyrics that reference New York City. A Jagger/Richards/Wood composition titled "Do You Think I Really Care?" actually has two sets of New York-centric lyrics—the original that can be heard on bootlegs and the new version with Jagger's re-recorded vocals.

Both versions feature a singer asking the listener, "Do you think that I really care / About a girl who's never there?" Yet despite how much the singer insists he doesn't care about her and how she is "never there," he rattles off a list of places where he sees her in New York. The song is a virtual travelogue of New York sights. It even includes a part about the singer looking for a yellow cab to get out of the rain.

The second song on the reissue that references New York, "So Young," actually had already been finished by the band in 1994 and was the B-side of the "Love Is Strong" single. Jagger re-recorded the vocals again for the 2011 reissue in a version that is closer to the original 1978 backing track. As the title suggests, the song is about a singer infatuated with a beautiful teenage woman, but who feels troubled because she's so young (which, if his reputation is to be believed, is not something that has bothered Jagger in real life). One line in the song is: "Well I took her down to Barneys, bought her a brand new set of boots." Barneys is the luxury department store on Fifth Avenue that many of the Stones, particularly Jagger, were known to frequent. Prior to 1993, Barneys was located on Seventh Avenue between 16th and 17th Streets.

While many were excited about the re-release of *Some Girls*, Stones fans knew that 2012 marked the fiftieth anniversary of the Rolling Stones. By now it was obvious that the Stones had mastered the art of exploiting their brand, and because the band's fortieth anniversary had been such a major media event with *Forty Licks*, the Licks Tour, and *Four Flicks*, it was expected that the Stones would make their fiftieth anniversary an even bigger celebration. Another band hitting the half-century mark, the Beach Boys, announced plans for a 2012 reunion tour at the end of 2011, which created further speculation that the Stones would be planning an even bigger party. But it would be months before fans found out how the Stones planned to celebrate and just how New York would factor into those plans.

CHAPTER 17

FIFTY YEARS ON...

At the end of 2011, Howlin' Wolf guitarist Hubert Sumlin, who had appeared as a guest at some Rolling Stones concerts, including the January 16, 2003, show at Madison Square Garden, passed away. Not only did Jagger and Richards pay for Sumlin's funeral, but on February 24, 2012, Richards took part in the "Howlin' for Hubert" tribute concert at the Apollo with other stars influenced by Sumlin, including Buddy Guy, Eric Clapton, and ZZ Top's Billy Gibbons. Richards performed "Goin' Down Slow," "Little Red Rooster," "Spoonful," "Wang-Dang-Doodle," and "Smokestack Lightin'."

The music of the Rolling Stones returned to Carnegie Hall for the first time in almost forty-eight years on March 13, 2012, when the venue hosted Hot Rocks 1964–1971, a charity concert featuring various performers tackling all twenty-one tracks from the twelve-times-platinum compilation album. The performers included Marianne Faithfull (who performed "As Tears Go By" and "Sister Morphine"), Ronnie Spector ("Time Is on My Side"), and bluesman Taj Mahal ("Honky Tonk Women"). The March 26 issue of *The New Yorker* featured an extensive profile of Michael Dorf, who organized the concert, including his attempts to convince Richards to attend the concert, though Richards never made it because he was "running late" after recording in a studio downtown.

Though it had been rumored that one or more Stones might drop in on the Carnegie Hall tribute show, it didn't happen. Nevertheless, both Jagger and Richards were in New York earlier that month—Richards was recording with the Winos at Electric Lady Studios, and Jagger was seen dining with Dave Stewart at the Lambs Club and then dancing at the Double Seven nightclub—and the pair met on March 10 to discuss what the Stones' plans were for the anniversary. After the meeting, Jagger and Richards told *Rolling Stone* they had no plans to tour in 2012, though they admitted that the band had rehearsed in London at the end of 2011 and even revealed that Bill Wyman had sat in on the rehearsals. Nonetheless, Richards did say something would be happening, noting that Jagger "is going to be living in New York too for a while, so we're planning to get things going with the Stones again." Richards also pointed out that since Watts didn't join the Stones until 1963, 2013 would be just as appropriate for a fiftieth-anniversary tour.

Still, the interview did little to stem the "will they or won't they?" tour rumors for 2012, especially since other band members were publicly as noncommittal. Wood had another art show in New York, this one of his portraits, called *Faces, Time and Places*. It opened April 9 at a studio space at 498 Broome Street in SoHo and closed on June 30. When asked by the *Daily News* about the Stones' touring plans, Wood was as noncommittal as his bandmates, saying, "We're not sure right now about anything going forward. We are just in the meeting up stage and enjoying getting together again really." Wood also appeared at a party at the Core Club on April 10 to celebrate the release of the book *Faces, 1969–75*, which celebrates the history of Wood's former band; both the Small Faces and the Faces were being inducted into the Rock & Roll Hall of Fame that year. Though Wood was also telling the press that the Stones would go into the studio to record an album, he quickly had to walk back on those comments when Jagger told him that it wasn't happening. Whatever the Stones were planning in terms of recording and touring, it was still a mystery, even though the band met in early May in New York and Weehawken, New Jersey, to rehearse. Of the rehearsals, Richards told *Rolling Stone*, "We played everything, really. We're just getting our chops together. It was like playing in the garage, a maintenance check, you know?... I thought I'd be quite rusty, after all we hadn't done it for a while, five years or something. But it sounded as fresh as you could hope for. It was a great week."

While the Stones wouldn't be touring in the summer of 2012, Watts had been playing steadily with his swing group, the ABC & D of Boogie Woogie, since establishing the band in 2009 with pianists Axel Zwingenberger and Ben Waters and bassist—and childhood friend—Dave Green (the first letter of the first names of the members gave the group the ABC & D moniker). In April, Lincoln Center announced that the ABC & D of Boogie Woogie would play its annual Midsummer Night Swing series in Damrosch Park on West 62nd Street on June 28. It would be the band's first US performance. Meanwhile, ex-Stone Mick Taylor was back in the spotlight in New York when he performed an extended run of shows at the Iridium Jazz Club on May 9 through May 14 (two shows a night). Located in the heart of Times Square at 1650 Broadway at 51st Street, the club was famous for hosting weekly shows by Les Paul from 1995 until his death in 2009. In fact, Taylor played the two shows on the final night with Paul's old band, Les Paul's Trio. He promoted the residency with an appearance on *Late Night With Jimmy Fallon* on May 9. Taylor performed "Can't You Hear Me Knocking" with the house band, the Roots.

The Iridium became a hot spot for Stones fans that summer, because the ABC & D of Boogie Woogie followed its Damrosch Park performance with a residency from June 29 to July 2 at the Iridium (like Taylor, the band played two shows per night). Richards attended the first show on the last night of the residency. Following Taylor's lead again, the ABC & D of Boogie Woogie performed on *Late Night With Jimmy Fallon* on June 29 to promote the residency at the Iridium.

With the other Stones busy with their own projects, Jagger decided to likewise perform on his own—but in a much more vis-ible venue than the Iridium. Jagger hosted the season thirty-seven finale of *Saturday Night Live*, which was broadcast on May 19, 2012. When asked why Jagger had agreed to host after his long association with the show as a guest star and musical guest, *Saturday Night Live* producer Lorne Michaels told the *Post*, "That's a question he's asking himself every day. I know him pretty well, and I think he'll be charming and funny, and I think people will see a side of him that they're not used to seeing. He's a very, very smart guy, and he's very, very smart about how to put on a show."

On the show, Jagger performed "The Last Time" with Canadian band Arcade Fire and "19th Nervous Breakdown" and "It's Only Rock 'n' Roll" with the Foo Fighters. In addition, Jagger sang the humorous song "Tea Party" about US politics during a skit, with Jeff Beck on guitar, backed by the Saturday Night Live Band. He also appeared in other skits, including one involving various cast members performing bad karaoke to Rolling Stones hits and one in which Jagger portrayed Steven Tyler as the host of a television dance show. The episode ended with Jagger performing "She's a Rainbow" and "Ruby Tuesday" with Arcade Fire to say goodbye to departing cast member Kristen Wiig. After the show, the cast and Jagger celebrated at the after-party, with Jagger performing "Miss You" and "Bitch" with the Foo Fighters.

Though all four Stones, plus Taylor, were active in New York during their fiftieth-anniversary year, the members still firmly denied any touring plans in 2012. However, that changed at the end of August when the Stones finally announced they would play a handful of shows as the 50 & Counting Tour to celebrate the occasion. The Stones would play two shows at London's O2 Arena on November 25 and 29, their first-ever show in Brooklyn on December 8 at Barclays Center, and then shows on December 13 and 15 at Prudential Center in Newark, New Jersey—the group's first shows in Newark since 1965. Initially the Barclays Center concert was to be the band's only performance in the US for 2012, but the Newark dates were added when the Stones decided to broadcast the December 15 concert live on pay-per-view. The Stones also announced a career-spanning compilation puzzlingly titled *GRRR!* featuring two new songs, "Doom and Gloom" and "One

More Shot." *GRRR!* was released on November 12 in forty-song, fifty-song, and eighty-song versions.

In between, New York saw the premieres of two Rolling Stone films—first, the rarely seen 1966 documentary *Charlie Is My Darling—Ireland 1965*, which had been filmed during the band's second 1965 tour of Ireland. The re-release features footage that was not in the original cut of the movie. *Charlie Is My Darling—Ireland 1965* premiered at the New York Film Festival on September 29 before its November 6 release on Blu-ray and DVD. To promote the film, Andrew Loog Oldham appeared at the festival and was interviewed by Steven Van Zandt. Six weeks later, the Stones made their first appearance as a group in New York since 2008 to attend the premiere of *Crossfire Hurricane*, a documentary that covered the band from its inception through 1981, on November 13 at the Ziegfeld Theatre. On November 14, the Stones appeared at the Museum of Modern Art to speak about the film with Tom Stoppard, and then appeared on *Today* the following morning.

* * * * *

New York City had faced storms of historical magnitude throughout its history, but Hurricane Sandy, which caused damage across the entire eastern seaboard of the United States in addition to the Caribbean, was one of the most severe storms in the city's history. As it approached New York in late October 2012, Sandy increased in size and became the largest Atlantic hurricane on record. When Sandy hit New York on October 29, it did severe damage to coastal areas in New Jersey, New York, and Long Island. Transportation services had been suspended the night before, and the subway system was flooded. Homes and cars all over the area were destroyed, particularly in southern Queens and along the New Jersey Shore, resulting in billions of dollars' worth of damage. While the area was still suffering and rebuilding and over a million New Yorkers remained without power, Mayor Bloomberg insisted that the annual New York City Marathon would go on as scheduled on November 4. His decision was controversial, because the immense law enforcement and material resources (such as hotel rooms and water) needed to operate the race could have been used as relief services instead. On November 2, Bloomberg announced that the marathon was canceled because areas in the city still suffering from the effects of Sandy needed these resources. Bloomberg's flip-flopping on holding the marathon was extremely unpopular, because to many New Yorkers it signaled his desire to put New York's tourism and image over the welfare of those who lived in the city, a common criticism of his tenure in office.

Two weeks later, it was announced that a concert to support the Robin Hood Foundation would be held at Madison Square Garden on December 12. The event, called 12-12-12: The Concert for Sandy Relief, was organized by the same production team behind The Concert for New York City in 2001, and several of the same artists signed up to participate—the Who, Bon Jovi, Eric Clapton, Billy Joel, and Paul McCartney. The Rolling Stones announced they would also participate. Being that the Garden is almost the halfway point between Barclays Center and Prudential Center, the stop was not an issue for the Stones' mini-tour. The concert was held in the midst of a three-year, $1-billion renovation of the Garden from 2011 to 2013, the second in this Garden's history after a series of renovations in 1991 that installed suite boxes where upper-tier seats had formerly been. The 2011–2013 renovations, which significantly reconfigured the seating of the Garden and updated the facilities throughout the arena, took place in the NHL and NBA off-seasons, so the renovations did not affect the 12-12-12 concert.

In pre-concert interviews, Jagger revealed that his New York City apartment was flooded with two feet of water and explained why the Stones had chosen to participate in the concert, saying, "Imagine you hadn't known it was coming. It would have been pretty dire. I think it's good to do events to support people in the area where you're very familiar with. I mean, I've been coming here for a long time."

At the concert, the Stones played just two songs—"You Got Me Rocking" and "Jumpin' Jack Flash," and although the first line of "Flash" made it appropriate for the occasion, it was odd that "Gimme

Shelter" wasn't played. Jagger also received some criticism on social media for a joke that he made between songs. He said, "This has got to be the largest collection of old English musicians ever assembled in Madison Square Garden. But I've got to say, if it rains in London, you've got to come and help us, OK?" Some said Jagger's quip was insensitive considering the magnitude of the hurricane's destruction, but the minor uproar was quickly forgotten.

* * * * *

Before 12-12-12: The Concert for Sandy Relief, the Stones made their first-ever concert appearance in Brooklyn at Barclays Center. Plans to build an arena in Brooklyn had existed for nearly a decade before Barclays Center opened in 2012, but various court battles over the arena's location delayed construction. By 2009 the plan was for the arena to become the home stadium of the New Jersey Nets, who had played at Izod Center (formerly the Brendan Byrne Arena, where the Stones had played on their 1981 tour) since 1981. Since the team had been founded as the New Jersey Americans in 1967, the Nets had bounced between arenas in New Jersey and New York, including Nassau Coliseum, where the Stones had rehearsed for the Steel Wheels Tour. Once it was decided that the Nets would be rechristened the Brooklyn Nets upon moving to Barclays Center in 2012, the basketball team made Prudential Center in Newark its temporary home from 2010 to 2012.

Naturally, Barclays Center was seen as an immediate rival to the slightly larger Madison Square Garden, as Barclays was built as a state-of-the-art arena (perhaps one of the reasons why the Garden was undergoing $1 billion in renovations); plus there was the growing popularity of Brooklyn as a place to live and the mere five miles that separate the venues. Barclays Center opened on September 28, 2012, with the first in a series of concerts by Brooklyn-born rapper Jay-Z. In an attempt by management to get the arena as much attention as a rival to Madison Square Garden in its opening months as possible, that fall saw a variety of rock concerts at Barclays, including shows by the Who, Bob Dylan, and Neil Young.

The plan worked—according to *Billboard* magazine, Barclays Center was the highest-grossing arena in the United States from November 2012 through May 2013, bringing in $46.9 million in non-sports ticket sales versus the $39.5 million brought in by the Garden, which Barclays touted in the media. Of course, considering that the Garden's renovations severely limited the number of available dates for non-sports entertainment, those figures were not an accurate measure of popularity. In fact, a year later the May 2, 2014, issue of *Billboard* took an extensive look at the growing rivalry between the arenas, noting that from October 2013 to April 2014, the Garden sold 35 percent more concert tickets than Barclays did during the same period. In terms of the rivalry, Barclays' getting Madison Square Garden Hall of Famers the Rolling Stones to play its stage instead of the Garden's on their fiftieth-anniversary tour was a huge coup, though the Stones' decision to play two songs at the Garden's 12-12-12 concert four days later softened the blow somewhat.

Anticipation for the three New York-New Jersey Stones dates reached a fever pitch after the Stones' November 25 and 29 concerts at O2 Arena in London. Not only did the band open the first show with "I Wanna Be Your Man," which they had not played since 1964, but the Stones were joined onstage by Bill Wyman for the first time since 1990 on "It's Only Rock 'n' Roll" and "Honky Tonk Women" and by Mick Taylor on "Midnight Rambler" for the first time since a one-off 1981 appearance. Furthermore, the band performed "You Can't Always Get What You Want" with a chorus, the London Youth Choir, for the first time ever. On the second night, the Stones played "Lady Jane" for the first time since 1967 and performed "Champagne & Reefer" with Eric Clapton.

Tickets for the Barclays concert reached as high as $18,000 on ticket reseller websites. A piece in *The New York Times* on the affluent make-up of much of the Stones' audience at Barclays focused on how the band was "once seen as dangerous, hedonistic and anti-establishment, [but] has somehow become the establishment, as their fans have aged and climbed the social ladder," as if this were a new revelation for a band that had been shattering concert ticket sales records for more than two decades already.

At the Barclays concert, the Stones performed "Get Off of My Cloud, "I Wanna Be Your Man," "The Last Time," "Paint It, Black," "Gimme Shelter," "Wild Horses," "Going Down," "All Down the Line," "Miss You," "One More Shot," "Doom and Gloom," "It's Only Rock 'n' Roll," "Honky Tonk Women," "Before They Make Me Run," "Happy," "Midnight Rambler," "Start Me Up," "Tumbling Dice," "Brown Sugar," "Sympathy for the Devil," "You Can't Always Get What You Want," "Jumpin' Jack Flash," and "Satisfaction." While Bill Wyman and Mick Taylor didn't join the band onstage in Brooklyn, the Stones were joined by Bronx native Mary J. Blige on "Gimme Shelter" (she also performed it with the band at the November 25 London concert), guitarist Gary Clark Jr. on "Going Down," and the choir of the historical Trinity Church in Lower Manhattan for "You Can't Always Get What You Want." In between, Jagger joked about arriving to the concert via subway and thanked the audience for fifty years of support.

Perhaps due to the short length, the tour featured one of the smallest stages and one of the smallest backing bands in the recent history of the Stones. The first four songs featured only the Stones, Darryl Jones, and Chuck Leavell, and when the only backup musicians on this tour finally appeared, they were Bobby Keys, Tim Ries, Bernard Fowler, and Lisa Fischer.

Rolling Stone called the performance sloppy at points, writing, "At times, the show seemed like a public rehearsal—less spectacle, more barroom, with some confusion over what went where in the set list," and recounted two moments during the show when Jagger or the band was unsure of what the next song was. But as in all other media outlets, the praise of the Stones far outweighed any criticism, though Jim Farber of the *Daily News* said the lack of appearances by Wyman or Taylor was "a particular shame."

After the brief appearance at the 12-12-12 concert, the Stones prepared for their concerts at Prudential Center. Like Barclays Center, Prudential Center was another recent arena compared to the older venues the Stones had been used to playing in Manhattan. It was built to serve as the home arena of the National Hockey League team the New Jersey Devils, which had played at Izod Center since moving to New Jersey from Colorado in 1982. Despite the Devils' popularity with New Jersey sports fans, the team was exploring the option of relocating again until the city of Newark agreed to build a new arena specifically for the Devils just ten miles away from Izod Center, though the arena has also been used for college basketball and was briefly the home arena for the New Jersey Nets before their move to Brooklyn. Prudential Center opened in October 2007 with a series of concerts by New Jersey native band Bon Jovi between the opening games of the Devils' season. It has been a less popular concert stop for bands compared to Izod Center (which closed in 2015) or Barclays Center, though its capacity is between that of Barclays Center and Madison Square Garden.

The set lists of the Newark concerts were largely the same as the Brooklyn concert's. However, the December 13 performance replaced "I Wanna Be Your Man," "Going Down," and "All Down the Line" with "Respectable" (featuring guitarist John Mayer), the band's first performance of "Around and Around" since 1977 and "Midnight Rambler" with Mick Taylor on guitar. The December 15 performance featured "Going Down" with both John Mayer and Gary Clark Jr., "Who Do You Love?" with the Black Keys, "Dead Flowers," "Midnight Rambler" with Taylor again, "Gimme Shelter" with New York-born pop sensation Lady Gaga, and "Tumbling Dice" with New Jersey native Bruce Springsteen. Both concerts again featured the Trinity choir introducing "You Can't Always Get What You Want." As advertised, the second concert was broadcast live on pay-per-view as *One More Shot*. After the second concert, the band went back to New York for an after-party at the Carlyle hotel, where the band held after-parties after each of their three New

York City-area concerts. However, this party was the largest of three, with over 150 guests.

As the Stones and their family, friends, and entourage partied at the Carlyle, fans wondered if the very short 50 & Counting Tour marked the final goodbye of the Rolling Stones, a band that previously wouldn't have let such a significant anniversary pass by without cashing in even more. As if anyone had ever thought that the Rolling Stones would end it all in New Jersey, at the end of the second show Jagger teased the audience by saying, "This is our last show," and then, after a pause, continued, "of the fiftieth anniversary tour. Hope to see you again soon."

"STILL SURVIVING ON THE STREET"

The 50 & Counting Tour and subsequent 14 On Fire Tour did not return to the New York City area after the December 2012 Prudential Center dates. Several shows on the 14 On Fire Tour were postponed when Jagger's longtime girlfriend, L'Wren Scott, was found dead in her Chelsea (New York) apartment on March 17 after committing suicide. Jagger presided over her memorial service at St. Bartholomew's Church on May 2. The Stones' short North American Zip Code Tour in summer 2015 that celebrated the reissue of *Sticky Fingers* got no closer to Manhattan than Buffalo. Nonetheless, over fifty years the Stones have performed to over 1.5 million fans in the New York City metro area. Few performers outside local arena favorites like Bruce Springsteen and Billy Joel have even come close to that number.

The Stones haven't stopped rolling, but they have slowed down. The one-hundred-plus show tours of 1989 through 2007 appear to be a thing of the past. The band has played an average of just eighteen concerts a year since kicking off the 50 & Counting Tour in 2012. Whereas it once seemed like at least one member could be seen in New York on a monthly basis—even more frequently when Jagger, Richards, and Wood all lived in Manhattan—their appearances in "The Capital of the

World" have been limited in recent years. While the Stones have yet to play the fully renovated Madison Square Garden, they are making their first New York-area performances in almost seven years in June 2019 with two gigs at MetLife Stadium, the massive football stadium that replaced Giants Stadium at the Meadowlands in 2010. New Yorkers are clearly still there for the band—the second show was added before the pre-sale had even concluded.

Still, the Stones have remained busy, especially in New York. In November 2013, Wood and Taylor teamed up for four gigs at the Cutting Room on East 32nd Street and ended their sets with "Going to New York," the same "I'm going to make it" blues tune that their Rolling Stones bandmates had played in London clubs in the early 1960s. Jagger and Richards have attended numerous film premieres and celebrity parties, and Jagger did most of the promotion for *Get on Up*, the 2014 James Brown biopic that he produced, in New York. Richards appeared onstage at Eric Clapton's Crossroads Guitar Festival at Madison Square Garden in April 2013, appeared on *The Tonight Show* and *Today* in September 2014 to promote *Gus & Me*, a children's book he wrote about his relationship with his grandfather, and introduced a musical performance by Paul McCartney on the *Saturday Night Live* fortieth-anniversary special on February 15, 2015. Most of his 2015 solo album, *Crosseyed Heart*, was recorded and mixed in New York City studios.

Despite all the jokes about the Stones' longevity over the past forty years, the Stones will play their final concert sooner rather than later. But long after they are gone, their music will endure in pop culture. The band's hits of the 1960s and 1970s have remained popular for decades, like the music of their long-gone contemporaries the Beatles, Jimi Hendrix, Janis Joplin, the Grateful Dead, and the Doors, and show no signs of disappearing even as the cultural landscape of America has dramatically changed. Many of these hits have a connection with New York, whether they were recorded or mixed in Manhattan or mention the city in their lyrics.

New York itself is also facing a different future. Bloomberg's twelve-year tenure as mayor ended on December 31, 2013. He was succeeded in office by progressive Democrat Bill de Blasio, the former New York City public advocate whose campaign rhetoric called New York a "Tale of Two Cities" and heavily criticized Bloomberg's pro-business policies. De Blasio's administration stands in marked contrast to the previous twenty years of Giuliani's and Bloomberg's administrations, and the era of corporate domination of New York City's economy will likely see significant changes. Critics of de Blasio's social policies are concerned that his administration is returning New York to the "bad old days" of the crime, grime, and homelessness of "Fun City" dominating the streets, the very environment that inspired some of the best Rolling Stones songs of the 1970s.

Over the past three decades, Jagger and Richards have answered those criticizing their advancing ages by suggesting that if they were old blues or jazz musicians playing in small halls well into their eighties, like many of their musical heroes, they wouldn't be targets of criticism for continuing to tour. Indeed, Chuck Berry, who died in 2017, continued to perform live until he was eighty-seven, and B.B. King, who died in 2015, played his final gig just a month after his eighty-ninth birthday. As New York City emerges from two decades of corporate-sponsored economic expansion, so might the Stones. Eighty-year-old musicians strutting on the stage of MetLife Stadium or Madison Square Garden might be unlikely, but the Stones would not be the first octogenarians to perform at the Beacon Theatre, Radio City Music Hall, or the Iridium Jazz Club. No sponsorship from a Fortune 500 company would even be necessary.

* * * * *

On June 10, 2013, Philadelphia mayor Michael Nutter announced that the Rolling Stones would be honored with Rolling Stones Week in Philadelphia ahead of the band's June 18 performance at the Wells Fargo Center on the 50 & Counting Tour. In the press release, Nutter announced, "The Rolling Stones and the City of Philadelphia have a long and storied history. Philadelphia continues to be a must-play city on Stones tours, including this current tour in which they are only visiting eight American cities. We're very fortunate that they continue to create music and perform here in Philadelphia for their many fans in our great city." Before the June 18 concert, Nutter presented the band with miniature replica Liberty Bells.

While the Stones certainly have lots of history in Philadelphia stretching back to 1965—the band opened the 1981 American Tour and the Steel Wheels Tour there, and Jagger, Richards, and Wood all performed at Live Aid there in 1985—they obviously have far more history one hundred miles up the New Jersey Turnpike, the highway mentioned in Chuck Berry's "You Can't Catch Me," which the Stones recorded in 1964. If the Stones get a week of celebration and ceremonial Liberty Bells in Philadelphia, what do they deserve from New York City? A Rolling Stones Month and keys to the city (perhaps keys that would open every bar, nightclub, and arena stage in the five boroughs)?

But even if the Stones have already played their last concert in New York—most would bet that they haven't—they have built an undeniably rich legacy across the city and the metro area in stadiums, arenas, theaters, and nightclubs. All of them can proudly tout that "The World's Greatest Rock 'n' Roll Band" or one of its members has graced their stages—that is, if they don't tout it already. And much like John Lennon's Strawberry Fields memorial in Central Park, it seems likely that the Stones are worthy of being honored with their own New York City memorial somewhere in New York when they finally call it a day for their contributions to the Big Apple.

Of course, perhaps the most fitting memorial to the Stones in New York will be the fact that their music will still be blasting out of every jukebox in every dive bar from the Bronx to Queens for decades to come. Even if New York never returns to the violent, yet creative, years that inspired *Some Girls*, it will still be a city of "love and hope and sex and dreams."

ABOUT THE AUTHOR

Christopher McKittrick's publications include five entries in *100 Entertainers Who Changed America* (Greenwood) and "The Secret History of New York Blues" in *Artefact* magazine. Christopher and his work have been quoted in *The Wall Street Journal*, *The New York Times*, *Newsday*, and CNBC.com.